FAKE IT, IT WILL COME

Kathy Gotz

Copyright © 2016 Kathy Gotz
All rights reserved
First Edition

PAGE PUBLISHING, INC.
New York, NY

First originally published by Page Publishing, Inc. 2016

ISBN 978-1-68409-373-1 (Paperback)
ISBN 978-1-68409-374-8 (Digital)

Printed in the United States of America

To my wonderful husband Michael,
and to my children David, Christine,
Karen & Eric and families.

Preface

THIS IS MY STORY, my perspective, and my feelings throughout my life. My objective in writing this book is to help people with any relationship that is a struggle, a madness, irreparable, unlovable, and about being totally lost, not having anywhere to turn. Throughout the dark night of the soul, I gave up all hope of survival. I do not know why I chose the very worst; only a few choose to go through this. I think that there is no comparison to just spinning in hell and extreme pressure and pain being added to that. I have met people that thought it was no big deal; they obviously did not go through the very worst. I am crying just writing this! Iouya told me that my goal would be to help people going through the dark night of the soul.

It is also not to blame or point fingers at anyone in my story—everyone is innocent. I can honestly say that I love all the characters of my book. After all, we are each other. Most of all, by telling my story, I helped myself. It was so hard to tell about my childhood when I knew the world could be reading it. It was a freedom to be liberated by bringing light into darkness. It feels like a huge boulder has been lifted off my shoulders. I feel lighter! This book is also not embellished in any way; I did not exaggerate my experiences. It is also not to say that I had it worse off than any other person did; it is not to parallel or make a comparison. I know there are many people on the planet that have had it far worse than me. So my only hope is the readers walk away with healing in their hearts and for the people that surround them.

Jesus did show us the way with his calm, non-attack method. He showed us how to resurrect out of suffering and pain. No one can say, "Jesus, you do not know what it is like to suffer." He did not attack his attackers. This was threatening to the people that crucified him. No attack is justified; we just justify that it is okay to judge and strike back. In fact, we think that we should judge and that it is our God-given right. All attacks are cries for help; there is no exception. If you love yourself unconditionally, then you could not possibly attack. It is that simple! Because you know what you give out, you get. The choice is always yours. So go forth and love yourself through the process of atonement. At one moment, become the stellar person that you are, and separate yourself from. Embrace life because time is of the essence.

1

The Dark Night of the Soul

I KNOW EXACTLY WHEN my "dark night of the soul" started: June of 1999. I also know that it started because I read *A Course in Miracles* and offered my relationships up to the Holy Spirit, every morning and night, concentrating on what I did, not what they did. That set the stage for what was to come. I never guessed what I would be in store for was called a divine order.

I do believe it was activated on Sunday, May 25, 1999, when Carl, Shirley, and I knelt down and joined hands. All three of us said our part… mine, I invited all the spirits and entities that loved me to be present and thanked them for coming. Then I said, "I choose to awaken and remember who I really am." During the blessing or being prayed over, I saw six angels swirling above my head, which looked like skeletons—several single different varieties of flowers, different colors, then I saw a stream of golden light coming down from heaven at an angle. All I saw was dull up until this point, but I saw stuff throughout. I believe that represented the old me dying, which is the fear based on Kathy. Last but not least, the tunnel we see when we die was crystal clear. It was a side view into the inside, which looked like a membrane, then out to the circle of blue light, like a sky. Felt a lot of energy during the event.

On November of '98, I had had a dream. I was outside, and I was extending my hand, saying to my dad that I would always be Catholic as I was going to be baptized in the Church of Jesus Christ of Latter-Day Saints; it was imminent. In my dream, I had on what they are baptized in—and I did not know what they were baptized in—that flashed twice. Then a huge "1999" flashed twice. I thought that a baptism meant a new beginning; I did not have a clue as to my new beginning. Because I do not usually remember my dreams, this dream stood out. Plus, the "1999" seemed most unusual; I thought that something was going to happen in "1999."

I do not know why both flashed twice, what that represented.

Right after the blessing, the three of us went to the Church of Today in Warren, Michigan. We had written a letter to Marianne Williamson asking if Carl could meet with her about spirituality and politics. So before the service, we were invited into her office to meet with her. Shirley and Carl both talked politics, while I just said that "Return to Love" had a big impact on me. Carl was interested in how he could incorporate spirituality and politics together.

Then we went immediately afterward to the service Marianne was giving. We sat three rows back in the middle right in front of Marianne. I sat next to Shirley on my left, and there was an unknown lady on my right. Immediately I was told to take the hand of the lady next to me. I figured out really quick that it was not going to stop. This was also not familiar to me, being told to do something in my head. So I told my sister Shirley that I was being told to take the hand of the lady sitting next to me. Then I simply looked at the lady to the right and said, "My name is Kathy. This is my sister Shirley. I am being told to take your hand, and I do not know why." She paused for a moment and said yes and that her name was Carol. The moment I took

Carol's hand, energy, which I was not familiar with, was flooding down my right shoulder, down my arm, and into her hand during the one-and-a-half hour service. I forgot to mention that the moment I stepped into the Church of Today, I was energized; the moment I left the energy was gone. It was truly an exciting moment, nothing on this caliber had ever happened to me before. After it was over with, I asked Carol if she could feel the energy. She said not only could she feel the energy, but my hand was vibrating as well, and she could not believe that it was my first time at the Church of Today because she felt like she knew me.

This is my theory, but I need to let you know now. I believe when that energy was coming down my arm that it was a healing gift given to me. I did not have a clue as to why I was told to take Carol's hand. Was she receiving a gift, or what did that represent? At the time, I thought it was Carol receiving a gift and I was the catalyst. All I know is when I started praying over people, things happened. So I believe on the day of the blessing, I received healing gifts. I was the one that had to become healed after I gave them. I had to release any outcome or attachment whatsoever. I had to get out of my own way. So in other words, I was the catalyst for Carol letting me know I had the gift, only it took me two and half years later to figure it out. I was also told two and half years later that all the flowers I saw, when I had the blessing by Carl and Shirley, represented something also. I cannot remember most of the flowers and do not know what they represented. I do remember one of the flowers—it was a white hyacinth. So it seems everything has a purpose and a reason.

Also during the service, I saw distorted men's faces flash every time I closed my eyes, then there was a lady kissing herself. I do believe that the distorted men's faces were my dad, whom I did not resolve my issues with, and possibly my husband, Mike, and that the woman kissing herself was me not loving myself. I also saw the light from heaven throughout. I also saw the statue of Abraham Lincoln illumed—I was thinking then, what did I have to emancipate?

One day, Shirley called me up and said she felt like she was pregnant and ready to give birth and asked if I would come over and help her channel energy. I said I would be happy to, even though I had never done it before. We said a prayer first. Entities laughed at us because Shirley laughed. We channeled from the center of the earth through our root chakras on out, like bubbles then circling around outside our top chakras. I felt like I was having an orgasm. That wasn't enough. I went home right afterward and decided to relax in the tub, when my rectum started pulsating. I called Shirley at my mom's house and asked her, "What is going on?" She said it was probably my root chakra opening up. I thought, *Maybe this is not happening*, so I put my finger down there, and yes, it was happening. Shirley did not know why for three days or that she was getting ready to deliver either.

When Carl and Shirley gave me the blessing, David, my son, was very strong. (She did not know why.) The next day, David was in a pretty serious motorcycle accident in Fremont, California, on the way to the nearby community college. He got a dislocated right elbow and left knee, which Ron my brother said was totally black. His knee and elbow cleared up pretty good and quick. Police called Ron, and my son Eric showed up while David was being put in an ambulance, and they would not let them go with them. They both suspected the worst.

During this time, I saw this purple weed that I have seen often when I closed my eyes. The name of this weed is blue bonnet. The flowers were illumined and in a different formation every time. I would see it day or night, and I couldn't remember how many days this went on, but I would say approximately three days. Did not know what to think of this, nor did it seem like anyone else knew what it meant. Shirley seemed to think that it was clearing different dimensions. It was amazing because I saw the actual weed in a field near my house, went up to it, and ate a couple of the petals, not having a clue to what it meant. Maybe it represented the three days to my resurrection, like when Jesus was in the tomb and resurrected on the third day.

I had another dream while I was in my bed at home. This time, I was seven months pregnant. Three out of my four children were with me in a little house. Even though we were inside the house, I saw a huge tidal wave coming at our house. My daughter, Karen, was told by the spirit world to go in the back bedroom and that if she did this, she would be safe. I got the message at the same time and ushered everyone back. I decided that because I was pregnant and I didn't think that I would be able to swim, that I wanted to get in the closet as well. Somehow I felt that by getting into the closet, I would be more protected. I passed this dream off as a weird dream. I went over to my mom's and told her about the dream. Shirley overheard us in the bathroom and told me there was more significance to that than I thought. So then I surmised that maybe whatever situation we were in, if we trusted, we would be safe and unharmed. I thought of this tidal wave as a mega tsunami.

During Shirley's stay of three weeks, Shirley and I did several blessings or praying over people. I did a little at the beginning while Shirley took over and did her deal. So although I participated, I was very unfamiliar with praying over anyone. Also it was very strong for me that Shirley and I should say a prayer for the lady who lived next door to me. Her name was Shelia, and she was pregnant. The doctors wanted her to abort the baby. He told her that the baby was way underdeveloped and would not make it full term. So she was set up to have the abortion. I told Shirley that it was very important that we do it immediately. She said that there wasn't any hurry, but I felt the urgency of doing it right away. She went into the hospital the day she was set up to have the abortion and told them she would not have the abortion.

When Grace was born, she weighed like three pounds, ten ounces and was a full-term baby. They called her Grace because she lived by the grace of God. She is now almost two, weighs nineteen pounds, and is perfect in every way. I had an opportunity to give her a little blessing. When I gave her back to the aunt, after only having her for ten minutes, she reached out both of her hands for me. She stole my heart. Hope to see her often. The only miracle is that she did not have the abortion!

When Shirley left, three weeks later, we joined hands on her bed while she said a prayer; she told me that I could now pray over people on my own and was capable of all the gifts of being a great healer. I had reservations about the whole ordeal. I lacked self-esteem and thought about what was I going to say and do. Nevertheless, I just started to do my thing, implementing the *Sedona Journal of Emergence: A Course in Miracles* and generally watching other people. At first I felt very self-conscious, but as time went on, I became more and more comfortable doing it.

2

The Bauer House

SHIRLEY AND I WENT to a healing meeting at the Church of Today. This is where I had my first introduction to reiki, cranial sacrum, therapeutic touch, angel readings, and healers in general. Reiki is laying on of hands, a touch healing system of incomparable ease and power and is a part of every one of us. It is a universal energy from the universe, which is the divine source. We sat in a large circle that was being held in the chapel. Each person was to give their name and tell a little bit about what they did. I was the last person to talk. I simply said that I am none of it and I am all of it. The crowd approved. I do believe I said the very least. Shirley even approved of what I had said.

This is also when I met Theron for the first time. He was an older man who would make a good father figure and used to be a minister. Brian sat next to Shirley and guided me to him, so I went. Brian is also an older man. I asked Theron what I should do with the rest of my life. He took both of my hands and asked me to tell him about two of my recent experiences. So I told him about this lady that I just had met at a funeral home. She knew that I was Catholic, and she was condemning all Catholics to hell with a bible in one hand. I told her that was not a good idea because Jesus said, "What you do to the least of my brethren, you do to me." She continued for a while, and I took on her pain. I literally had to walk a couple of miles to get rid of it. Then this man across the street who was dying from leukemia and who I used to joke around with, he would wave to me wherever I was at. I told him that he was brave with a smile on his face all the while he had this disease and that he should cross over being brave with a smile on his face. I gave him a hug and told him I loved him. Theron told me that I had all the qualities to work for a hospice. Brian also guided me to the Bauer house by showing me where it was.

At the Bauer house, Pam did a cranial sacrum, and I was advised to go to her; I found her to be delightful. I went to Pam because I had a bad neck from some very serious falls, but nothing much seemed to happen during the visit. It is important to tell you a little bit about my falls at this time. When I was in the seventh grade, a boy was chasing another boy. He hit me so hard I hit the blacktop and was knocked out for a couple of hours and had a grand mal seizure. The boy chasing the boy that hit me I later married. He had to put up with endless stiff necks and all I had to deal with. Around the same time, I flew up into the air on ice skates; I did not get knocked out, but I saw stars. When I was about forty-two, I ran downstairs because I thought the laundry tub was overflowing. I did not take the time to turn on the light. I was also barefooted. When five feet away from the laundry tub, I flew up in the air and shot like a bullet, feet first underneath the laundry tub. I thought that I must be dead. I did not become unconscious, but I knew my head had to be cracked open, and I lay back. The hair hanging from the back of my head was unbearable, and I could not touch the back of my head for a month. So now my neck is going in the opposite direction, plus there is almost no cartilage between four of my vertebrae, for I felt each of them touch each other.

So because of this, a neurosurgeon wanted to perform two neck surgeries where you fuse a piece of bone from my hip to my neck. The neurosurgeon wanted to do this surgery in January of 1998. I was a week away from having this procedure done, when a friend of mine while we were kids called and said that she had been hounded for the last three days by the spirit world, to give me a call and tell me about her biological dad. His name was Ed, and he belonged to the Church of Jesus Christ of Latter-Day Saints. She told me that he did massage with pressure points and to at least give him a try before going for surgery, for I had nothing to lose. I felt like the heavens were intervening, so I called up and canceled my surgery appointment. My first visit when I was getting off the table to leave, I felt like a truck had hit me and told him so. He also told me that my back had calcified itself for protection and that he would break it up and my body would get rid of it itself. I went to him for like seven visits, where he worked as long as three hours at a time. His wife also worked on me for like a half hour each visit at the same time. At the end of the seventh time, I noticed a great deal of energy leaving through my right shoulder. I was really quite astounded in the amount of energy being released. So I took it that it was time to go to a chiropractor.

I also went to Doctor Rosenblaum at Henry Ford Hospital in Detroit. My primary care physician thought it was in my best interest to have a second opinion. Dr. Roseblaum, who is the chief of staff of the neurosurgery department, said he would not give me that surgery unless I was dying. But the truth was I felt like I was dying. My quality of life was gone; it was hard for me to get dressed. He told me to go out there and find anyone that could make me well. After going to Ed and Dr. Easton, I wrote him a letter thanking him for telling me not to have the surgery. He wrote me back and said although that was his profession, plus he knew the doctor who was going to perform the surgery, he did not casually do that surgery.

I went to Dr. Easton out in Waterford, Michigan, quite a jaunt. He told me my neck was going in the opposite direction. He took moving x-rays of my neck and promised me that he would get me pain-free. He was a Jack Mormon and quite spiritual. His goal was to genuinely help heal his clients—he was out for them not to come back. I could not believe how painful it was to get out of pain. It was also hard to believe that I would ever be out of pain. Much thanks to Doctor Easton for saving my life. I am grateful. I went to Ed and Easton throughout the year of 1998. Doctor Easton told me many times that my recovery was faster than most and was amazed with my progress. I was told that I agreed to go through these neck problems because in a previous lifetime, I had clobbered someone in the back of the neck and killed him. You get what you give out!

The next time, I went to Brian for reiki at the Church of Today. Nothing much seemed to happen. They spend a half hour on you for a love donation. The following week, I wanted to go to Nancy, and she wasn't there, so I went back to Brian. I told him that I was experiencing a lot of pressure in my temple and jaw area. So while he was doing reiki to the sides of my head, all of a sudden, all the emotional pain of my whole life was coming up. I just started crying. Actually, I tried to control it by keeping it under control because I was having reiki done and I wanted to really cry. It wasn't anything specific; I just knew it was emotional pain. Don't ask me how I knew. Brian told me that he could feel my pain. He also started crying, and his tears were falling in my hair. He told me that he was being advised to tell me to have my blood pressure checked. I told him my blood pressure was always low. He said just have it checked. Then he told me that I was being called to Utah and that Shirley wasn't just my sister but my soul sister, plus she needed me as much as I needed her and that I should call her tonight. He told me then that I was in the process of healing myself and that I should go home and have a good cry. The pressure never went away.

So now I am back at the Church of Today. I told Brian that I had taken his suggestion and called Shirley. She said it was the weirdest thing, that she had been guided by the spirit world to this house. She knew this would be the place for her healing center. They directed her which way to turn. She had seen the house previously but did not have a clue as to how to get there—geographically, that is. We drove by the place several times while I was there in Utah.

Then I went to church and cried throughout the service. I felt like the service had been written and sung for me. As usual, I was sitting next to a lady named Carol, whom I did not know. Well, from that day on, I had a lot of pressure in my jaw and temple area that did not let up. I was drinking a glass of red wine a day, for pain in my neck and generally on my right side, and I could have become an alcoholic very easily. There are times that you get a break and you think that whatever was causing it has gone away, only to find that it comes back with a vengeance. Initially I thought I was releasing something but really did not know what was going on. I did not know what I had done to deserve what I was getting, thinking maybe it might be many lifetimes. The right side of my head felt the worst, felt like it was going into my brain.

The next person I went to was Steve. After the service, I met him outside at one of the entrances to the church. We sat down on the cement forms available, perpendicular to each other. He asked me to say my full maiden name three times slowly. He said Mike, my husband, and Crissy my daughter were connected in a previous lifetime.

He said I was a pink rose within a rose that was strong at the stem and root but weak on the outside. He said I went back and forth, plus I was in the process of healing myself. He said Crissy was a smaller yellow rose. Karen was a taller, willowy purple rose and had come into this family to help us. Eric was gray, and we should just let him have space and let him know that there was room for him when he was willing to come around. David was dark with brown leaves; he said I had kept him bound because I had worried about him so much. He said that because I had spent so much time worrying about others, I needed now to go within and concentrate on healing me. He said David would be okay but that I may not consider him okay. That saddened me. He said the whole family was in the process of healing ourselves. He also told me about three different lifetimes.

He said one time I was a man who lived in a rural area and that was a recluse, that I had a difficult, lonely life because I tried to commune with the nearby village and was unsuccessful in doing so.

The next time, I was a woman who literally ran through that lifetime, not taking any time to smell the flowers. The next life, I was a woman gymnast but not what I would think a gymnast would be. He said I was in a wheelchair and my arms were strong.

I asked about my dad. He repeated for me to go within. Heal myself! He also told me to see how those lifetimes were a reflection of this lifetime.

In correlation to those lifetimes to this lifetime, I have been quite impatient with almost everything. At a couple of jobs, I felt ostracized by my coworkers, so much so that I cried. I was even asked to leave. Because of the conditions of my family life, I felt like a loner in many ways. But I could say through it all, I tried really never giving up. Most of the time, I am always in a hurry—have to do this and have to do that. I also have been an impatient driver—however, not by honking my horn or giving hand gestures. I can definitely see the reflection of those lifetimes in this lifetime. We can pray for patience, but ultimately, we must be patient by giving patience to ourselves, by changing our minds. I can also be slothful, not moving hardly at all. I am a very fast painter, a little sloppy, but when the job is done, it looks great. I can start a monumental job, and I will not stop until it is done, no matter what it takes or how much pain I am in, so finishing a project is not a problem.

    I was driving home from the Church of Today, and I thought I could really feel bad about holding David bound and continuing to hold him bound, or I could make a conscious decision to not do so. At that very moment, I had made a conscious decision to not worry about him ever again. I also went to Higgins Lake, up north Michigan, and said, "I release you, David. From this day forward, I will only send you love." That is exactly what I did. I could really feel guilty about all of it and continue the madness, but I chose to let it go.

While Brian was doing reiki on me, he told me that there was a Divine Order and that I should have patience. I told him that I had spent most of my life playing the submissive role to a controlling husband and father. He told me I had to take a stand and move to Utah. So many people told me so many things; I did not know what to do. In my heart, I was not ready to do anything, so I didn't.

Then I called Carol, who was spiritual psychic. She said I was pink on the right and purple on the left. She said that was very good. She saw me working with either a red-haired or hot-tempered slender man. Appearance means a lot to me. A celebration was coming my way. Very good changes—clairvoyance—and I would be very busy as a gifted healer. Just talking to people would heal them. She saw an older woman—glasses, heavy and wavy hair (teapot, large bubble money). She said it would be great in the beginning of August. She saw me in a large white house on or near a lake with the letter *M*—she didn't know if that meant Michigan. She said if I would go to Utah, she saw me back in Michigan in five years. She also said to go with my gut feeling. She said a lot of healers were being called to

Michigan. She did not think that Mike would want a divorce. She thought my children would be fine. Mike would see a spirit… so he would be convinced that I was on the right path, but he would not go on my path. I would have a lot of happiness. She said when I prayed to ask spirit guides and angels to vibrate at my level for strength and then thank them. I would get a wish but would be disappointed.

Again I was at a service at the Church of Today, sat next to an Ann Marie. I sat down to an aisle seat that was available and asked her if she happened to be a Carol. A few minutes later, she asked me, "Why, do I look like a Carol?" I said no, that the four previous times that I had been there, I had sat next to four different Carols. She said she could not come often and that this was like her fifth time and that she had seen me there before. I told her I gave my money at the Bauer house and told her she should go. I told her that she should see Nancy and Sherry. A cute gal was happy to guide her. She was reading a course on miracles. She said she had known I had something to offer her as soon as I sat down and was waiting for me. I was amused with that.

3

At Roscommon

I HAD HAD A dream while I was up north in our trailer. Dreamt that I was taking a test and drawing a complete blank. So I ran up to this lady and asked her, "What are the gifts the witches are given?" She said, flinging her head to the side and back in disgust, "Up the Ante." I said, "Up the Ante are the gifts the witches are given." So I surmised that I should not limit the spiritual gifts that I was given. To me, I was already saying that I was everything, just as they wanted me to say that I was god.

Also while I was up north, walking on my property in Roscommon, Michigan, I had this experience that only took a few seconds. It was during the daytime. I felt like I was on the ship, like when Jesus was asleep and the storm was coming. Everyone was panicking but me. I was so calm that I could not figure out what was their problem. I do not know what happened, if I tapped into Jesus's life or what. At the Deepak Chopra seminar I went to later, I believed he said you could.

Saw the stars up north, and they're spectacular, brilliant, a canopy display. We put a roof over the other trailer. I still need to paint it. We have two travel trailers that are old, which we have restored. Tyler, our shih tzu, loved it up north. The dog across the street must have died. I called him Daniel Boon. His name was Boon, and he was a golden lab. He would come over and stay with us all the while we were there. One day my sons, David and Eric, were walking over to the people across the street. Boon would not go across the street. He stayed on our side of the street. The owners would have to tie him up so that he would not totally stay with us. Needless to say, we enjoyed him very much. He would lie at our feet while we were mesmerized, sitting around the fire with the darkened serenity enveloping us.

I went to the art fair they have in town and bought a couple of fairies to put in my flower garden in front of the porch at home in Taylor. We brought our Sea Ray boat to use on Higgins Lake.

Higgins Lake is my heaven! It is the sixth prettiest lake in the world and the most pristine in Michigan, in my opinion. It is so inviting that you want to jump in its cold, refreshing, crystal-clear water. The reason the water is so clean is that it is a spring-fed lake, so there is no silt to stir up. The water has an incredible bluish green color, which I have never seen in another lake in Michigan; you can see way down in the water its pure essence and elegance. Higgins Lake is over a hundred feet deep in some areas, with a couple of sunken islands and an island. I love up north with my whole heart and soul. That is one thing that Mike and I both had in common: we loved our property, the city of Roscommon and Higgins Lake. It was literally magic for me! Our creation was a labor of pure love.

On Wednesday, July 25, 1999, I went to the Bauer house and saw Nancy, who does angel readings. She said the first entity was Jesus or God but of that caliber. She thought Jesus. I do not remember everything she told me. Jesus said to seek and I would find that he was always with me, even in my darkest times. I should have paid attention to that. He told me during my darkest times if I had paid attention He was holding my hand. She proceeded to tell me that I had three Indian guides dancing in a row. A man dressed in white with a white headdress, a woman at the end, and a boy in the middle. All of them dancing in elation for me. She did not tell me why. Eagle popped into my head, so I thought *Gray Eagle*. I had read a book, "The Eagle and the Rose" by Rosemary Altea. Rosemary's guide was Gray Eagle, and I asked him if he would be my spirit guide as well. So you can see how I was surprised that he was. She also said I had a spirit guide named Toshi, who is oriental and a llama, who bowed initially and, at the end, also was in elation for me. I did not know why, nor did she say.

Immediately afterward, I went to Sherry. She said I would have prosperity with abundance and be happy, that I should go away with Mike, my husband, this weekend. She said there might be a reason I would not want to go and that I should go. She said we would be selling our house in two months or two years. She described the house as being light, with big windows, fields to either side, and with lots of trees in back, plus a big willow tree in the front. I do believe that was the house that Shirley had been guided to; I had visited it while I was in Utah. What is unusual also was there being a big willow tree in Utah—there isn't enough moisture for it there. She told me I had six angels encircling my head, which

I saw when Carl and Shirley gave me the blessing. We sat under the tree in the backyard, with shoes off, on the earth, looking at each other. Both Nancy and Sherry acted like my life was just beginning.

Shirley hypnotized my daughter Karen. It was very special and exciting. Her grandma, Frieda, who died when her dad was fifteen, was present throughout and holding her hand. The message was very clear, that Mike, her dad, was her joy and light, plus the firstborn, and that she did not abandon him. She felt greatly saddened that Mike had blocked her out and that she saw him not healed. She showed Karen three different scenes with her dad. One, he was in the hospital, and she said she was not concerned about him physically; she told her he wasn't healed. She also showed her two different scenes while he was at work, and the same thing—he wasn't healed. She asked Karen if she would just love her dad, that she had tried with the other siblings to get through to no avail. She also showed Crissy, my other daughter, on the bed and how sad and lonely she was, and Karen felt her sadness. She said, "Crissy is your only sister" and to love her. Then Shirley said, "What about Karen's brothers?" Grandma laughed and said they had a stronger bond than either one of them realized and that they would be fine. Grandma told Karen that she loved her and gave her a hug and a kiss and told her she could not get on the elevator and kind of nudged her in.

Shirley and I met up with Mike at the bar and told him about the whole experience. He just looked ahead, listening intently to every word. Mike felt like his mom had abandoned him at the age of fifteen and that she no longer existed after she died. Mike, throughout my twenty-eight years of being married to him, had only spoken only a few words about his mother. We have gone to her grave but mostly when we were there at someone else's funeral. I have always felt that she would be there when I was crossing over.

I asked Shirley to hypnotize me while we were at my mom's house in the guest bedroom. Shirley did her usual; she let me choose what I was going to go down in. I chose a yellow Volkswagen. Plus I took Tyler, my little shih tzu, with me. All of a sudden, I saw myself from the back with Tyler, and I was at the entrance of Oz. Tyler was Toto. I was so surprised that I opened my eyes and I said, "Shirley, I am at the entrance of Oz." Shirley said to me, "You're not hypnotized." We stopped right then and there. Theron later told me that my Dad and

Mike were the wizards twisting their hands back and forth. I knew that I was hypnotized; it was a full picture in color. The next morning, when I awoke, they told me that I was already home. They were the spirit world. Could I have been my higher self? I think the reason they told me that was I had spent my whole life wanting to die as far back as I can remember. Shirley is an advanced hypnotherapist. Never before, when she had hypnotized me, did I have a full-color picture like that. I told Shirley the next morning about what was said to me.

Well there aren't any accidents or coincidences, but I thought it was very strange that when I went to the following time to the Church of Today, the theme was *The Wizard of Oz.* They had colorful cardboard stand-ups of the characters in the hallways. I found this quite remarkable, just having had this experience with the hypnotism. Dorothy did not need the magic red slippers; all she needed was to believe. And that is all we need—to believe! It is two and a half years later, but I can tell you, I believe. I am ahead of myself here. And you will say, "In what?" I believe that we are all one, that all negativity is an illusion, and that love conquers all. I believe that we can have heaven here on earth. I believe God does not want us to suffer. I also believe that Jesus showed us how to resurrect out of pain and suffering. I know there are many Catholics that believe in sacrifice and suffering; my dad is one. Our father in heaven is the same as our father here on earth. Can you imagine your father saying, "I want you to suffer and endure much pain and have hardship"? I think not! My dad used to tell us to believe in ourselves, but he never showed us how, either in his own life or in ours. I thought it was peculiar that he would even mouth those words, when it seemed like he would knock us down whenever he could. That certainly gave me mixed messages, an oxymoron, if you will.

On Sunday, August 15, 1999, I went to the Bauer house and saw Pam, whom I had seen the first time I was there. She said she saw me spending time in Utah but not living there. She said David, my son, wasn't doing well but that he would be great. She told me that I had held him bound because of Mike and my anger. She told me that I needed to change the way I responded to Mike's anger. That I should say ouch! He did not know how to feel and I needed to teach him. Of course, she said that we agreed to go through this, which I knew. She said Mike had not had his needs met as a child.

Afterward, I went to the service, and I went to the back, where I was crying to myself. I asked to be sent someone to help me. A lady walked in, and I extended my hand because we were saying the "Our Father," during which everyone holds hands. She said she was not supposed to be here and felt that she had been guided to come. She asked me why I was crying. She took me to the chapel. The lady, whom I had never met, asked me what I wanted to pray for. I told her for my son David, that it was a mother's prayer. Several people put their hands on me, and this lady said the most eloquent mother's prayer. I do not know whom the prayer was for— me or David. I thanked them all and felt so much better.

4

Meditation Group

Now this was the first time I was going to this meditation group, and my mom came in with me—her first time also. I saw Theron. I asked him if he remembered me from the healing meeting. He said yes. He stuck out his hands for me to put mine on top of his, which I did. After a little bit, I asked him to do my mom. He told her that she was an anchor for the family. Then he took me aside and asked me if I could help her lose weight and that he saw her only having four more years. He told me that I would be going to Utah at the first of the year and that it would be pertaining to the movie, plus it would be a powerful experience. A lady came up to me and said that I would write a script and it would be in the *Phenomenon News* with my picture in it. Another lady, Martha, told me that I was no stranger, that she knew me from another plane or dimension. This meditation group meets every Wednesday. They described the spirits released and walking into the light. Michael the Archangel was there. The Blessed Mother was white, holding a white rose. She said the rose on the table was not white but to offer us all a petal. We were all also given a rock to hold. Also, the man who founded the church, Jack Boulen, was also there.

On September 5, 1999, I went to the service first. Marianne did a good talk as usual. I did not send anyone to the Bauer house. Afterward, I went to the Bauer house, and Pam did cranial on me right away. She diligently spent a lot of time doing mega balancing. She said my left hip was pulling to the right and that my left hip had to work harder to overcompensate for a damaged right hip. Pam also told me that I shouldn't work so hard. Afterward, she said that the fire that was in my neck had moved to the middle of my back; she said that was good because I was processing it. She also said I was improving since the first time she had worked on me.

Now I was talking to a lady in the bookstore who took me to the chapel to be prayed over, when out of my peripheral vision, I saw a black lady carrying a baby girl, with my hand on the little girl's back. So I finished my conversation and decided to hunt them down. I found them and asked the mother if I could put my hand on the baby's back. I told her she was an angel. I did not know why I was supposed to do this; I didn't question it. I went back to the Bauer house and saw Lynda and gave her a hug, and then she hugged me again and told me she loved me. After that, I went back into the family room and saw Brian. I gave him a hug.

On Wednesday, October 8, 1999, I went to the meditation group. Earlier, Shirley had called me up and asked me if I would write something about her movie. This seemed a little strange when I almost knew nothing about it, other than that it was spiritual and metaphysical. So after I got off the phone, I had written this out like I was writing a letter. I called it a riveting exercise. I called Shirley later on that evening and read it to her; she found it quite remarkable. So now I gave it to Theron to read at the meditation group. As Theron was reading it, he told me that I had channeled it. He told me Harrison Ford might be in the movie, which was what came to him.

A Riveting Exercise

The juices are now flowing feverishly to Shirley. She can barely Dictaphone it fast enough. She perseveres relentlessly to accomplish the grandest version of the greatest vision that this movie can reveal to all. There is a vortex in her home that has opened up many doors and a limitless explosion of expression and thought-provoking ideas. The most qualifying light workers step forward to do the acting. The singers do a heavenly, angelic sound echoing out throughout the universe. This movie cries out to all denominations and no denomination—it is unparalleled to any previous movie because it is clear and concise so that people awaken and remember who they really are. They see themselves at the grandest version of the greatest vision of who they really are. This is a very exciting, energized, and effervescent time to be alive. Amen!

All you have to do is imagine yourself being the unimaginable.

Within a short time of writing "A Riveting Exercise," I am again feeling sorry for myself and decide to use my imagination and write something for me. It is in the evening, I am on the couch in the front room, and I am the only one at home. This is how it went.

Kathy

I am going to travel the world, meeting all kinds of whole, marvelous people. My experiences are unparalleled to any previous experiences. I also travel in space, in a spaceship, seeing other galaxies and cosmoses and extraterrestrials of higher dimensions and readily understanding their concepts and makeups. Even though I am primitive compared to them, I enlighten them anyway. I readily take in and understand all they have to offer effortlessly.

I am soaring to the highest mountains. That is minuscule compared to what I am capable of. I am truly limitless and relentless. Nothing can stop me or get in my way. No negative forces or comments slow me down, for I am a pillar of strength that is untouchable. Every day is new and exciting. I think that sometime it might become mundane, and it augments and enhances the previous day. I am truly a shining star that is emanating and radiating throughout eternity. I am capable of seeing through a bird's eyes and other animals' eyes, seeing their vision and their thoughts. I can heal people and spirits on the other side of the planet—seeing them and where they are.

Meanwhile I stay centered, balanced, and humbled, never, ever forgetting every moment and appreciating all that I have and am. I am very happy and love myself, and I am complete in and of myself. All the power is within me! I love God.

5

I Went Dancing

I WENT TO THE Burton Manor in Livonia with my friend Jo Ann. I met the lady I had seen on and off throughout the years at the check-in. She said she knew I was coming before I walked in the door because she got a surge of energy. I really don't know if she knew it was me specifically or just someone she knew. I asked her if I could sit at her table. She said yes. I saw her talking to the lady next to her while I was sitting at their table. I suspected she was talking about me, even though I was sitting quite a ways away.

    She walks up to me, and I asked her if she was a psychic. In my wildest dreams, I do not know why I said that. She said no, but because I asked, this is what she said. I would not be married much longer. I asked her if I was getting a divorce or if my husband would die. She said she would not tell me that. Then she proceeded to tell me that I had justified it in my mind to drink a small amount of wine every day. She told me that I was in too much emotional pain, too fragile, and I could not handle it—on a deeper level, I knew what she was saying was true. She told me my father's father had the gene for alcoholism and so did I. I started crying. She said if I was going to cry, she wanted me to go to another table. I knew she wasn't being mean to me, that she was just trying to help. I asked her what I should do to get rid of this. She said to dance.

When a man asked me to dance, my first thought was, *I am not in the mood.* Then I remembered what she had said and said yes. I found out his name was John and that he also went to the Church of Today. Anyway, I had a ball dancing. JoAnn told me that she saw a side of me that she had never seen before. She said that I held myself like I was rich and that I looked young. Jo Ann was my biggest support system in helping me rebuild my self-esteem.

Wednesday, November 3, 1999. I didn't know it, but it would be the last time I would be at this meditation group for a year. It was being held at Sherry's house close to the church. I said that I was reading *Seat of the Soul* by Gary Zukav, and it said that you have to have reverence for all life. My daughter, Karen, screamed about a spider being on the kitchen counter, and I immediately went in and killed it. She said I wasn't supposed to do that. Then I said "I forgive myself" about the thoughts of Elaine and asked for forgiveness. Ingalor said that my voice was small and that I thought I was in all this pain, and then Cindy joined in and agreed. Theron jumped in and said, "This isn't what this is supposed to be about." I cried during the rest of the mediation. I felt very vulnerable and very embarrassed and totally exposed. I felt like I wanted to throw myself on the floor and start screaming. I described it like I was nude in front of them all. I drove home thinking I did not want to ever return.

At this time, I was literally spinning very deep in hell, so much so that I was surprised I was able to stand. The last few times at the group, I would leave feeling very bad. I couldn't figure out why I was going to a meditation and feeling so bad. Before this, I had some really bad times at night. One night I went to bed, and the pressure in my temple area was so bad I felt like I was dying. The angels were kind to me, and I fell asleep in a short time. When I am in pain, it is rare that I fall asleep, let alone quickly.

I did not sleep much during these months and had some wild, not believable times with my stomach. One night I thought there was an extraterrestrial ship above my house that took my stomach away; it felt like a cavity. Around the perimeter of where it was taken was extreme pressure. I was not afraid; I was totally numb. I did not touch my stomach—I just plain did not know what to think or do. I had gone into another bed so as not to disturb my husband.

Another night, my stomach was in so much pain that I thought, *You either take this pain from me or you take me.* That very second, my pain was like 75 percent numbed. They call this spiritual Novocain. I was impressed with the control of the situation. I do believe, however, that you are better off if you just endure the pain; it will expedite your process. Oftentimes, when I went to bed, I think, *What am I going to be in for tonight?* The very worst part is when you are in the void, cast away from God and everyone else. Like you are out in space, by yourself, away from everyone. As I recall, the void does not last very long, but it is pure hell. The truth is that you are never alone. In fact, the further you go into hell, the more you are protected from the world and negative forces. I think that is why I was told Gray Eagle was on a horse with a bow and arrow. I believe he was protecting me. I also know that God directly protects you, especially while you are in the void.

One day after the meditation, a group of us went to a restaurant near the Church of Today. I was sitting next to Theron. After some small talk, I said to Theron very slowly and calmly, "I need help!" By this time, I really did not know what was happening to me, and I gave up all hope of survival. It was so crazy that I no longer thought I was in my right mind and definitely did not know where to turn. Theron said nothing; he did not even ask me why I needed help. I was sinking fast, with all the pressure and things that were happening to me. I was in pure desperation, like I was going under the water for the third time and giving up all hope of survival. Theron and I agreed that I would come to him when I was ready to come to him; before that, I wasn't ready.

Called Carol, my spiritual psychic, and asked her about my impending trip to California. She told me that it would be all that I thought it would be and that a lot of healing would take place. She said she saw a white, blue, and green light, and that was good. Then she said she does not usually recommend a divorce but that Mike would not change. She said, "Don't get one because I am saying it though."

6

California Trip

IT IS NOW THE day of my trip to Fremont, California, Friday, November 19, 1999. I did not realize how important this day would be. In the airplane from St. Louis to San Francisco, I was reading the *Sedona Journal of Emergence*, minding my own business, when all of a sudden, I felt like I lit up the whole airplane, plus I felt limitless. So I thought, *Is this what it is all about? Do these people on the airplane see my light?* It was quite an experience, seeing as I had been in so much pain for so long.

When I arrived in San Jose, California, I told my sister Shirley about what had happened on the airplane. She seemed to pass it off, so I did as well. She had already arrived before me, from Salt Lake

City, Utah. During my eight-day stay, I slept like a baby, plus I was pain-free throughout. Sleep deprivation and pain were normal these days.

My brother Ron was having our parents over as well for Thanksgiving. It was the first time that I would be visiting his house, and it was beautiful. While driving in the car, Ron told me that what I was doing was dangerous. I told him that he did not know what I did, how could he say it was dangerous? Then I said that I could see how he would think that extending pure love would be dangerous. My son, David, is living with him and going to college. His bedroom is in the front of the house, and it looks like he has his own private apartment set apart from the rest of the house.

The next day, Ron, Shirley, and I went over to my brother Gary's house, which is a few minutes away. Gary and Mary are very estranged from one another… hardly ever in the same room together and communicating through their two boys. I asked Gary, "Where is Mary?" He said she was upstairs in her room. I headed upstairs, signaling to Shirley on the coach to follow. I just knocked on her door, not knowing what to expect. She was lying on the bed, fully dressed, doing some schoolwork. We came in and did some small talk, and then I just simply asked,

"Could Shirley and I pray over you?" Because she is oriental (from Taiwan), I did not know her religious or spiritual beliefs. I did not know how she would respond. She immediately was very receptive. The moment I sat on the bed, my hands started vibrating. I told Shirley that, and she said, "Let's go." We had her sit in a chair next to the bed. I started off as usual; Shirley really did the majority of it. But Shirley also told me that it was my deal, not hers.

From that moment on, during the rest of our stay, we saw a new Mary come forth. Four days into the trip, Ron came into the family room where Shirley and I were at and said, "I do not know what the two of you have done, but you have created a miracle." He could not believe the difference his relationship with Gary, plus Gary and Mary's relationship. By the time we left, a transformation unfolded right in front of our eyes. My mom asked me what I was doing. I said, "Tapping into love." That was the closest thing that I could come up with.

The ending of 1999 seemed like I was no further ahead, but I was sure I had progressed. I surrendered everything. I was ready to do Jesus's work.

New Year's Eve, Mike had to work nights. Again, I was feeling sorry for myself being alone. So

I decided to go out to the Church of Today. I had the best New Year's Eve I had ever had, and it was at church. The place was packed, the energy was incredible, and I didn't know anyone. Marianne did an outstanding job, and so did the choir. There was so much energy that you could not help but feel good. There had to have been at least two thousand plus people there. The choir sang songs throughout the millennium; each person sounded like the artist that sang the original. Even though you feel like you have not progressed in the dark night, your greatest progress is when it is the worst. At midnight, when the lights did not go out, we realized that Y2K probably wasn't going to take place. I think the reason that I thought I had not progressed is that I was in so much pain. This is more incredible than it sounds.

    I went into the backyard behind my garage. I faced the west, extending my arms out and willed myself to be on top of the tallest mountain. And I yelled at the top of my lungs, with every fiber and ounce of my being, with joy and ecstasy, "I fuckin' made it!" Please excuse my French. You cannot imagine how good that made me feel. I really felt like I was on top of the tallest mountain—which is probably hard for someone to understand. After spinning in hell for so long, it sure felt good to do that. You cannot imagine how good it felt unless you were I and had been through what I had been through. I never felt that I would live through it—physically, mentally or emotionally. It felt like the heavens gave me a standing ovation! A performance undoubtedly very hard to match! I called up Shirley in Utah immediately, telling her what happened. She really enjoyed the moment with me. She was always there for me (a much-needed soul sister).

So the next time a person comes along, feeling less than impatient and somewhat a pain in the ass, know that magnificence and elation is screaming to come out. Much thanks to Brian for all his reiki; he truly extended himself and co-created—for this I am grateful. (I cried when I said it because he was there during several of my lowest times.) For Theron, for putting up with my multitude and myriad of questions and for sticking up for me when Ingelor and Cindy were saying my voice was small. I do not know why, but I feel connected to him somehow. For Shearry, just for being so sweet. For Nancy, for helping me and giving me one of the best times during this garbage can—by telling me about my spirit guides. To Carol P., for giving me a reason to live, by telling me that I would be happy and a gifted healer—I felt like she pulled me out of hell by the head of my hair for that moment. To Carol, for giving me good reiki and to Steve, for the reading. I will continue to keep in contact with Brian, keeping him updated on what is happening.

I was told that I could not go to the meditation group anymore. This totally destroyed me; in fact, it took over my life and almost all my energy. How could these people whom I thought were so high-leveled do something like this to me? So much so that I called Brian and told him how he really hurt me. I was put on a rack for two days, from head to toe; I knew exactly how it felt. I went out into the backyard and offered up my thoughts of this meditation group to the Holy Spirit, and it finally went away. I felt like I needed them all so badly, and they were turning me away. The truth is I knew I was that bad. I knew in my heart that I should not be going there because I was that bad; I just did not want to admit it.

Thursday, February 17, 2000, I called up Carol P., and this is when she told me that I have a "golden cherub." She said she had never seen this before, that she was taking it as special and so should I. She also said that they wanted me to know. My spiritual path would be starting; she thought it will be healing. I told her that everything she said about California was true.

Now it was Thursday, March 2. I went to the Church of Today for a Deepak Chopra seminar. I went early enough so that I sat in the middle, right in the front of him, third row back. I decided that I would try to communicate telepathically to him. So I said to myself a few times that my name was Kathy Gotz and "I have something for you." Then I surrendered it because of the volume of people there. During the break, I was standing near the table where he would be signing books, when all of a sudden, he slightly nudged my shoulder. I thought, *Here is this enlightened man, invading my space*. Then I thought that maybe this would be the only contact I will have with him. I did not even bring my book in for him to sign because of the volume of people there.

As I was walking out, down the corridor of the sanctuary, Deepak got up to me and walked the rest of the way out shoulder to shoulder with me. As soon as he was walking with me, I knew then and there I had communicated telepathically. What impressed me the most was, I was sure a lot of people were trying to, and he listened to me. I told him I had something for him; I handed him "A Riveting

Exercise." Then I asked him if I could shake his hand. Told him that I had enjoyed his books and watching him on TV. Meanwhile, he said nothing to me. I drove home with my jaw dropped, wishing I had brought my book in for him to sign.

The next morning, when I was waking up, a voice said, "You did communicate telepathically." I had learned how to do it in the *Sedona Journal of Emergence*—a monthly magazine from Sedona, Arizona.

I decided that I would give Theron a call from the meditation group to see if I could go to counseling with him. I planned on never seeing him again because I planned on never going back to the meditation group. When I called him up, I asked him why he did not tell me what I was going through. He said I must not be through with the dark night of the soul if I was blaming him. He also told me that he had not been counseling me. I actually had a lot more to go. I told him that all the pressure was gone, but now I had all this pain. I felt like that I had tumors in my head, cancer in my throat, and God knows what to my stomach. I did not know what to do. He could not fit me in that day and said that we would meet on Tuesday.

7

Little Rose Chapel

MARCH 30, 2000, I went to the Little Rose Chapel on Mortenview in Taylor between Goddard and Wick. I walked into the attached store and looked around. I decided to go into the chapel, when Mother, the nun, asked me if I wanted to be prayed over. Then two other women joined in, Dian and Helen. They did a much-needed blessing. My husband had lunged at me the night before. He was sitting in the La-Z-Boy asleep, and I was lying on the couch. I asked him if he wanted to go to bed—that is when he lunged at me. I felt like I was destroyed at that very minute. I pulled the afghan over my head for protection, like that would have protected me. It is hard to believe that I could feel that way when he did not lay a hand on me. Theron told me later on that in a previous lifetime, I had been lunged at and, of course, killed. Everything seems to happen for a reason. It took me several days to feel okay again. The other two women left. Helen stayed seated. She asked me if I would show her what I do. I said sure and did. When I got through, she asked me, "Did anyone show or tell you what to do?" I said no, that I had made it up on my own. She told me that most of my pain was from stress. She told me that she did reflexology and that she did not take on new clients but she would take on me for free; plus, she told me that she would help me with my marriage.

I went to Helen for reflexology at her home in Southgate. She said she saw the desperation in my eyes, and that is why she decided to take me on. She also said that I was a mess, that most of my pain was stress-related. She started with my feet—I thought I was going to go through the ceiling. Everywhere she went was pure pain. I do not know what I would have done without Helen; she helped me in so many ways. I gave her a candle in a glass container. I will be doing things with Helen. She will be my teacher.

On that same day, I went back to the little Rose Chapel and brought Dian and Mother a candle for appreciation for them praying over me. I put my hands on the heart of Jesus, which is a statue. Dian had told me that something would happen, but she did not tell me what. The Jesus statue was in the corner on a pedestal, so I had to stand on my tiptoes and reach. All of a sudden, the statue became real. I was swaying with the statue. I could feel the breathing, and it no longer felt like a statue but now human. I gently slapped myself in the face, asking myself if I was dreaming or hallucinating. I knew all along that it was happening; I just had a hard time believing what I was experiencing. I went back into the store where Dian and Mother—who, by the way, is Dian's real mother and also a nun—were and asked them if that was what was supposed to happen? They said, "Yes." Dian said that I could also levitate. None of this was meant for magic or for people to come and witness magic. I guarantee you, if that is your motive, it will not happen. Dian also told me it only happened once where the statue became alive; again, I think this is to let you know that it is no magic show.

I went to St. Mary Magdalene's in Melvindale, Michigan, with Helen and Debby for the first time to go to the Light of Christ prayer group. They sang songs, and did a little talk on scripture, then you got to say something at the end in front of everyone. Helen knew I was having a very hard time with my husband. I was sitting next to Debby and asked Debby if it was okay for me to get up to tell my story. She said yes. I got up in front of the mike; the instant I did this, extreme pressure took over my entire body. Here I was, standing in front of fifty people whom I had never met before, telling them about my angry husband. It took an inner courage that I had never dreamt that I had. I couldn't believe that I could barely open my mouth. I just must have been barely audible. I know during that speech, I was in the dark night of the soul. Debby told me that I could not have done it in a better place, that now I would be bombarded with prayers. I cannot imagine what those people thought about me, at that moment. After that, we went into the prayer room, where two people prayed over me in tongues, plus English.

On Thursday, April 13, 2000, Theron came over to give me the second attunement into reiki. It was a most remarkable few hours. We discussed the Bauer house, Elaine and Sandy, the meditation group being a part of my dark night of the soul, and my experiences, like when my stomach felt like it was a cavity. Theron went around, clearing negative energy out of every room of the house. I showed him a picture of Freda, Mike's mother; he said immediately how bad she suffered. I gave him a blessing. He had helped me out so much that I wanted to give back to him. He told me that when I was through, he did feel a bright light. He talked to me about clearing fields and graveyards out west. While he was doing this, my floor in the corner of the kitchen, like a computer simulation, started moving a few inches up. This happened several times while he was talking. I do believe the spirits were letting me know that what he was saying was true. He told me that he had wished that he had seen it happen. It floored me—no pun on words intended.

I also went to the Little Rose Chapel for a healing mass that Helen had recommended. Mass was said out in the yard underneath a canopy. The sun was starting to set. Helen, who sat next to me, kept asking me if I saw the red all over the sky, to which I told her yes. After mass, they had three groups of two healers. I went to all three groups.

The first group was a man and woman. The man told me that I was Jesus's disciple and that it would be hard. I think he was referring to the dark night that I was still in. He told me that he saw me in Utah but did not know the duration of my stay. He also saw me being in Venezuela. I told him about Shirley's movie, about which he told me to practice discernment. The next set I went to was Judy and Tony. She told me that I was following in Jesus's footsteps and that I would suffer. I still think she was referring to the dark night again. She asked me how old I was. I said forty-eight. She told me I was a mess! I know she was referring to my organs and body on a whole, not my appearance. I was in a whole lot of physical pain that I thought was truly happening to me. I did not think I was going to live or be out of pain. Now looking back, I think it was all the dark night of the soul. She also asked me about what surgery I was having. I said I had my appendix out. She said no, some other surgery. Then I said the neck surgery that I did not have. She said yes and to not have it. I told her I did not plan on having it.

8

Dark Night of the Soul

This is how I got the book. I went into the bookstore at the Church of Today and asked if they had a paperback book that was very detailed on the dark night of the soul. A man walked up and went immediately to this book. I am very grateful for this book and would definitely recommend it for anyone going through it. I feel like a lot of people think they are going through it because of drama, trauma, or some sort of depression (divorce, death, or whatever). Mike asked me for a divorce with four small children, for whom I did not know how I was going to provide. I spent a whole year crying and having diarrhea. That was not the dark night; that was depression. I believe the prelude is the distorted faces of whichever parent or person you did not resolve your issues with when you were young. That purple weed was unique to me—clearing dimensions and different parts of me. The dark night of the soul is a total breakdown of the old self and a rebuilding of the whole divine-like self. The dark night of the soul is an "inventory of your part of the play."

I paced in my driveway, morning and night, offering my relationships up to the Holy Spirit for six months before I started the Dark Night. It was easy for me to do while reading a course in miracles. You could not help but want to make that a regimented part of your day. The course said if you do not see the innocence in your brother, you will not see the innocence in yourself. So it went hand in hand that I should want to offer my relationships up every day. There is probably a multitude of reasons that the dark night starts; that is just why mine started.

I have thought, how could I help someone if I knew they were going through the dark night of the soul? First of all, I would recommend walking every day, at least a couple of miles, which will help you in all areas mentally and emotionally. I would tell them that no matter what they think, they are never alone. I would tell them to get up every day, asking the Host of Heaven to assist you throughout the day. I would say that they are not going crazy and to try to go within and look at every part of them, accepting and loving every part of them. Usually, the right people will come along to assist. I would say to not give up hope. Last but not least, I would tell them to find a way to serve mankind. That will expedite their dark night, when they think of others. Mine, I gave blessings; it seemed like people would come my way. We are here on this planet to serve mankind. We just usually get caught up in materialistic whatever. Everyone else is us, so we are giving to ourselves. I felt like each person that I would pray over or extend I was literally healing a part of me.

Then I thought, would I have been better off had I known at the beginning that I was going through the dark night of the soul? I thought all along that I would have wanted to know. Actually, I was probably better off not knowing. You might say. It is that horrible and awful that it might be definitely to your advantage to not know. I probably figured it out six months after I was in it. I was at the Jean Houston seminar when she briefly tapped into it. In any case, I said to myself, "That is what I am going through." When I first figured it out, I thought the meditation group that I had gone to was laughing at me. Then I thought that they knew what you give out is what you will be getting.

You physically have problems as well. Besides your blood pressure, I had a lot of diarrhea. I forget where I read this—may have been the *Sedona Journal*—that you do not take medication to stop this. I do believe it is part of the cleansing. I thought my bowels would never make it through this. There are also times that the slightest thing will send you in a tizzy. It is greatly amplified, hard to explain. Also, one of the greatest things that you will have to do is let go of all the pain! You would think that you could easily release the pain and the hurt, the abandonment. But it is extremely difficult to let go. You think, why would you want to hang on to it? All of it is very hard for me to do.

You feel so alone and that no one is assisting you. Looking back, I had many angels sent my way. I definitely did not go through it by myself. The distorted faces spinning in hell, the void, are all a part of it. Mine was the worst because mine did all of that plus much pressure and pain. So much so I never thought I would live through it. I also spent my whole life, as far back as I can remember, wanting to die. I was told that that was my protection so that I could live. Well, it was the same thing through the dark night; I just wanted to die or I just figured I wasn't going to live anyway. Then there were times that I just plain do not have the words to describe. I had never taken drugs, and I wanted drugs. Theron told me that I did not want to be a zombie. And I said, "Yes, I do want to be a zombie." He simply told me that I would still have to go through it regardless. It is especially good if you go for a walk during those extremely desperate moments. This can go on for years, even a decade. You definitely want to expedite your process if you can. It is when you are helping others that you help yourself. Can't say it enough—"Go within." Everything begins and ends with you. Proportionately equal to what you go through—you have gifts and opportunities waiting for you on the other side.

9

Reiki

On Sunday, May 28, 2000, I went over to Mom and Dad's to do reiki on Mom. I was sitting in a kitchen chair, leaning over to do reiki on Mom, who was sitting in a La-Z-Boy in front of the room, when she realized that I was the mosaic charm that she had been given by God in her dreams some thirty years ago. She said I looked young, and it was the first time she saw it while looking at anyone. My mom had been talking about this dream for all these years. She thought that it might be my daughter, Crissy, but really did not think it was she. I never thought that it could possibly be me. At that time, she was given two other gift—a golden dress and she cannot remember the third—she thinks it is a pair of shoes.

On Thursday, June 14, 2000, I went to the Texas Steak House with Lupita, Joe, Kaye, and my mom. Lupita's cancer was back after two years. I asked my mom about giving her a blessing in the restaurant so they knew that I wanted to do it before we got there. There was no place else to do it, so here is how it went. I asked them all if they would participate because we are healers. I was sitting across the table from Lupita, and I took her two hands in mine. Then I asked if the rest would also take hands, that we all be joined. I did the blessing, and after I was through, Lupita said she felt the warmth from the top of her head to the tips of her toes. It felt really good to co-create and extend like that. It was so unusual for me to do something like that out in public; it was now becoming a regular occurrence.

Now I was at the Holy Ghost meditation group. I had wanted to help these people out with my message. I told the Holy Spirit that I would wait for a clue as to whether I should give my speech or not. So I told Mary about what happened with Lupita at the restaurant, and she told me that I should share it with all. I took it that that was my clue that I should give my speech. This is how it went:

I thanked Helen for guiding me to this wonderful group. Then I thanked my four teachers, Pat, Mary, Don, and Jerry. Then I said I would like to say a little bit about myself, not my family. This is how it went: I told the group that I was totally fear-based—that if I did not have something to worry about, I literally made something up, that I did not love and accept myself. And I told them that the world was going to hell; everything indicated that to me. Then two falls ago, because I had been reading *A Course in Miracles* every morning and night, I would go out and offer my relationships up to the Holy Spirit. Twelve months ago, I had the privilege of starting the dark night of the soul. Then last Thursday, my mom's friends were at a restaurant. I told them that her friend Lupita got cancer a couple of years ago. At that time, I sent her a card. I did not just sign my name; I wrote the card out. She was too sick to have visitors. She read my card every day, and that was literally what got her through the first episode. The doctors told her that he would buy her a couple of years but took a lot of her insides out and did not leave her much. Well, the cancer was back, so I gave her a blessing with all of us connected. After I was through, she looked at me and said, "I felt the warmth from the top of my head to the tip of my toes." So I paused and said slowly, pausing between each word, that I would bask, bathe, and teach Psalm 23 and I would walk in faith for the rest of my life.

When I sat down, Pat my teacher was sitting behind me. She tapped me on the shoulder. I knew that meant that she approved of what I had said. I gave much thought to this speech. I wanted to give them a message without any form of attack. I knew if I attacked, I would immediately lose ground. They believed in the scriptures of the Bible, even the fear. I just wanted to let them know, that Psalm 23 said it all. I was walking in faith, with courage, with Jesus at my side with his rod and staff.

The following week, at the Holy Ghost meeting, everything that was said was a reflection of what I had said the previous week. I was proud of myself, and I felt like it was a huge success. It was not my nature to get in front of people and give a speech like that. I waited for the Holy Spirit to let me know when I should give it. Then I released everything or surrendered everything. I had fully accomplished what I had set out to do.

One day, while I was at the Holy Ghost group, I was being prayed over by Jim and Carol—a man and wife. Jim always stands behind with his right hand on a slant above your head. Even though he did not touch me with his hand, I always felt the energy coming from it, very strongly. One time in particular, I felt like he was sucking my brain out through the top of my head. I think this happened several months after I was going to this group. I now think that the demons were sort of being pulled out through the top of my head by the Holy Spirit. I asked Mary what it could mean, and she said it was negativity being pulled out. Things often happened that I did not understand.

10

A Vacation out West

MIKE AND I ARE heading out west to the wild blue yonder. This is my trip also to waking up and remembering who I really was. We drove to Pike's Peak in Colorado Springs, Colorado. Mike was quite angry several times, so I thought I would give him some reiki in bed, hoping it would relax him. This was Sunday, July 2, 2000. I bought purple quartz from the summit – plus I took two rocks from the outside. It was sleeting, raining, cold, foggy, and windy while we were up there, and on the way down, it was extra crowded because they were holding races like the next day. So people were camping and getting ready for the event. I was all too happy to get out of there—seems like we had just made it before the congestion started.

As soon as we left Pike's Peak, we ate at a bar called Crystola. Mike had on his Detroit Edison cap on, when a man told us he was from Michigan. He sat around the corner near us. We struck a conversation. He said he lived in the area and such. Then I said we would be going to Sedona, that Mike wasn't on my path, but I was going there for spirituality. He said that if I liked that, then I should go Ojo Caliente, New Mexico. He said it was a spiritual place that was not well-known and not many people knew about it. He said four different waters came together—iron, lithia, arsenic, and soda. I figured I definitely wanted to give it a try.

Now we were in Monument Valley, Valley of the Gods, Utah. I saw Mexican hat rock—Mike pointed it out. He usually doesn't miss too much, even when he is driving. We stopped and ate lunch there. We ate some Mexican food at a little resort of sorts. They had a couple of gift shops with a river running alongside.

At Page, Arizona, we went to go for a swim in Lake Powell. We stayed at the comfort inn and could see Lake Powell from our room. There were lots of people, because it was the day before the Fourth of July. This was our second visit here, and Mike and I enjoyed it very much—enough to live there. I do not know what it would be like to live without grass and trees, though.

We went swimming in Lake Powell. There were a lot of people everywhere; it was hard to even find a parking spot. I decided to swim out to a little island nearby. I knew if worst came to worst that I could rely on floating. Floating doesn't take very much energy at all. Well, I definitely ran out of energy and asked a lady if I could hang on to her raft. Mike told me that I was on my own when I got back, because he would have never made it out there in time. The sun had started to set; it was most enjoyable.

The next morning, we toured Antelope Canyon—quite extraordinary. A guy walked you out to this little hole that you were supposed to descend with iron stairs. Never would I have believed that this existed. I said you expect us to go down into that. I didn't think I would fit let alone Mike. It was all quite breathtaking. Mike did not go through the whole thing, but I did. You went into some pretty small areas. We took a lot of pictures of both.

We spent the night in Page, Arizona. All Mike talked about was moving here. He said he had really liked it the first time we went here, and he did not change his mind. We just got out of the hot tub—great!

We were now on our way to Sedona, Arizona. Went through Flagstaff—it was big but not great. Loved Sedona and meeting Carol from the meditation group back in Michigan. She had since moved down here with her husband Steve. She took me to stores to look for my golden cherub. The Unity store lady told me that she had gotten three yeses, and that was the picture I was supposed to get.

On the way back, Mike and I both climbed Airport Vortex. Quite a view from the top—we took a couple of pictures. After that, we drove to Boynton Canyon, where I did the best I could by myself to climb. Then I decided that I wanted to visit this little Catholic Church nearby. I walked around the outside and inside, and that was it. As far as I was concerned, I would have liked to stay longer but figured Mike wouldn't. I think he liked swimming in the pool the most. As far as I was concerned, I went to the main vortexes. So we decided to leave the next morning.

I absolutely loved Ojo Caliente mineral springs—arsenic, iron, lithia, and soda. I went for a massage—it was expensive, ninety dollars apiece. We spent the night in our own little cabin. I got two rocks climbing the mountain behind it. I fell a couple of times and decided to quit going up. It gave me a nice and different view of the whole complex, one that I would never have had if I did not go up.

Tony Gold gave me a massage. His name is fitting because he is as good as gold. He started out by saying that he knew me in a previous lifetime. He said that when I left him in this previous lifetime, he said that he had been sad but I told him that I would be seeing him again. He said this twice. He told me that I was a master and that people did not know how to handle me. I do not know what he meant by that. Then he proceeded to tell me about everything that was wrong with me and that he was correcting it at that moment. He said that not only was he a massage therapist but a healer as well. He told me that I was healing and that I had a pink aura. I have not come across too many people that see auras. He said he knew I was a healer by my aura. He also said that when he saw me earlier in the day, he knew he would be giving me a massage that evening. I asked him if he was taking on my pain. He told me he was but that it was okay. He told me that he had nine brothers and five sisters. He said I had to kneel down every night and say the rosary with a passion. He said his father was dead at ninety-three and that his mother was still alive. When she prayed, her prayers were answered.

So I asked him to ask his mother if she would pray for me. He told me he would. Many thanks to Tony—it was one of the most enjoyable, pleasurable moments in my life. He called me his sister, which was the highest compliment that he could have given me. He also told me something about my relationship getting easier, whatever that meant. He said something about a yellow house; he first thought an apartment, with a tricycle in front. I do believe that was my mobile home in which I lived in Belleville, Michigan, for the first four and half years of our marriage.

When I left Tony, I went into the mineral water and said to the people that I was in heaven! A man spoke up and said, "I thought we were in New Mexico." Then he told me he could see I was in heaven by the look in my face. Tony also told me that spiritual people did not come from Michigan and asked if I knew any. "Yes, of course, I do plenty." His hands were also hot. He said I was scattered and that now I was more focused. While I was there, the name of my book came to me: *Fake It, It Will Come.* Tony also told me to look up in the sky. It did not matter if my eyes were closed or open. I could see it as a TV and change the channels if I did not like it. He also gave me some exercises to do daily. It only took a few minutes a day to do. I do believe that when Carol told me about the pink light she saw, she was talking about my experience with Tony. The whole trip was worth being in Ojo, Caliente. Thanks to that woman and man right near Pike's Peak for recommending that incredible experience. We headed for home.

11

My Trip to Utah!

Our extended family went camping at Jordonelle's campground in the mountains of Utah. I decided to go for a walk with Larry along the boardwalk, where there is a river. Larry had listened to me about my dark night of the soul, so now he said it was his turn. He talked about all the pain he had experienced with his dad's death. Then he also talked about his wife, Shirley, how she wasn't there for him at his dad's death and about their relationship. I truly felt his pain. I kept saying to myself, "This is an illusion, it is not real." I was hoping that the river would take the pain with her from us.

With great trepidation, I asked Larry if he would like to see what I did. First of all, I told him that I was afraid to ask this. Larry is an elder in the Church of Jesus Christ of Latter-Day Saints and gives blessings himself. Fear of being critiqued was definitely on my mind. We were off the beaten path, but I think Larry was afraid that someone would see us. Nevertheless, I proceeded. So I basically did my usual deal. I also said all the spirits and entities that had loved Larry, especially Ralph and Phyllis, his deceased parents. As soon as I called in everybody, I had my eyes closed, looking away from the sun; I saw a little circle of bright light. It was like a blank black painting where the sun would be to the left. After I was through, I drew the reiki symbols on Larry's forehead and heart. Then I stood behind him and gave him a little reiki to his head. When we got up to leave, he said, "That was beautiful, but don't tell Shirley." Then as we walked a little further, he said, "That was so beautiful you can tell Shirley." Women do not pray over people in the Mormon Church; only men do. Larry said after what he had gone through, he would accept good wishes from anyone. He also asked me if anything had happened. I told him about the bright light. He said that must have been the sun. I said I was not facing the sun. I asked him if anything happened to him. He said the rose was his mother's face. He said more happened but did not share it with me.

The rest of the evening, I went into the tent to relax, while the rest sat at the campfire. Shirley said that Larry was euphoric for the rest of the evening and that he told her how beautiful the blessing was. I was happy to extend to Larry. I do feel close to him. I was exhausted from the stress that had taken place.

What Carol P. saw when she was giving me a psychic reading was red all over Utah. Was Utah on fire? There was smoke all over the valley because the surrounding mountains were on fire. She also said it could be anger too. Was I going to anger? There were a couple of flare-ups, but that was it.

Saturday, August 5, 2000, my brother-in-law David and his son Shaun and I set out to climb the back of Timpanogas. You could see the shack from off the deck behind his house. He mentioned it a couple of days earlier, and I told him he was out of his gourd. When he mentioned it again, I took that as my clue that it was part of my growth. The day before we were going, I spent it in fear. I thought that I was afraid of heights, plus how would I physically take on this trek? Nevertheless, our journey began. They carried everything, even my camera, plus water. I was doing a good job carrying myself.

    I struggled with my breathing all the way up and had to sit down regularly, one thing they recommended not doing. David and Shaun were very patient with me, seeing as they were at least six feet and I was only five feet two inches. They let me lead so I would set the pace. I am sure they struggled going so slow. I told David that I would be writing a book, so at the beginning, he told me to feel the experience. I thought that was thoughtful of him. My left sides hurt pretty much all the way up; my knees hurt pretty much all the way down. About three miles into the trip, we ran across a moose with her baby near the path. A few people ahead of us had also stopped. Finally I said, "Let's go" to the man in front of me, and he went, and I followed. Nothing happened; they kind of continued on their way. Not too much further, we came across a llama, this time resting right in the middle of the path that we scooted by. Again I said to the man in front, "Let's go." He went walking right next to me and I followed.

    The hiking never seemed to end. The further we got up there, we saw several varieties of brilliant colors of wild flowers. I was mesmerized by the amazing, iridescent brilliance of purple, red, yellow, and white, all standing out to be gazed upon. About three fourths of the way up, I decided that not only was I going to sit down, but that I was going to lie down as well. I put my hat over my eyes, trying to be in the moment. David walked up and said, "Kathy, look up." I tipped the brim of my hat to David taking my picture. Once we got to the saddle, we rested. David took my picture overlooking Salt Lake City; it was an awesome view. Looking up the saddle climb, it looked scary to me, so I said to David, "Be honest, just how scary is it?" He said, "Not any worse than what we have just come through." I didn't believe him because my twin sister, Carol, had told me how afraid she was, doing the whole saddle. So I asked a few people that were descending. I got "Not bad" from some, and a girl said differently, that she was afraid.

The mountains off in the distance were incredible, in a mystical grayish blue color. Even though I was in pain the whole trip, I knew it was a wonderful growing experience. One of the difficulties was walking on all the rocks. I had on a good pair of Reebok tennis shoes, that fared fairly well, and so did my feet from blisters.

When we could see the shack off in the distance, we stopped to drink some water. I drank with gusto. David said, "You will get sick." Instantly I felt like my head was spinning and that I was going to throw up, pass out, and got pins and needles throughout my body. I think I was hyperventilating. Just lay back on stones, so it wasn't too comfortable, but I had no choice. I told David, "I couldn't go any further." About ten minutes later, I got up and said, "Let's go to the shack." As soon as we got to the shack, I signed the book, on which there was only one space left, at the very bottom of the back of the last page. Plus we took a couple of pictures. I did not want to stay any longer because I knew the length we still had to go. It amazed me that I no longer had my fear of heights. None of it bothered me. I thought that maybe going down and looking down would be different, and it wasn't. I remembered that I wanted to get a rock at the top—too late. David pointed one out, and I took his suggestion. It was little and easy to carry.

Met three old men at the top—say about, seventy—and was amazed at their agility and speed. They had climbed several mountains together before Timpanagos. Lots of young girls climbed as well. Saw a few old women; all of it surprised me.

It was quite an undertaking at best. I do not think it would have been so bad if you did not have to do it all in one day. Nine miles up makes nine miles down, no matter how you look at it. Somehow you think that it will be less going down; you just know it. Even though we hardly talked on the trip, I bonded with David and Shaun. It is hard to explain that type of bonding, but our spirits merged. It took us six hours to ascend and four hours to descend. I think the only reason I made it is no one coaxed me into going or not going. They only said when I was ready to turn around, they would. In their not coaxing or commenting, it gave me the courage to do it.

I had climbed the front of Timpanagos when my daughter Crissy was five months old. Larry, Shirley's husband, dropped us off at the front and left us. We could see little specks of people off in the distance, never dreaming the walk would be that long. When we got up to the caves, they were cold. I had nothing to wrap around my baby, and someone offered me something to wrap her up in, which I thought was nice. My mom, who was quite heavy, made this climb, and in my wildest dreams, I do not know how she did it. We were able to drink water while we were in the cave. Did the best I could to feed Crissy out of a cup. My brother Greg had pushed her all the way up and all the way down. I was doing good to get my body up there and back.

Doing this trek reminded me of the dark night of the soul. I told David, as we were descending, that I wanted to jump off. He said, "Do you really?" I said, "Yes, to get out of pain!" When you are in the worst of the dark night, you do want to die, just to get out of pain. So it was a process. Your greatest progress is when you are at your worst; however, you do not think you are progressing. The whole thing reminded me of Shirley MacLaine's also, because of her treks that I have read about. Plus I wore a similar hat that she wears.

The next day, Larry came to pick me up with Shirley and Shara. I was in so much pain I could hardly walk. I slept very little; I did not even take aspirin. I took a hot bath, but it wasn't enough. The four of us were en route to Shirley's house, when all of a sudden, we saw the most awesome, breathtaking, ineffable rainbow unfolding before our eyes. I had never in my life seen anything remotely close to this, and Shirley said she hadn't either. It was a little ways up in front of the left mountain range and grew to the right mountain range, fanning out like a fan in an incredulous, panoramic orchestration. I wanted Larry to stop the car to take a picture. My camera was in the trunk; otherwise I would have stuck it out the window. He was mad at Shirley, and I didn't put my foot down, should have. It was so brilliant; I wonder who else saw it. Was it just for us? It would be embedded in my mind forever. It was magnificent in every way. I do believe that a rainbow means creativity. What will we be creating? Shirley felt that the clouds were trying to say something as well.

Shirley and I went to visit Edie Roberson at her house in Salt Lake City. Although her home was in the city, you would have thought otherwise. First of all, she had her doors wide open for anybody to walk in. The house was old, but she was restoring and redoing a lot. Although you could tell she was an older lady, she looked very good. She taught the Avatar, plus she was a three-time wizard. Not sure what a three-time wizard was. Told her that I had just been through the dark night but that I definitely had a lot more to go. She congratulated me when we were getting ready to leave. I said, "For what?" She said, "For going through the dark night of the soul." She was the only one that had. We talked for an hour or so in her courtyard. That is where it seemed like you were out in the country. In my opinion, she had the ambiance of the country, right there in the city. It was a joy meeting her. I hope I do again someday.

Today I am leaving SLC; it seemed like I was gone forever. First, we went to Tanner's flat campground. Then on our way to Snowbird, we had coffee and bought a couple of things. I had been there before but enjoyed going back. All in all, I have probably been to Utah on twelve different occasions. On the way back from Snowbird, we stopped along the side of the road and climbed this huge boulder that was on the banks of the stream going down the mountain. We both sat down, joining hands, and had an awesome meditation. We both felt good about saying prayers for friends and family and giving thanks for everything we could drum up. I really enjoyed my trip to Utah and being with my family. I also really enjoy my sister Carol. We do not have much in common because she is Mormon and definitely not on my path. Plus she, of course, does not approve of reiki metaphysical anything, so just everything that I represent. But she respects me, and we have more or less agreed not to talk about that aspect of our lives. We were so close the first twenty years of our life. She was my buddy in every way.

On Friday, September 8, 2000, I am now up north, by myself. I have the electricity and water turned on and the fire going, and it is an awesome evening. I missed Mike as soon as I got up here, just looking around, looking at our creation. It is incredibly peaceful, but will I be able to stand being with me for four days? I am looking forward to wondrous possibilities and probabilities. Nobody understands how much I miss the meditation group. I think that Theron is fed up with me, and I can't say that I blame him. It came to me that the reason I enjoyed this property so much was I have been on it for many lifetimes. I said, "In this exact spot?" They said, "Yes." I do believe that it was Gray Eagle that told me this, and it is sure my heaven.

12

Baby

This took place in the summer of 1988 or thereabouts. One day, Eric brought home a baby robin. I told him that it would not live and to take it back where he found it. Well, we just couldn't help but give him some food. So I got a piece of wheat bread and poured a little milk over it and put it in the microwave for a few seconds to warm it up. He gobbled it up. We kept him in a deep bucket with a towel on the bottom of it. Then he got tired of being in the bucket after a couple of days, and I set him out on a branch of my shrub outside our front door. He would just stay there, and we would feed him and give him a little water from a small cup for him to drink. Never before had I dug for worms or held one, but now I was doing both. I would sit on my front porch and talk to the baby robin, which I called Baby, and he would just listen to me. I was his mom for all intents and purposes.

Now, by the fourth morning, I knew Baby would live because on the other attempts I had tried, they always started not eating or moving too much. This one showed all the signs of life. So after Baby being on the bush during the day and the bucket at night for a week and a half, he wanted to check out more of his world and wander. I had a couple of big shrubs behind my house, and Baby would stay there, out of the sun and hidden somewhat from predators.

One day, Aunt Barb and Uncle Fred came over for a visit. I wasn't home, and Mike was working on an engine in the garage. So Barb took a seat near the family room door wall. She heard a bird and looked over to see Baby at the screen on the floor in the family room, trying to get out. She said, "Mike, are these birds supposed to be in your family room?" He says, "Yes, they are." Well Aunt Barb was a little surprised. When I got home, I brought Baby out on my finger and told Aunt Barb about him.

Our dog Higgins would go up and nudge Baby and bark at it, plus it had plenty of opportunity to eat Baby and didn't. One time in particular, we left Baby on the window ledge in a bowl while we were gone. Baby flew down to the floor, they were together for a while with no one around, and Higgins didn't eat Baby. The barking Baby would ignore. Higgins would not care about Baby trying to fly on his back, but Baby kept trying. It was so funny, watching Baby trying to fly on Higgins's back.

One day, Karen, my daughter, had Kristi, her friend from school, spend the night. They were sleeping bags on the family room floor. Baby was in a bowl with a towel in it on top of the stereo. That is where Baby spent the night. I got up and was watching Baby watch when Kristi would be opening her eyes. Just as she opened her eyes, Baby flew down right in her face and looked her eye to eye. Could you imagine waking up to a baby robin staring you in the face?

So now Baby decided that he wanted to check out even more of his world by going in the surrounding yards. I would go in the backyard and call Baby, and he would come walking through the fences over to me. Baby was so cute. Sometimes he would not hear us because he would be too far away, so we would have to go in the surrounding yards to find Baby. I would walk around and show Baby to the neighbors. The lady across the street's daughter, Joyce, came down to her house and asked her, "Whose bird is that?" She said, "Oh that is Kathy's bird across the street."

One morning, Crissy my daughter went out to dig Baby a worm behind the garage. She dug up one worm and decided to leave. Baby said, "That not enough," and flew on the shovel, saying he wanted more. Baby would fly at the front door when he wanted to get in. He would follow me around the house with the pitter-patter of his little feet hitting the kitchen floor. Kids in the neighborhood would come over and bring worms. My father-in-law would stop over, dig a worm in the backyard, leave, and not say anything to us.

This went on for a few weeks when finally I saw a mother robin fly down with a worm in her mouth and give it to Baby. I decided that we should let Baby go and be in his own environment. I thought to myself that I would not see Baby again. After Baby had been gone for two nights now, and I was cleaning out my waste paper basket in the backyard, I heard what I thought sounded like Baby. So I called Baby. He answered again. This went on a few times, and I stopped and decided to look up in the Maple Tree located in the adjacent yard. I could not see him. So as I was bringing my eyes down, I spotted Baby sitting on the fence looking right at me. My eyes went wide, and my mouth dropped. I was so happy to see Baby. He came to me, and I brought him in the house and set him on the floor. He immediately lay down; we petted him and lovingly talked to him.

Then I had to go to the store, so I set Baby on the speaker in the bowl, where he went to sleep. When we arrived home, Baby woke up, and I took him out to show a few more neighbors. Baby took off, and that's the last I saw of Baby. Baby brought a lot of enjoyment into our lives. It was a very special moment for me, one I will never forget.

13

Beginning of My Marriage

DURING THE FIRST YEAR of my marriage, when I was twenty-one, I started having what I thought was a heart attack. In fact, I went to the emergency room. This scared me very badly; I did not know what to make of it. The doctor in the emergency room told me that it was a muscle spasm and to go to my regular doctor. When I went to see my regular doctor, he told me it was a muscle spasm and that it was caused by stress. Each and every time I had one, I would get more afraid, and that would cause more pain. It was definitely a catch-22, and I did not know how to stop it. He gave me heat treatments, and after a couple of months, they stopped. I believe that that is how stressed out I was during my first year of marriage. It was a very frightening experience. I did not even know I was stressed out.

When I was getting ready to have my fourth child, I decided that my first three births were too difficult and I did not want that for my fourth. The truth was I was afraid to go through it. So I decided that I would take the three older children downstairs to play while I paced in the basement, thinking on just how I wanted my birth to go. My husband was working afternoons, so I did this in the evenings. Plus it was winter and not conducive to going outside anyway. I practiced and envisioned in my mind over and over again just how I wanted my birth to be. This is how it went. I decided I wanted three contractions and I would have to leave to go to the hospital. I decided that as soon as I got to the hospital, the doctor would tell me that the baby was ready to be born. So in other words, the baby would be born a half hour after I got to the hospital. I had been in labor for three days with my first, so this would be too good to be true.

After Mike and I got to the hospital, Mike said to the nurse, "What about my wife?" She came back and told him that I was in the delivery room and that he better hurry and get a gown on if he wanted to be in there. Mike got in just as the head was crowning and proceeded to pass out. (We had rushed so fast that he had not had time to eat the spaghetti dinner he had made after we had just sat down to eat.) The doctor and I both watched as he was standing at my side and plummeted backward. There was nothing he could do; he was busy stitching me up. He had to be put on a gurney and lay there for a half hour, so he could not call anyone to tell him or her we had a baby boy.

That delivery went exactly as I had planned to a T. I had had exactly three contractions, and I had told Mike it was time to go to the hospital. Luckily, he had not given me a hard time by telling me that I was rushing. I remember driving to the hospital, and the little deviations in the road killed me. As soon as the doctor came in, he told me to tell him when I was ready to bear down. As soon as he left, I called. I marveled at the fact that I had orchestrated exactly what I had wanted and got it.

As I said, Eric was my fourth child. They did not lie any of my children on my stomach. I wished I had asked—too afraid to, I guess. While I was on the delivery table and Eric was in the bassinet near me, I had this special feeling come over me that I had not felt with the other children. I thought I had named him appropriately because Eric means "leader." I figured he would be a leader of good and would be doing God's work. This same feeling happened again two months later when I got him baptized. And again I did not experience this with my other children. I have told him about this, but he does not want to hear it.

Art Linkletter had a show, *Kids Say the Darndest Things*. This was brought to mind thinking about my son Eric. When Eric was starting kindergarten, I was getting ready to take him somewhere in the car, when this is what he said to me: "Mom, don't you think it is about time to teach me how to drive?" I started laughing, like it was a prerequisite for all kindergarten children to know how to drive. That was a hoot! At that time, he also stood up as a ringbearer in Mike's brother's wedding. When it was time to return the tux, Eric asked if he could wear it to kindergarten. He looked so cute decked out in his tails and matching the other men standing up. I also thought he thought he was a stud muffin in his tux. He was so little and adorable.

Right after we had gotten back from one of our trips out west, I had what I think was a mini breakdown. Luckily it did not last long. At twelve o'clock at night, I rode to the Detroit River on my bike. The best way I could describe it is it was like I was in a drunken stupor, only I had nothing to drink. I looked straightforward and down. Cars were honking their horn at me. I paid them no mind. It was like I was in another dimension or like in a tunnel. I thought, *Nobody cares about me, not even complete strangers*. I did not care if I lived or died. I rode back home after I got there and went directly to bed. The next morning, my friend Joan called me up and said, "Kathy, I was so worried about you all night. I wanted to call you all night." At that very moment, I knew God cared. It meant a lot to me that the heavens let me know that they cared. I do not know if I was catatonic, closing down, breaking down, or what. I have never experienced anything like that before or since. I think of that prayer "Footprints," and I think Jesus carried me.

14

Trouble with My Dad

I HAD A GREAT deal of trouble with my dad. It was an ongoing and never-ending struggle. I wasn't the only one in the family that had this problem with him. I have seven brothers and sisters, all of which struggled with him. A few of them decided when they became adults not to have anything to do with him. I tried over and over again, but it was madness. He would push your buttons. You would attack back. Then he would attack. He would tell you, though, that he never attacked, that he was an innocent victim and persecuted unjustly. Iouya and the group consciousness told me that in a previous lifetime, I did a really good job of pushing buttons and gave them the gifts. She used those words—*pushing buttons*.

    Thinking back to Christine's graduation from high school. My dad, mom, and I are at the restaurant. I tell my dad I have her enrolled in Henry Ford Community College. He says, "you've got to send her to the University of Michigan." I explain that she has an average grade point average and that they would laughed at me and also it was too expensive. He said that it was cheap. He would not let it go. I begged him to stop. Finally, I said, "read my lips, they would laugh at me." Then a man comes over looking at my dad and says, "Excuse me sir. I could not help but overhear your conversation. I am a U. of M. scout and you sir, are wrong." I brought my arms up in elation. My dad proceeded to throw his coffee in my face and then immediately threw his water in my face with disgust. I then threw my water in his face. Maybe I could have taken the coffee, but the water was too much. My mom immediately went out to the car. I left in a hurry and went out to their car and opened the door. She was in the front seat. I told her I never wanted to see him again as long as I lived, went to shut the door, hitting my head in the process, and cried all the way home.

One day I was visiting my dad. He was sitting on the love seat and I was in his La-Z-Boy across from him. He is not mad at me. Out of the blue he says, "You were vile all the while you were growing up." I was in shock! I took a moment and said to myself, *Holy Spirit, what do you want me to do now?* I know without asking it was to give love. (I know this is an untrue statement). So I went over and gave him a hug and said "I love you," and cried all the way home.

So you can see that the course in miracles was truly meant for me. I was a "classic case." Now is the time to tell you how I came upon the course. I had read Marianne's book *Return to Love*; she had talked about the course in miracles in it. I thought at that time that it was just that, a course that she had taken. One day, November 28, 1998, my sister Shirley called me up from Utah. She had been reading the course for a couple of months. She said, "You must drop everything right now and go out and buy *A Course in Miracles*—no author. It is a hard-covered blue book that cost like thirty dollars." So I did just that. The first bookstore I went to had it. The course is not for everyone. I know people that just could not get into it. I knew it wasn't an accident or coincidence that I was reading this book.

From that day on, I read with a passion and vengeance. I read almost all day, every day. I simply could not take it in fast enough. You could spend an hour just reading one paragraph, for there is a lot to digest. I just read and read. Some of it, I will have to admit, I read, and when I got through, I did not know what I read. Then other times, it literally came down like lightning bolts. I felt like I was in the college of evolution. I had not gone to college at all, but I sure felt like it while I was reading it. I want to say that it took me about four or five months to read the first seven hundred pages. There are three books in the one book. After that, I read the third book. It is a manual for teachers, which is where I read about giving blessings. It said that the words were not important; what you did was not important. What was important was making up what felt good to you and extending love. It did set the tone and the ambiance—just use your imagination. All that is important is that you are pure and that you trust. We are all healers. You can do it with a smile, a kind word, and gentle touch!

Before I started reading *A Course in Miracles*, I read spiritual, metaphysical books for, like, fifteen years. I had no desire to read a novel of any kind. I wanted to devour everything I could get my hands on, from near-death experiences to psychological books. Although these books were certainly great, I just could not seem to implement what I had learned. So although I was growing in knowledge, doing was a different matter. The course gives you the blueprint on what you must do. It truly is what the title says. It is a course in miracles!

In my particular case, because I did not resolve my issues with my dad, I married my dad. Both of them were controlling and very hard to deal with and manage. I do believe that I projected a lot of my problems with my dad onto my husband, Mike. I was afraid of both. Both were big men, and I was a little woman. Mike's masculinity was what attracted me to him; that was the very thing that I began to hate. Throughout most of my marriage, I was emotionally divorced. I felt like Mike had disdain and contempt for me, and I did not know how to change it. What you fear, you attract! I was bankrupt; I did not have anything to give.

So this is how it all started. Reading the course and going out, probably morning, noon, and night, offering up all my fears to the Holy Spirit. I had gone to a Catholic school and really did not know what the job of the Holy Spirit was. During this time, I could not talk to the Holy Spirit enough. Never did

I think that that would cause me to start the dark night of the soul. Truly, if I had known what I was going to be in for, I do not know if I would have done it. I do consider it a privilege to awaken and remember who you really are. Every part of me was dying. Before I started the dark night, I felt like all my organs were closing down.

It is very important for you to go through the dark night while you are in body form. I guess you can go through when you are a spirit, but it is far more productive because you can rectify by loving and forgiving the people you have karma with. *The Dark Night of the Soul* is not an easy read because it was written long ago in that lingo. But because I could relate to it so much, I understood what it was saying. That book was the main reason I was able to let the meditation group go, knowing that they only played the parts. In fact, I should be grateful for the gifts that they gave me.

15

Forgiving

WITH MY EXPERIENCE DOING reiki on people, I always tell them that they have to forgive. Most people say they have already forgiven or they have no one to forgive. I thought the same thing. I thought that I had forgiven my dad and my husband, and likewise, I had no one to forgive. Until I started reading *The Course in Miracles*, that is! Actually, it was going through the dark night of the soul that I realized I had toyed with the situation. I did not face me, every facet of me. I was still the victim; they, of course, were the perpetrators. When you are at the breaking point, you finally surrender out of pure desperation. Then you realize the importance, the value, of this gift of walking consciously.

Until then, you are asleep. This doesn't mean you are perfect. It simply means that regularly, you offer relationships or whatever up immediately, that you take a minute to act instead of react. Last, but not least, you look inside you, concentrating on you and not outside of you. This also means you love yourself unconditionally. I think we are the hardest on ourselves. There is an old saying: "We are our own worst enemy."

This is my perception, but I do believe that I was tested throughout the dark night. I do believe that I was given opportunities to either act in faith or fear. Fear is anything that isn't love. Of course, I cannot prove this; I just feel that that is what happened. An example—one day, I saw an ant on the landing. I killed it. The next day, I saw just one ant on the landing; this time, I picked it up and carried it outside. My perception is that they did not want me to kill the ant. Then I was just awakened out of a sound sleep. My daughter, Karen, who did not live with us, was screaming in my right ear, "Mother, mom," and "Mom, mom…" in a panicked voice. It seemed to go on forever; I thought I could either act in faith or fear. I chose faith and stayed in bed with hands out, sending my daughter love. I wanted to jump out of bed and call her, but it was 12:00 p.m.

You won't believe this—I went back to sleep. I wasn't able to talk to her till a few days later, for she had left the next morning for up north for the weekend. I left a message on her machine for her to call me. When she returned, she called. I asked her if she had anything peculiar happen to her last Thursday at twelve o'clock. She thought for a moment and said yes, that she was having a dream that her dad was being killed or she was witnessing his death in any case. She said it also seemed to go on forever, and she was calling for me. In my whole life, I had never experienced anything like that. I was tapping into her reaction to her dream. In any case, it definitely could have been a fearful situation, to which I reacted in faith. There were other situations as well; they cannot infringe on your free will. Always it is your choice.

One evening—I believe February 2000—I was by myself and going to go on my regimented walk. I put my Sony Walkman on to do my couple of miles. While I was putting my shoes on and getting ready, this incredible feeling came over me. It is hard to explain, but I knew I had made it. In fact, I said just that: "I made it." I did not need the response; I knew that I had made it. So my entire walk was spent in elation. I twirled and spun, basking in my own light. As soon as my walk ended, so did the elation, but I will never forget about it. I passed off the airplane experience and Carol telling me that I had reached a certain light and I would not be going back. But I was not going to pass this off. The spirit world—or you could say the heavens—communicates with you directly.

If you do not have someone to talk to, a portable radio is great substitute. You can put your favorite station on or listen to a cassette or CD.

On November 11, 2000, I was at my mom and dad's house looking out their front door, when all of a sudden, I saw a perfect stickman shaped in cirrus clouds—the head at the west and the feet at the east. You could see the whole shape of the body. It was perfectly detailed in every way—the face was even filled in. I do not know why I decided to tilt my head to the right so that I could marvel at what I was seeing. There was no other cloud around. Had I not tilted my head, I would have missed it as well.

I also went to the first sweat lodge that I had ever gone to. Anthony, who was orchestrating the performance, did an in-depth ceremony before we entered the man-made lodge—made out of layers and layers of blankets. I truly have never sweated so much in my life. I flung my hand; to my amazement, sweat flung from all my fingers. It was a neat experience, which I would like to do again sometime. It is supposed to resemble when we were in the womb. A while later, Theron told me that he got that my dad would be dying. When he told me that, I decided henceforth I would only give my dad love. Whenever I left their house, I would give him unconditional love, and he returned it. I told my mom that I showed her how I loved Dad and that she should too. When I told her about his dying, she said that she was releasing some of her perceived pain. So I am grateful for those clouds for sending that message because it helped me to grow up. When I loved my dad unconditionally, I loved myself unconditionally. It's called growing up.

It was my father-in-law's seventy-fifth birthday, and I got it in my head that I would like to go over there and give him a blessing, if he would let me. I called up Estelle and asked her if she thought that would be a good idea. Estelle was his wife, but they did not live in the same house. She knew about my metaphysical path and agreed with it; besides, she loves me. She told me that I had nothing to lose and, by all means, to give it a try. So I called him up on the phone and asked if I could come over.

He told me to go ahead. For me to entertain the thought of going over to his house and being with him by myself is incredulous. I walked in the door and sat down at the kitchen table and said, "I am not going to beat around the bush, and I am going to get right to the point." I calmly said, "I blamed you for my husband being so angry. I was so afraid of him, and I wanted a divorce my entire married life. I apologize for blaming you." All the while I was saying this, I was pretty near tears; it was extremely arduous at best. He also said that he was sorry.

I told him that for his grandchildren to be healed, I proposed that he allow me to give him a blessing. He said he has his own way of praying. I said that was okay. I told him all his grandchildren were angry and asked if he wanted this perpetuation to continue. I told him we could end the anger. So I told him that I had to go over to my parents' and got up to leave. He said, "Go ahead with the blessing." I was shocked. So I went ahead and did my usual blessing. When I got through, I asked if I could draw the reiki symbols on his forehead. He said yes. I do believe at that time, he would have taken anything I had to offer. I gave him a hug and told him I loved him. I went home and spent the rest of the day crying. I was happy I did that before he died. I believe I was successful because I was calm, didn't attack, and presented my case with sincerity and passion. Estelle could not believe that I had stood up to this man successfully. She said she had never known anyone to do that.

This is a little hard to explain, but I will do the best I can. I do not know how long this lasted, but I would say maybe several months. I would go outside to meditate and close my eyes—I would see billowing, puffy, tinted-in-red clouds, which would sometimes be flowing over, like a waterfall. Other times it would be going into a circle in the center or two circles horizontally and symmetrically centered, which only happened once for me. I saw this often and many, many times—even throughout the day. I think it could be that I was burning karma. Although I am not sure why this happened, if I was burning karma, I sure burned a lot of karma. It has ceased doing this, but it happened on a regular basis. It was like a still moving picture—very unusual. Never saw anything like it in my life. I did burn more karma every now and then.

On December 28, 2000, I read in the *Sedona Journal* that you should balance the north, south, east, and west in you, plus you could ask them to share their wisdom. So I had been going out in the snow, facing each direction and touching my forehead to the ground in humbleness. I had done this several days in a row previously. As I was in my driveway facing the sun, which is not too bright at this time of year, closing my eyes, I saw a sword trimmed in black with a long, narrow blade pointing toward the ground and a detailed handle that was brilliant, iridescent indigo. Nothing else was in the picture but this sword. Then I saw two more in succession—same thing, indigo. After that, I saw a mint-green one, which I think was for my health. Right after that, I saw a circle trimmed in black, brilliant indigo, that was like the sun rising. I actually saw it rising without moving my head. I believe the three indigo swords were my mental, emotional, and psychological, all being cut and set free. The circle represented me being unbound and set free. I learned that my karma with my dad and Mike are fulfilled... that is why I was told they died.

I knew as I was seeing these symbols that there was great significance but did not know what they could stand for while I was seeing them. I ended the year 2000 being set free. So in other words in a metaphysical state, since I was starting out the new century being set free. Could you possibly imagine how good that made me feel? I felt like I worked so hard taking on each step with courage, tenacity, perseverance, and relentlessness.

I asked a few people what that could mean. Theron said the sword was for cutting and power; I surmised the rest. I was lying in bed, finding it difficult to go to sleep, when I came up with the answer. I have seen other shapes doing the same thing, and I still don't have a clue what they are. I have surmised that they might be gifts and that I do not have to know what they are. I do believe that there is a purpose in everything that we do and what happens to us. There are no coincidences or accidents. Everyone that comes in our path was intended to come in our path.

I cannot remember when I stopped having my flying dreams. I do believe that it was before the dark night of the soul started. I know I said I did not remember my dreams at the beginning of my book. You have to know that those flying dreams went on for about six years, and it was like breathing for me—second nature. I would go to bed, and on a regular basis I would be flying. Always, there were people on the ground, standing around, not paying any attention to me. I was impressed, but nobody on the ground was. Sometimes I would be in a gymnasium flying around the beams. Sometimes it would be dark and the streetlights were on and I was zooming around, nobody commenting or caring. I felt all along that it meant something but did not know what. I did not have a backpack on; I just flapped my arms. Sometimes I would wake up during this dream and go back to sleep to continue my flying experience. I think that maybe I was getting ready to fly in real life—standing on my own two feet, seeing clearly.

16

St. Elizabeth's

THE FIRST WEDNESDAY OF every other month, they offer a healing mass at St. Elizabeth's. I had been going a couple of times, and nothing seemed to happen, although I went backward. With the falls that I have had, that is not something I do easily. This one time, I went up to Father Charles, and I went down. I went back to sit in my seat and got back up and asked Father Charles if I could do that again. He said, "Can we do that again?" So he did his usual. As I was going down, just as he went to touch my knee, I was slain in the spirit. I did not want to get off the floor. The best way I can describe it is you vibrate at a higher level. I really thought that was something, but it has not happened like that since.

I went back to where Helen and Ken were sitting, and I thought that was quite incredible.

For approximately three weeks at the beginning of this year, my stomach was doing some flipping and cramping, and I had some horrible painful experiences—so much so that I decided to go to the doctor's. He sent me to have a colonoscopy. It got so bad that I really thought I was dying. I did not think that anybody's stomach could be doing what mine was doing and live. Then one day, ironically, my husband took it away. He gave me a massage. I was lying on the floor in the family room. When he walked away, something happened. It reminded me of being slain in the Holy Spirit, but it was a little different; it appeared to be more above my body than in it. From that day on, my stomach was doing a lot better. Do not know what happened. All I know is there was a release. I do believe that that was the end of my dark night of the soul. I have thought that it ended—oh at least a million times.

I went over to my mom and dad's to watch *Finding Forester*. In the movie, Sean Connery is an author named William Forester. He tells a young black student how to write a book. The first key to writing is to write, not to think. He says, "Write the first draft with your heart, and rewrite with your head." The student ends up helping the teacher—for the teacher and student are one. This message came at a good time because I am presently writing my book. On the way home from my parents' home, I was inspired to write the next paragraph.

In high school, you are often asked, "How will you leave your mark on the world?" I pondered and gave thought to that question, but nothing came. I figured that I could not possibly make a difference, and if I could, what would I do?" I could say that I would get married and have children, but everyone does that. How could I really leave a mark on the world with millions and millions of people on it? One that would stand out, be unique, and be challenging! I feel now that I am leaving my mark on the world, because I have stood up to a mountain and to the three main men in my life, and I have faced myself. In anybody's book, that is truly an accomplishment. Most of the time, the hardest person to look at is ourselves.

My brothers, Ron, Gary, and Paul, also came in from California. I had taken Gary over to my house to show him my house, and we were by ourselves. I have wanted to give Gary reiki or pray over him, and he always declined. We sat down at my kitchen table, and he said that he had done a major booboo at work and felt his job was in jeopardy. I asked him if I could pray over him; he said, "Not now." I said, "Why not now?" He agreed. I took him into the living room where I give my blessings. I had him sit in the desk chair that swivels. When I got through, he thanked me and told me that he had really needed that. I told Shirley about it; she could not believe it either. Gary is definitely one of our favorite brothers.

My brother Paul only came in for two nights, so time was limited. It was about a half hour before he was leaving for the airport. Paul was the youngest in the family, and I do believe the hardest out of all of us. He was not disciplined and had some serious problems. We were all sitting in the living room, and Shirley said in front of everyone, "Kathy wants to pray over you." I totally did not think he would respond in any way, but to my surprise, he went into the bedroom with my dog Tyler. He lay down on the air mattress, and I followed him in. He had just yelled at my mom because she had asked him again if he wanted something to eat. Shirley said with the mood he was in, she would not have gone near him. I lay down on the mattress too and asked him if he minded. He said, "Go ahead." So I thought that it did not matter what position he was in and guided him through the meditation. When I was through, he also told me thanks. When I told Shirley that I had prayed over him, she said, "You are courageous" and that she found that hard to believe. Paul left in a much better mood; I was very grateful.

17

Pauline's Visit

SHIRLEY HAD CONTACTED A lady called Pauline Larson, who channels iouya and group consciousness for the *Sedona Journal of Emergence*. She lives in Ephraim, Utah, not that far from where my sister lives in Draper. We had tried to contact her last summer while I was there, but she had just left for New York. Shirley left a message on her machine, and her husband called back and said she was in New York. Anyway, when she returned, Shirley did get a hold of her, and they started doing activities together. So I had an opportunity to talk to her, and she channeled iouya and group consciousness for me. This was before Christmas. I was told that I had been with Pauline in several previous lifetimes.

Also that I had played the role of Joan of Arc several times and that I was burned at the stake. She said I might have been Joan. I tell her about meeting the Redfields and Deepak Chopra at the Church of Today, and she said that she would very much like to come to Michigan to visit Marianne Williamson. Shirley was planning a trip to Michigan in April. So I called up Pauline and asked her if she would like to come likewise. Shirley also called her and asked her if she wanted to come. So now Pauline was set up to come to Michigan.

Shirley was not available, so I went to the airport to pick up Pauline. I had seen a picture of her face in the *Sedona Journal*, but that is all I had to go by. I pulled up to American Airlines, and I saw a lady who might have been Pauline standing with her luggage right out front. So I pulled over and got out of the car and said, "Pauline?" She said she was looking for both Shirley and me. I took her to my house. Although I had talked to her on the phone, it still was a little bit strange being with a stranger. When we got to my house, I asked her if she wanted the third attunement. I gave her a blessing first and then the attunement. From that moment on, we did really well together.

The next morning, we had an appointment with Marianne Williamson at the Church of Today. We got caught in traffic in Detroit, but Marianne ended up being a little late herself. It was the four of us—Shirley, Pauline, Marianne, and I. I asked Marianne if she would read my book because of the church and herself being a big part of the book. She said she would. Mostly after that, we joined hands while Pauline channeled iouya for us. Pauline said that she would like to buy her book, *Healing the Soul of America*. Marianne said she could have that one and signed it for her as well. Then the three of us went to the seminar that they were holding.

That evening, I took Pauline to the Holy Ghost meeting. I explained to her ahead of time that there might be some fear-based messages but to overlook them because they were very loving people. She very much enjoyed every bit. She could feel the Holy Spirit very strongly. Pauline said it was interesting seeing the Catholic religion from the perspective of someone of the Mormon religion. A couple of people prayed over her at the end, which she enjoyed. She said she could tell that they extended pure love. She did not sing and thought maybe that would affect me. I just thought she was enjoying the energy and did not think about anything. She did not think her voice was good enough. Pauline has a wonderful voice.

The next morning, we took off for our property up north. Pauline and I went together and David and Shirley went together; they arrived later than us. As Pauline and I were attempting to drive into my driveway, we got stuck in the snow. Because we were going downhill, we got stuck pretty well. So I went and opened up the shed, where we got a couple of regular tall shovels out and started shoveling behind each tire. A couple of times, I started the car, and the wheels just spun. After the third attempt, I was finally able to drive forward and get out of the drift that had accumulated over the last snowfall. Pauline also made a path to the trailer and to the fire pit, which made it nice. In the meantime, I brought in our bags of stuff that we would be using. I did not have to take much because we had pretty much everything up there—all we needed were clothes and accessories.

After we took care of business, we went into the trailer, and Pauline channeled iouya for me. I asked about the purple weed, which she said was clearing different dimensions and different parts of me. She said the purple was royalty and that now I saw the weed differently. Like now I was looking at myself differently. When I told her that I ate a petal of the weed, she said I knew the weed and I were one. I also asked another question but do not remember what else I asked. We thought this would be on tape but found out the tape recorder was not working. We ate a scrumptious bacon, lettuce, tomato, and cheese hamburger at the local bowling alley called Fred's. They have good food there, and we have eaten there often. After that, we went to Glenn's market to get a few things we would need.

We started a fire as soon as possible. I brought up plenty of newspaper to get the fire started. We also collected some brush to ensure our success. I still did not want to take any chances, so before I lit the match, I also doused it with gasoline. I mostly did that because of the moisture, although the wood seemed dry. We got the fire started uneventfully. We mostly stood up, tending to the fire and just having some small talk. I did bring out a couple of folding chairs for us to sit on. We had plenty of wood stacked up, so running out was not a problem.

The only thing I turned on was the electricity. I did not know how to turn the heat tape on, and I wasn't going to take a chance of the pipe freezing. I also did not turn on the furnace; I was going to wait for David to do that, although I could have read

Mike's directions and done it myself. We put on the small portable electric heater that helped take the cold out to be at least bearable. It would have been real nice to have water. Dave and Shirley did not show up till it was 12:00 p.m. We thought maybe that they had decided not to come. I immediately got the other end of the trailer, ready for them to sleep. They saw our fire as they were rounding the corner still blazing away. I was happy that they had found the place at night using Mike's directions.

The next morning, the four of us went out to my favorite little breakfast place, called Baum's. Actually, I called it the Slanted Floor. They had since corrected the floor, but the wall was still greatly slanted. Before the correction, your plates or cups could roll off the table if you did not hang on to them. Somehow, I just liked the ambiance of this little restaurant. Mike and I have talked to the two waitresses, who are sisters, for about twenty years or so. Dave paid for breakfast, which was nice of him.

After breakfast we walked to this little gift shop that was next to the Dairy Queen located around the corner from Baum's. It is a cute little shop that Nancy, our waitress, said we would enjoy, even though I had been there many times. Pauline bought me this crystal shaped like a sun in the middle to hang in my window. It definitely looked metaphysical. She also bought a crystal for herself; I pointed out the one I wanted her to buy for her. I do not think Dave or Shirley bought anything. It didn't take us long, and we headed for Higgins Lake, north end State Park—my heaven!

Higgins Lake was engulfed in a mystical fog, so you could not see out very far. You surely could not appreciate the magnificence and beauty of this lake. We walked along the shoreline in the sand. Pauline picked up a leaf, pinecone, and stone to bring back with her as a keepsake. Then the four of us joined hands, and we all said a few words. Pauline again channeled iouya for each one of us. I attuned David into the second attunement into reiki while he sat at the picnic table overlooking the lake. I also did Pauline again, just to do it again with this kind of ambiance. I did not write down what was said because I thought it was all on tape—Pauline does not think it was taped at all. Tyler ran around, even going out of sight. Normally he is not allowed on the beach, so this was unusual for him. Even though you could not see much of this beautiful lake, everyone enjoyed themselves anyway. In fact, I think Shirley would definitely call it magic.

After we spent time at the north end, we decided to go to the south end of State Park. We walked around the lagoon. I remember when we were teenagers, being buried near the lagoon. I was buried in so much sand that it was hard for me to breathe—it scared me a little. Tyler again followed along while we walked along the shoreline. We did not stay there very long, but it all was a most enjoyable afternoon. Then we just decided to head back to our property. When we got back, Dave and Shirley said they were going to take off. Dave started a fire and put the bed away before they left. Pauline channeled iouya for all of us once again. We all asked several questions. They asked us if we wanted to go out to eat with them, and we said no. After they left, I was sad that they left. Pauline and I started dancing around the fire. We started doing the pure love symbol in our dance. We danced a form of Hawaiian. While we were dancing, we said, "We freely give and we freely receive" over and over again. We tried to be as creative as possible, just really enjoying the moment. Shirley told me later that she saw Pauline and me doing that dance at the fire in the airplane going home to Utah and again when she was home in Utah.

We just played around at the fire a while into the darkness. Shirley had wanted me to engrave Pauline's initials and date into the wooden bench that Mike had made. A lot of our guests in the past had left their mark on the bench. I told Shirley that it was time-consuming and that you had to press quite hard doing it. Pauline tried for a little while and gave up. We finally had enough and just decided to go to bed. Tyler peed blood again, so I know that he was sick. In the morning, Tyler squeezed between the side of the trailer wall and me. We lay around for a little while, and then we packed up everything to leave. There was not much to do because the only thing I had to turn off was the electricity. We did not even vacuum like I normally always do. We did not stop to eat breakfast; we just headed to Frankenmuth, a little German town that is quite popular. I had never driven to Frankenmuth and was not sure how to get there. Fortunately, we made all the right turns and made it to the restaurant. Their specialty is chicken dinners. During the summer months, you could wait in a long line going quite a distance outside the entrance to the building.

The sun started coming out just as we had arrived and cleared things up so we could at least see. We were seated immediately in a small room near the front. Our waitress was quite old—seemed like she would have spilt my coffee with all the shaking she was doing. But she managed, in spite of all of it, to not spill a thing. We were hungry because we did not stop for breakfast. I ate with gusto. One thing is for sure—when I am really hungry, I cannot wait to eat. We both got two pieces of chicken with mashed potatoes and coleslaw. After we were through, we decided to walk around a little, going to the nearby shops they had available. Pauline bought a gift for Susan, a neighbor that she walks with. I bought a couple of things also. Most of the shops have Christmas ornaments and decorations that you can buy.

We thought about going up to Mackinaw Bridge and possibly even the Tahquamenon Falls in the Upper Peninsula. It would have been a lot of driving, and it was foggy everywhere, so we would not have seen much anyway. I even thought about taking a hovercraft over to the island of Mackinaw if it was running. We figured out that we just plain did not have that much time to do all of that driving. Then Pauline could say she had covered a lot of Michigan.

Pauline and I, after giving Mike a little reiki, decided to go for an evening walk. As soon as we stepped out, we could see lightning randomly going off in the southeast. We stood on the sidewalk at my next-door neighbor's house and were mesmerized by the panorama view. My neighbors stepped out also but then, shortly afterward, went back in. We never did hear any thunder; it was like a symphony orchestration from the heavens for us to gaze upon. I would describe it like *Close Encounters of a Third Kind*, when the spaceship was getting ready to land. It is really important to notice the gifts that are sent your way, to smell the roses. I asked iouya, if that was meant for us; she said yes, that your neighbors didn't stay to enjoy. Shirley and Dave likewise viewed this symphony orchestration of the heavens from my dad and mom's house.

The next morning, Pauline and I went to St. Elizabeth's in Wyandotte for mass. We were asked before mass had started if we would bring up the bread and wine up. Pauline was totally unfamiliar with anything in the Catholic religion; I told her that she could handle it and to just follow me. Pauline thought that was an honor to do that, thinking that they would not have asked her if they knew she wasn't Catholic. I told her it did not matter. I also asked Father Charles if he would pray over Pauline, seeing as she was leaving for Utah the next morning. He said he would after mass was over with. After mass, Father Charles did pray over Pauline, and Pauline was very grateful and appreciative that he did. There was an old man named Carl sitting at the entrance lobby of the church making a pyramid out of the palms because it was Palm Sunday, the Sunday before Easter. I asked him if he would make one for me, then I asked him to make one for Pauline, which he did as well. He was sitting out there because he did not feel well. Pauline, likewise, was very pleased that this total stranger would make this for her.

After church, we went to Bishop Park at the Detroit River. Pauline said if this river were in Utah, they would call it a lake. We took several pictures separately, and then we asked a couple if they would take our picture together. We walked along the walkway and down to the end of the pier. We stood at the end of the pier, gazing upon the fishing boats nearby and the sparkling sprinkles of light resting upon the water. A little boy had thrown a Frisbee in the water, and the nearby fisherman raced to retrieve it from his boat and threw it back for the little boy. I felt like the boy had deliberately thrown it in because his mom and sister were there.

As we were walking back along the boardwalk, Pauline and I stopped again to gaze upon the water. I read that all light reflections on the water are fairies. So we looked down, with our elbows on the railing, gazing at the reflection of lights right below our feet. We stared for some time, then Pauline pointed out the brilliant iridescent blue lines that curved; as soon as she said it, I also saw them as well. Then I pointed out the yellow haze, and she saw it as well. I do not remember how long we stood there gazing in that spot, but I know it was for quite a while. We both thought that it was magic and it was for us. I told the fairies how much I appreciated their performance.

We came home, and I asked Mike if he would barbecue us a meat-and-vegetable dinner on the grill. I actually wanted to go to Greek Town in Detroit for a lamb, spinach, and rice dinner. I do not do a good job driving around Detroit; there are a lot of one-way streets, and I did not want to take a chance. Finally, Mike made the dinner as asked. It was heaven; Pauline liked it very much as well. My famous saying is "It is better than going out to eat." My children will never forget that saying because I say it anytime that we make a good dinner at home. Mike is a good cook and performs his expertise often. He has watched many, many cooking shows and takes some of his work from there. Mike was a little put out that I paid attention to Pauline for the rest of the day. He told me he never wanted me to invite a total stranger in our house again; I said nothing.

The next morning, Mike went to work, and this would be our last moment together. I wondered what we should do. First we went out for breakfast and got a Southern omelet at the Real McCoy's restaurant. We both enjoyed it very much. Then we came back home, and I decided that I wanted Pauline to channel iouya one last time. I asked iouya many questions like were my experiences real, those that I thought were real? She told me yes. Even though I know they were, it is nice to be validated by another source.

I asked if I was courageous, going through the dark night of the soul. She said yes, that people committed suicide going through less than what I did. I asked if my dark night was expedited because I gave blessings and reiki. She said yes, that I knew in my heart that was the thing to do. I asked iouya if I did a good job as far as my dad was concerned. She said,

"You did not do a good job, you did a great job!" I really enjoyed the whole experience; it seemed so relaxed and informal. No one else was around to bother us in one way or another. I am very grateful for Pauline and the whole experience. We ate lunch at McDonald's and got a small sundae—I got caramel, and Pauline got strawberry.

Before we went to the airport, we stopped at the Little Rose Chapel that I had talked about previously. I had told her about my experiences with the Jesus statue becoming alive. She knelt down in front of the Jesus statue because the chapel had been redone and now was not on a pedestal nor located in the same place, looking into Jesus's eyes. She told me later that she saw a white aura around the statue's head. I asked Mother if she would pray over her, and she did. Pauline thought that she had taped the whole thing and found out again that it did not work. I took a picture of Pauline with Mother and a couple of pictures in the chapel. We also took a picture of me in front where the entrance was.

As far as I was concerned, I had taken Pauline to most of my favorite spiritual places. I do think that she is a mature person to enjoy another religion as much as she has. Soon after she arrived back in Utah, her father passed away. It is really hard to tell anyone how sorry you are when someone they loved dies. Most people would rather say nothing at all, in fear that they might say the wrong thing and hurt someone's feelings. Her mother was not doing well before she came here to Michigan, and her father up and died. They were both close to ninety, if not ninety. Now her mother wants to die because her husband wasn't there any longer. So Pauline was trying to help her out. How do you tell someone how to die? Pauline had been very involved in helping her mother, and she hadn't had the time to get the pictures or the tapes mailed off. When she talked about her childhood, it sounded like a fairy tale.

18

My Childhood

That brings me to my childhood, which I feel was not a fairy tale. My mom had seven children by the time I turned seven and a half years old. Paul, the youngest, was born when I was twelve and a half. My twin sister, Carol, and I were left in charge when we were seven. My dad would set us down and tell us that if anything happened, we would be responsible. I swore when I had my children that I would never say those words. My sister Judy, as an adult, asked me why I was so bossy. I told her that I had to be because of what Dad had told me. She said she remembered Dad saying that but paid it no mind. I was fortunate that Carol and I were twins, so we at least had each other.

We lived in a very small house—just two bedrooms and no basement. It is so hard to believe that ten people lived in a cracker box. Most of the time, there were wall-to-wall people. My parents would jokingly say, "Would all the neighbor children please go home?" One day, we went out to a park and mistakenly left Shirley when she was quite young. She sat calmly on the picnic table, saying that she knew we would return. From that time on, my parents would have us count off so that would not happen again. We went out to Kensington Lake almost every Sunday. We would even take neighbor children, and my aunt and uncle often came with their children. My dad had bought a sailboat, and we did quite a bit of sailing on that lake. One time, during a quick wind, the boat capsized. I was thrown out into the water. Luckily, I did not hit the mask or anything else. It certainly caught me off guard. We all enjoyed the picnics and swimming; we did not enjoy all the work of carrying everything and taking and putting the mask up and taking it down. It was a lot of work. The place where we would set up the picnic was quite a hike from where the car was parked. Plus we had to carry the freezer chest over a hill. My mom was quite heavy and the whole thing was hard on her, but she felt it was worth it because of living vicariously in all the fun we had.

This is hard for me to say, but here goes. Our house, most of the time, was a dump. My dad would always tell us to be proud of our home; I could never figure that out. There often were tools all over our kitchen. The kitchen table had junk all over it—we were instructed that we could not touch a thing. It also had food and garbage that you could not just wash off. Newspapers and magazines filled the whole corner of the living room. I was totally petrified if I thought someone might be coming over for any reason. We certainly could never have neighbor children or friends from school over. One time, the man I had been babysitting for showed up at our front door. Someone let him in. I came out of the bedroom to see him standing at the front door with a Christmas gift. I wanted to go ten feet under. I never babysat for them again after that incident; I believe they moved. I grew up horrified if someone entertained the thought of coming over. I would have much anxiety over this problem throughout my whole childhood. My dad said we could vacuum in the middle of the front room and we could not touch anything. Our stove had so much cooked-on grease in the oven and on the top of the stove that you could barely tell what it was.

For a year or more, the bathtub did not work, and we were unable to take a bath. I do not know what people thought of us. We filled it with clothes that got mildewed, and we had to throw them away. The walls in the bedrooms were also quite mildewed. Carol and I would try as little girls to push a lawn mower. Even with the two of us, it was too hard to do. I do not know if it needed to be oiled or what. The garage was filled with junk. Later on, after the kids left, the whole house was filled so it was a labyrinth. There were only a couple places to sit down in the whole house—the toilet and bed were a couple. All the kids later grew up, and when they had homes of their own, they kept them clean. All of us were anxious to not store junk either. If we wanted a blouse washed or ironed, we did it. That was okay if you did not make yourself breakfast or lunch—you just did without. I must say that dinner was always made for us. It was first come, first serve—definitely survival of the fittest. My mom never begged us to eat nor did she take our orders. We ate and we were happy to have something to eat.

One thing I will have to say is that we always had nice holidays. My mom's Thanksgiving dinner was the best I had ever eaten. There were times that we would eat our Easter dinner on the front lawn. We always had a Christmas tree that in my eyes was magnificent. Of course, I personally hung a lot of the tinfoil and ornaments. I would be mesmerized every year just staring at the tree. We, most of the time, did not get many gifts, but we were happy with what we got. There was one Christmas I got all the gifts that I had asked for. My twin sister, Carol, told me later when we were adults that she was jealous and felt she did not get the equivalent. To top it all off, she asked me if she could play with them, and I said no. I felt bad that I had said no. We also decorated around the archway with lights, garlands, and Christmas cards. One year, my mom made us all flannel pajamas, which for her was a lot of work. Then another year, she helped us all make our own stocking to hang on the fake fireplace.

My mom slept a lot, and if she wasn't sleeping, she was playing cards at the neighbors'. I do not remember my mom being with us much; she escaped in any way that she could. My mom also played quite a bit of bingo. All of it was a form of escape to get away from her responsibilities. When my dad came home, we all had to be quiet while he read the newspaper or watched TV. There were loud noises at his work in the factory at Kelsey Hayes in Detroit. I don't blame my dad. He worked a lot of overtime, and he was an electrician. Meanwhile, while Dad was at work, anything went—total chaos. My four brothers fought morning, noon, and night—I felt very strongly that they even fought in their sleep. Needless to say, I never thought they would reach adulthood. I thought they would kill each other first. To this day, when they are together, they don't fight physically, but they cannot get along most of the time.

My dad came over to my house, which was a mobile home in Belleville, and asked me why I didn't keep our house as clean when I was at home. I told him because Mike let me; in fact, he highly recommended it. I have to admit when I had my four children in less than five years, there were times that my house was a mess too. But it was not dirty. There might have been toys all over and the dishes weren't done, but I kept it clean. My oven and stove were always wiped and cleaned and the floors washed and vacuumed. I just could not understand my dad. If we wanted to weed the flower bed, he would tell us we could not do it because we might pull out a flower. So of course, the weeds would take it over. He would not trim the bushes, and boy, you better not do it either. Carol did one day, and boy, did she receive hell. I also had the audacity to wash down the kids' bedroom and paint it a light purple, a color I chose. I received hell before, during, and after. I thought I had made a brand-new room out of it. I was sixteen years old; I thought I did a great job.

I told Pauline about a lot of this on our trip up north. She just looked at me and said, "And look how good you turned out." So that is how our childhood went—us trying to make the place we lived in human. My dad looked at us as making decisions and controlling. He always told us to come to him and he would show us how, but we all knew he would never show us how nor would he do it. Because Carol and I were the oldest, we had a lot of confrontations with him. Judy and Shirley didn't even bother attempting to try. So most of my problems with my dad were that I wanted to clean, and he didn't want me to. Try telling that to most parents. Although when I had children of my own, there were times that I would rather they not do stuff either if I thought they would destroy or whatever. My dad often told us kids that he was giving us constructive criticism, and he would say whatever was on his mind, no matter how it hurt.

One thing I enjoyed immensely was camping. We had a high blue-and-white wall tent that the boys and Dad slept in and a smaller green tent that the four girls slept in. My mom slept in the station wagon front seat; she could never get comfortable sleeping on the ground. We did not go camping until I turned thirteen. It was the only time in my life that I was not ashamed to bring anyone over. For some reason, there was discipline when we went camping. We had to clean the tents every morning; the dishes and pantry were always clean. Ironically it was the only time in my life that I did not have anyone over. I mean from the campground. We oftentimes took neighbors and even kids from school with us. Here we were with ten of us, and we often took more. One day, when I was playing baseball while camping, I was the pitcher, and a boy was batting. He hit the ball with a line drive into my left boob. I was very embarrassed because I caught it. I thought, *What is this going to do to me?* For several years as an adult, I thought I had something wrong with it. I would not go and talk to the doctor about it; it just hurt. I breast-fed my children, and I thought that would correct any hurt that was caused to it. They said if you breast-fed, the chances of getting cancer were slimmer than if you didn't. During the dark night of the soul, my heart also hurt at the same time.

I debated as to whether I should talk about my childhood, but then I felt they would not get the whole picture. All of us children had had a hard time dealing with our childhood. When I got married, before I walked down the aisle, I told my dad that I was sorry for what I had done. I did not know that I was jumping out of the frying pan into the fire. When it came right down to it, does anyone have bed of roses? My dad would always say that my mom did. I never understood that part. I would have never wanted to take her place. One thing I did learn was just appreciation for everything. I took nothing for granted. Well, I am sure there were things I took for granted, but you know what I mean. Because we wore shoes with holes in them and cardboard in the bottom so that we would not touch the ground, when we got a new pair, we did not take it for granted.

Looking back, our childhood was far from perfect, but I know we were at least a family that loved each other, even if we had a hard time showing it. We often would have water fights or we would get people down on the ground and tickle them. I personally did not care for it because I would hurt my sides from laughing, but I know it was the glue that stuck us together. Through it all, I also knew that my parents loved us. They didn't tell us, and I just knew it. I am very proud of my parents and brothers and sisters; I love them beyond measure.

19

House is Being Restored

THE HOUSE THAT I grew up in is now in the process of being restored. The man that bought it lives next door, and he restored that house as well. I really can't wait until it is totally done. This man is very creative, and this house will be incredible when he is done. We had only finished emptying it last fall. I feel that we all had a huge burden lifted when it was finally taken care of. I personally helped carry some stuff out, so it was a cleansing. I was told that our whole family was in the process of healing itself, and I do believe that that is true. My parents are wonderful, and I do love them very much. I do not know how they will feel about me writing my truth; I hope and pray that they understand.

My parents presently live in a brand-new beautiful home. They do have a lot of stuff stored in the basement on benches that my brothers have made. It is truly a gorgeous home. I guess it is a little redundant to say that I wished we had grown up in that home. I am happy they are spending their last few years in what they would have definitely called a palace. I have to admit that when they first bought the house, I was a little jealous and did not think they deserved it; now I do. They still fight over whom does the most work. My mom resents that she has to wait on him, and he resents that he has to do everything else. I hope my husband and I do not fight over who does the most work when he retires.

When I was, like, nineteen, I was coming home in the evening when my dad told me very calmly he was not mad at me. He told me that I would not amount to anything, that I should not marry or have children, that I would never have any friends. I did not respond, but I thought, *This is coming from a man that is supposed to love me*. Quite a few years later, I found out that he gave that little speech to quite a few of my siblings. The biggest thing that bothered me is he did not say this in anger; he gave it much thought. Then I thought that maybe that was how much pain he was in—for him to say those cruel words.

One day, Theron and I were doing the two-chair; at least that is what he calls it. He sat in one chair and pretended to be my dad; I sat in the other and was myself. Because he had been counseling me, he could fake it quite well. All of a sudden, he started channeling my dad and I was forcing him in the closet. He also told me how he felt about me being the only one that had stayed here and how I had stayed to hurt him. I thought he was being facetious at first and did not believe him, and then I realized what was happening. I had been a worse perpetrator in a previous lifetime than he was to me in this lifetime. His dad also came through—because he did not think he was strong enough, he was mean to him and physically abused him. See, we think we are victims, only to find out we did that or worse in a previous lifetime. What you give out picks up speed and momentum and loops around, right back at you. Even knowing this, it is still hard to let go of the illusion; it is a process!

My mom is well read and is wise, plus she writes poetry. I think she wrote poetry because her stepfather would give her the option of doing chores or memorizing a poem; she always opted for memorizing. She was short (five foot two) with brown hair and brown eyes. She did not attend college; in fact, she did not complete high school. She went to Central High School in Detroit, which was predominantly a Jewish school back then. She only had a couple of months to go, but she figured that she did not need a diploma to have children. Her stepfather offered a trip to Europe if she did not marry my dad, which of course she did not take him up on. Her mother escaped by actually leaving with men regularly. My mom did not like it because she was never there for her. In fact, my mom, at nine years of age, literally raised her brother Paul, who had just been born. Luckily, they lived in a neighborhood that the other children were called in, so they went home. Even though my mom hated that her mom was not there for her, she repeated the process. The very thing you hate being done to you, oftentimes you repeat and do the same thing. My mom constantly wrote on the chair in the front room with her finger "This too will pass!"

My dad, as I said, was an electrician; he was also well read and smart. He was tall—six feet, two inches—with blue eyes and handsome. He never swore or used foul language of any kind. He taught us values, to tell the truth, to not take things that did not belong to us, to pick up papers, and to not litter. He did not drink much—almost never. We went to church every Sunday and holidays, although my mom almost never went. He worked a lot of overtime to provide for our large family. He never hit me or physically hurt me in any way. He went to the University of Detroit for a couple of years, which was a struggle for him to pay for. He was getting too old to be on the apprenticeship program being offered at Kelsey's, but because they had just started it, they opened it up to everyone. He went in to take the test, sick as a dog, and scored one of the highest. He could have been anything he wanted. I think he did so well because of his knowledge from U of D and all science magazines that were current and up-to-date that he read.

When I was in the seventh grade, I asked my dad what I could do my report on in school. He told me that I should do it on John Glenn, the astronaut. I did a real nice report, and I got an A on it as I recall. I remember two teachers standing at the doorway looking and commenting on my report. Then when I was in junior high, ninth grade, I asked my dad again what I should do my English report on. He told me, "The tides of the century in France." I also got an A on this report, and my teacher called me up to the class and told me he liked current-events stories. We had since thrown away our newspaper, but the lady next door luckily had it and gave it to me. There were times my dad definitely came through for me. I really do feel that they did the best they could with what they had to work with. My dad has said often that there are some people who should not have children—I always thought he was one of them. When my children were young, if something ever happened to Mike and me, I did not want my dad to raise the children.

When I was in eleventh grade, my dad took us every Friday roller-skating. Actually, he would drop us off then come back to pick us up. I got so good at roller-skating that I could skate as fast going backward as I could going forward. There was a group of us that went, and it was a lot of fun. He did do a lot of toting and fetching with all of us eight children. My mom did not do a lot of driving to our activities. When we got older, friends would often pick us up. There were a few friends that I would let in the house, not many. Mike, of course, was one.

20

When I Started My Manuscript

I STARTED MY BOOK at the middle of April of 2001. I really felt that the heavens were letting me know that they were going to assist me in my writing. First of all, I had no desire to write a book; I did not think I was smart enough or talented enough. I was also in the mist of painting most of my house and getting new carpeting. So my mind was on other things. The first day, I typed out a page. That is not so unusual, but I heard my song, "In the Arms of an Angel" by Sarah McLachlan. I do not hear that song on the radio that much. The next day, I turned on the computer, my book immediately came up, and I did not save it. It is like a ten-year-old computer; when you switch everything off, if you do not save it, it is not saved. I also heard my song every day for the next three days—four days all together in succession. Every day throughout the week, the same thing—I did not save it, and my book immediately came up. Also, the space bar was not moving the word forward—it was deleting instead, and then there was something else not working. I thought, *If you want me to do this, why are you giving me a hard time about correcting my mistakes?* Shirley said they were letting me know, without a doubt, that the spirit world was working with me. I was quite amazed and impressed that I was being assisted.

I also told the spirit world, if they wanted me to start my book, to give me a sign of some kind. I was talking to Pauline on the phone one day, the day I started my book, and this is what I said. I said, "I know exactly when my dark night of the soul started." Pauline said, "There you go, Kathy, that is your first paragraph." I figured that that was the sign for me to start, even telling me how to start it. A lot of that first information I had written down in my journal, so basically I copied it. So I actually did quite a bit of typing that first week. We bought a new computer, and nothing unusual has happened with it at all. Also, while I was typing a riveting exercise, I had it double-spaced. As I was printing it, I saw the screen go from double to single right before my eyes. Again, that was impossible unless you manually did it. So I thought they want it single-spaced. The spirit world has its ways of communicating—sometimes it's through books, TV, or people that you run into. Or it could be your thoughts that you think are your thoughts but aren't. I still thought my book was going to be too mundane and nobody was going to want to read it. Somewhere along the line, I started getting excited about the book.

My daughter Crissy brought Christopher, who is four years old, over to spend a little time with me. My daughter's boyfriend is Chris, and he has the two boys from a previous girlfriend. He has full custody of the two boys because the mother was found to be unfit. I never thought I would love two boys that were not of my bloodline. Christopher stole my heart, and this is how. One day, I was sitting in my family room on the floor. Christopher was sitting perpendicular to me. I said, "Christopher, do you see angels like that one on the coffee table?" He said, without skipping a beat, "Yes, that picture of you up there." I felt like Kathy Lee. I brought my hand up to my mouth to bite it like she does on Regis and Kathy Lee.

Before this, I decided to attune both Cory and Christopher into reiki. Cory is five years old. Chris's father had committed suicide when Chris was quite young, and both boys were having trouble dealing with their biological mother. I felt very strongly that the boys would benefit from this attunement. Besides, I loved them dearly. So the three of us were in the family room, and I gave them a blessing. All three held hands in a circle while I did this. Afterward, I went to right into the attunement. Christopher giggled a little bit during the blessing; both cooperated fully. I thought this was supposed to be a joyful experience, so I continued. While you give the attunement, you draw four symbols in their hands and tap three times after each one. They both enjoyed it so much that they said, "Can you do that again?" It is okay to do it again, so I did. Again they said, "Can you do that again?" I figured out that they would continue all day. A few months later, Christopher remembered it and asked me if I would do it again. So I did give them both another blessing and the second attunement, which, of course, they wanted me to do again. I felt like I was with two little angels. The joy was a treat and pleasure, extending it to these two little angels.

I met Mary, Chris's mother, a very delightful, pretty woman. She bragged and bragged about my daughter Crissy. She told me the youngest boy had stuttered before Crissy came along. She hounded the two of them to get married. I have never told Crissy to get married or even asked if she was. I figured if I did and it did not work out, she would blame me. I am sure they will get married when they are ready. My views on marriage have changed since I have gotten older. Besides, I have been married for twenty-eight and a half years, which should say it all. No one should make those kinds of decisions for someone else. You can give your perspective or advice. I just figured Crissy would know when she would be ready.

Around the same time that I wrote "A Riveting Exercise," I also wanted to see Mother Earth healed, so this is my attempt of visualizing this. My mom gave me a couple of suggestions, so I did get help.

Mother Earth

Thank you for Mother Earth being cleansed—the toxins and chemicals are dissipating. The oceans and seas are being calmed and are serene. The lakes, rivers, streams, and tributaries are healed and cleansed. The volcanoes are becoming inactive, and the bubbles are subsiding. The tectonic plates are relaxed and still. Thank you for Mother Earth being healed inwardly and outwardly. The skies are bluer, cleansed and tranquil. The people's hearts are full and also healed. This is purifying the atmosphere reverberating out into space. There is much gentleness with all the animals and insects. This truly is a new world for all. It is the grandest version for all. Amen!

My Declaration of Independence

While reading the Declaration of Independence, I thought that was nice altruistic talk about everyone being equal and all, but I did not think we were all equal. After all, some people were disabled, diseased, deformed, crazy, etc. How could they say we were all equal when I did not think it was so? Now I know we are! We would like to blame God, the devil, our parents, and just everyone outside of ourselves. And we see what we want to see. We do not see that we create or make our own reality. Plus, authentic, genuine living is taking full responsibility and accountability for your life. The love we hold back is held back from us. The innocence we do not see in our brother is the innocence we do not see in ourselves. We will be forgiven exactly to the degree that we forgive. The only regret or pain we will have when we die is the love we did not give freely to all.

Respect and celebrate each other's differences. It would be awfully boring if everyone were the same. Maybe everyone's individual expression is their truth for them. Maybe that is what the Declaration of Independence is all about—freedom to choose your joy—and isn't that what America was founded on? When our rights are taken away, so is our freedom. Only in freedom do we really learn, not if we are coerced or forced. It is your freedom to choose the right decision in faith or fear. Fear is everything that isn't love—only love is real! So the next time you are involved in any situation, ask yourself, are you leading with love? To even ask that question, you probably aren't, because you know when you are leading with Love. When you are involved in an arduous, tumultuous situation, laugh a lot. Lighten up! Then it gives it an all-new perspective or outlook. You've got to ask yourself, do you feel lucky? We make our luck and joy!

21

More Experiences

It is now Tuesday, May 29, 2001, and the sun is starting to set, I am standing behind my garage facing the west. I am able to look at it, and then I shut my eyes. I see something similar to my billowing clouds; this time, they are curved lines, crisscrossing each other, going slowly into a center. I see this rectangular-shaped corridor. I am viewing it as it is extending out horizontally in attached different sections, quite a ways, then it stops all of a sudden, and I sense that it starts coming back at me. When I see it, it is in the form of an eye still in the corridor. The eye is not outlined; it is a little illumined. I do believe the sections are different dimensions. I believe it stops at my third eye. I am viewing the sun through leaves from a branch of a tree. Then parts of it turn a bluish green color and flashing through the branches seems to be outlined in black. I believe that it is an extraterrestrial communicating subliminally to me.

Then as I am still looking into the sun with branches, I see what I think is Jesus's face. I stand out there behind my garage and alongside the patio for about a half hour. I also see other stuff but cannot remember or describe it. One looks like it could have been a blade of some sort with no handle. Then there is something long and rectangular running parallel to the ground—I do believe it is all black. I have seen the bluish green before in a similar situation but did not suspect that it was an extraterrestrial communicating with me, though. I very much felt it this time. I enjoyed it all very much; it was a time to reflect and enjoy. I felt that I had witnessed what I was supposed to witness, but I wondered if I should have stayed longer.

Mostly, when I would be lying in the bathtub with my eyes shut, I would rub my eyes for some reason, and I would see a brilliant light. The more I rubbed, the brighter it got, and then it seemed to vibrate for a little bit. One time, at the Holy Ghost meeting, it happened, but most of the time, I had to be in water. It seemed like, when I wanted it to happen, it didn't; it happened when I was not suspecting it. Although one time I wanted it to happen, and it did. Before the dark night of the soul, I never saw that brilliant bright light. I just lay back and enjoyed, suspecting it was the divine light.

I went to my meditation group with the Holy Ghost people. I had planned to give my little speech tonight if it presented itself. When I walked in, I had seen a lady that I hadn't seen in a while. I started telling them that Jesus was in all religions. Lillian said, "But Catholic is the true religion." I said that I had been at Baptist and Mormon churches and felt Jesus there. Then I said, "What you do to the least of my brethren you do to me, and judge lest thee be judged." I told her that I had enjoyed watching her, that she gave praise joyously in her singing. This gave me all the more reason to want to give my long-awaited speech. Jerry said, "There will be no talk this evening." I raised my hand and asked if I could share something. He said no, that there would be sharing afterward. I said, "Okay." Then he told me I could get up. I feel like the Holy Spirit had come through for me. So I read my two previous paragraphs on the Declaration of Independence. After I was through, I said, "Is the heinous of the heinous our brother? Is there any exception to who is our brother? Are all denominations and those of no denominations brothers? What you do to the least of my brethren, you do to me." I reiterated this sentence from the paragraphs that I had read. The only pain or regret that we will take with us when we die is the love that we did not give freely to all. The first will be last, and the last will be first.

I had successfully done what I had set out to do. I waited for the right moment and the right words to come. After I had finished those two paragraphs, I knew those were the words that they needed to hear. I do believe that it was because of them that I was inspired to write them in the first place. They had given so much to me that I wanted to give back to them. I also wanted to say that you could meditate all day long, but if you do not love your brother, you aren't making it. I went up to the two ladies to be prayed over and asked if there was anything that they wanted to tell me. She said that she could sure tell the Holy Spirit was working through me, that her mother had died and it had helped her. She also told me that she wanted to be last. I was amused by that.

I went over to my mom's the next morning and told her what had happened and said there was not anyone to share it with. She said, "Kathy, you have given your power away your whole life. The only one you need to prove it to is you, by taking your power back." I gave my power away to anyone who would take it. I put all my energy into being a victim. Guess what, that is what I was. Is that what I want to be? Wherever you put your energy, that is what you get, so put your energy on what you want and not on what you don't want. But if you put it on wanting, you will get more wanting. Fake your dream. Dream the impossible dream. I do feel for the first time in my life that I am now claiming my power back and living authentically. You do not need to be big or act powerful to claim your power. All you have to be is genuine to yourself and love yourself unconditionally.

If you love yourself unconditionally, everything else will fall into place automatically. "It is hard to figure out what is your truth, but when you do, it is hard not to do what is your truth." Know that everyone is equal—nobody is less than, no one is greater than, and what he or she thinks of you is none of your business. Face your inner demons. What you look at disappears. Live that one authentic dream to the fullest; that is meant just for you. The one you were born with. You don't make your life happen;

FAKE IT, IT WILL COME

you let it. Get out of your own way! Practice your dance, feel your dance, and focus on your unique dance. There is one perfect dance that is in perfect harmony with nature. Look on the world with soft, loving eyes. We see what we want to see, and we find what we want to find. The meaning of it all is there is no meaning. Play the dance; dance your dance. The one you were meant to play, the one you came into this world to play. My mom has been my support system, and likewise, I have been hers.

A part of this last paragraph, I got from the movie *The Legend of Bagger Vance*. It is a golf movie with a metaphysical spin pertaining to golf, and I thought it was most appropriate to put my spin on it. Plus it fit in this paragraph. Then "It is hard not to know what is your truth, but when you do, it is hard not to do your truth" is from the movie *Confessions*. Again, it seemed most appropriate in that paragraph. Everything I have written is an accumulation. I put in my tone and my context from my experiences, what I have read, and what movies I have watched. I do believe that that is so with everyone. Just letting you know that some are not my words, but the context that it is written I believe in; it resonates with me. The only pain you will take with you when you die is the love you did not freely give to all. I got that from the movie *Always*. I saw that movie a long time ago, but it had a big impact on me. You have got to ask yourself, do you feel lucky? That is from a Clint Eastwood movie called *Dirty Harry*. You know where he is spinning the barrel of the gun to shoot? That just kept popping into my head over and over again at the end of that paragraph. So I put it, and yes, I do believe it fits.

When I was young, I would occasionally walk home from St. Cyril's, my elementary school, by myself. I can remember feeling like I was in my own little world and how it felt like heaven. I feel as though I did some spinning and twirling, enjoying heaven and all that heaven had to offer, even talking out loud, not knowing that the spirit world would be listening. There was an occasion that I remember again feeling like I was in heaven and twirling and spinning in the middle of our street, coming home from the side street at the corner. The streetlights were on, and I was only hoping that nobody was watching me from their windows. The next day, our next-door neighbor at the time, Elsie, said to me something along the lines that she knew there was a special little angel yesterday evening, gliding and strolling down the street. My first impression was that I was very embarrassed, that anyone was watching me. This lady virtually never talked to me. Although she was a good friend of my mom, it was quite unheard of that she would say something that eloquently to me. She did not touch my life at that moment, but I did appreciate it years later.

22

More Problems with My Dad!

THIS IS EXTREMELY DIFFICULT for me to put in my book, mostly because I do not know what really happened to me. Abraham from Shasta, California, told me that my kundalini had been messed with when I was little, by my dad. Kam Yuen, whom I met at his seminar on Chinese energetic medicine at the Church of Today, asked me when my neck hurt, when I was still or when I was moving. I said it hurt when I was still. He said, "Your dad is making you be still." Then when Theron was channeling my dad when we were doing the two-chair, I asked my dad, and he said yes, along with most of my brothers and sisters. I have no recollection of what happened or what he did. I never ever suspected that he did anything sexually to us. One time when I was a teenager he asked me to sunbathe nude, either with no top or nothing in the backyard. I found this peculiar coming from my dad. I felt ugly and ashamed—of my body, that is—and I did not know why.

I think that is what hurts most of all is he has told us all what a great dad he was and how he was better than most dads. When I told my mom about this, she told me no, that did not happen. I said that is what most spouses do is, deny. I am writing this in my book for my healing, for my letting in light in, regardless of what happened. I have never asked my dad; I guess I figured that he would deny it. He told me that I was his favorite; I wondered if maybe I was his sexual favorite to play with. I know I was not the perfect mom. I remember slapping my kids when they were little; I feel very ashamed. I did it once or twice to my two youngest. I do not know about the two oldest, but I am sure I hit them. I was not perfect. I have apologized to all four of my children. My daughter Crissy told me that if I did hit her, she said she was sure that she deserved it.

When I had four teenagers at one time, it was very hard on me. I did not know if I wanted to slice their throats or mine. Mike worked a lot, so I had to do most of the raising. I remember my two oldest fighting over the telephone. I went in the kitchen, ripped the phone off the wall, and threw it outside. Also, when they were teenagers is when my self-esteem was totally in the gutter. It was so far in the gutter that I could not help myself, let alone deal with four teenagers. I had been taught badly, I taught badly, my parents had been taught badly, and their parents had been taught badly, etc. We spend our whole adult life trying to get over our childhood.

We all have our map, which is our paradigm that we work off of. My dad throws the past in your face; it usually does not take long after you arrive. This is called projecting and scapegoat. He tells you how you attacked and how he didn't. In particular with me, he said he had not seen such anger and coldness on anyone's face ever. I said, "Yes, Dad, I did attack—I am sorry—but so did you." I wanted to tell him that he hadn't looked himself in the mirror. He had told me repeatedly how vile I was all the while I was growing up. I told him I would never do to my children what he had done to his. He said, "Then why do you?" He said I said that he talked about love but did not give it. Then he proceeded to tell me that I bend over and give him a kiss and a hug and tell him that I love him while he is sitting on the couch and that I thought that was showing love. At this point, I did not know what to do; I just wanted to leave. So I went over, bent over, and told him that I loved him and left. I thought to myself, *What would the Holy Spirit want me to do?* I left feeling that my mom had to be an out-and-out saint. I know that I was probably being tested throughout this ordeal.

They say that while you are on the edge of a cliff and a tiger has you cornered that you should enjoy a strawberry that is in reach by eating it. I felt like my dad was worse than that tiger because I cannot imagine why he liked to hurt so much and then blame the whole scenario on me. He seemed so bright in science, English, math, etc., but totally illogical. Many times he has told me that he is a master of common sense, logic, and organization. He said organization when his home was a labyrinth of pure garbage. Garbage that was so high in the middle of the front room you would be doing good to see over it. When I was leaving, I thought I might as well be leaving my enemies. My mom told me that she did not think I was humble and that she thought enlightened people were humble. All of this also reminded me when I was at that meditation group and Ingalor said that my voice was small and that I thought I was in all this pain.

One day, they asked me to go over and water their plants while they were gone at the old house. I had done it and was going back the second time when I noticed some stuff in the path and wondered if someone had been in the house. Then I finally realized that I inadvertently must have knocked something over the last time I was there. I wondered, with my mom being so heavy and all, how she had made it through. She must have been very careful. When we were cleaning out this house and garage, you could see billowing smoke and fumes going all the way down the driveway. My neighbor told me that she could smell mildew two houses away. My Uncle Paul, my brothers Gary and Ron, and I could not believe what we were witnessing.

I could not believe how hard everyone worked. They didn't think I did anything at all, but compared to them, I didn't. I talked to Shirley in Utah quite a bit using Ron's cell phone. She told me what a healing it was for all of us. I thought she should have been there healing with us, being a little facetious. We filled up two huge Dumpsters that were the length of the driveway, and that was not enough; we could have done more. We had all the windows open, and you could have passed out from the fumes alone. I do not know how all that mold did not affect them very badly all those years that they lived in it. They had been taking the stuff out that was worth something for two years before we attempted doing this. As it was, my dad said we could not get any Dumpsters. Ron did this without him knowing about it. I think in his subconscious that he did know. My dad would want stuff done, but then he would thwart any attempt on your part of doing it and then blame you if it wasn't done. There was a lot of accumulation at the new house in the basement that they could not part with. It is all in the eye of the beholder as to what is your treasure. I told my mom when I left that no matter how you, slice it this was an obsession.

While I was watching *Good Morning, America* one morning, they talked about people being obsessed with hanging on to garbage and hoarding many of the same items that they could not let go of. I forget what they called it, but I think they were referring to it being some sort disease, that they really could not help themselves. At least I knew that others had this problem and my parents weren't the only ones. I know some people are big collectors, but you don't come across many that are of garbage.

My dad and mom went to estate sales, garage sales, and auctions. I do believe that they bought a lot of other people's garbage. I know it is one man's meat and another man's poison and that it is in the eye of the beholder, so of course, that is my opinion of what is garbage. These items were their treasures. I was amazed at the empty boxes that were in the house that had nothing in them. I guess they had kept them to put stuff into and forgot about them. The labyrinth reminded me of huge anthills that came to peaks. I was so amazed at how my dad precariously stacked their items, almost like an art form.

I told the two of them that this was a reflection of their mind and spirits. People that have this problem should seek professional help. They work on the people in baby steps. My mom is a huge collector of pottery. She believes that she was a potter in a previous lifetime. I have heard of other people's houses being like my parents, but I have never seen anyone's. They would both blame each other, saying they had collected more treasure. My dad had to have had a hundred oilers that you could see periodically everywhere throughout the house. He had enough tools for ten men. He was a photographer and had thirty different tripods—all the same thing. I think a lot of people during this generation were hoarders. They were either in the Depression or whatever and had an enormous need to collect.

Probably, I would say, the greatest sadness that I witnessed my father do was to my youngest brother, Paul. When he became a teenager, he encouraged him to abuse my mom, my twin sister, Carol, and myself with abusive language. He would take pleasure in witnessing Paul act up and out. My mom said to my dad one day, "Are you willing to sacrifice your son at my expense?" He acknowledged, yes, he was. So this was with thought. He took pleasure in watching our anguish. He figured that my mom had turned all the children against him and he was out for revenge. Finally, my mom told Paul that this was not healthy for him, and she managed to change it around some, but the damage had already been done.

We went to St. Cyril's for elementary school, and the school told my parents that he could not come back unless he went to counseling through Catholic social services. They went as a family, and then my dad went by himself. Well, he did not like what they told him, and he never returned. My mom never found out what they told him but guessed that they blamed him. Paul was a chronic liar about everything and a stealer. By the time they got to Paul, they gave him virtually no discipline. He destroyed anything that was given to him, even if it was a brand-new bike given to him by his grandfather. He would call me *witch*; I tried to stay away from him as much as possible. He would be nice to Crissy and David, my two oldest, one minute, and mean the next, when they were little. They had a dog named Dinky that was a miniature collie, which never knew if Paul was going to be nice or mean. When he was mean, he could be very mean.

Another sad time for me to witness was when we were at the family reunion in the summer of '93 at SLC, Utah. Before we left to drive out there, I knew that it was very important for me to go, but I did not know why. My dad set out at this reunion to get revenge against my sister-in-law Suzanne. She tried very hard to stay away from him, but before it ended, he managed to be successful. Ron and Suzanne's marriage was estranged anyway; my dad succeeded in triumph by ending it. I could not believe what I was witnessing; I was in shock. Many years later, I asked him if his intent was to totally alienate Suzanne, because that is what he succeeded in doing. I thought would I totally want to alienate an in-law child; of course, the answer would be no.

It would be too long a story to tell the whole thing, but I left feeling sad and crying all the way home. He felt like he had lovingly told Suzanne off on several different occasions, in front of everyone. When she was getting into the car to leave to go to the airport, he made his final scene. I couldn't believe my brother Ron said nothing. I went to my dad and told him what he had done was heinous and left to go upstairs, not believing what I had just witnessed. I do believe I put my hand to my mouth as I was going up. When I got into Shirley's bedroom, we were making fun of my dad, and I guess you could say that I took pleasure in it. I had to laugh because it was better than crying.

When I arrived home, a letter came from my dad in Utah that he had been inspired to write while he was at church one Sunday. I called up Larry, Shirley's husband, on the phone and read the letter to him. He said that I had made this huge scene as I was clutching my throat and running upstairs. No one was there when I did it. He disowned me in the letter, all of which completely destroyed me. After reading it, the angels were kind, and I fell asleep for a few hours, which normally I never can do during the middle of the day. Mike and I went up north to our property, and when I got into Higgins Lake, complete calmness came over me. That is hard to believe, but it did. It took me a couple of years to get over that reunion and that letter he wrote me. I have spent most of my life never wanting to see him again as long as I lived. I cannot imagine why I never moved out of state or just stayed away altogether. All the other seven kids moved out of state—I do believe to get away from him—so I felt like I was responsible to help him. I may as well been banging my head against the wall—it has been arduous and tumultuous at best just to have anything to do with him.

23

Sibling Reunion

There was a reunion in 1985, which was held in Las Vegas, Nevada, that only the eight kids went to, and maybe a couple of spouses. Most of the time we spent at the reunion was on complaining about our difficulty getting along with our dad. None of us could understand the method to his madness. He blamed everything on my mom and her mom, Alice. He told us often that he was just a paycheck. That my mom waited on him hand over fist, hand over fist, because that is what she said. I do not know why I agreed to all of this. I do not remember the previous lifetime where I had given it to my dad. Boy, if only you all knew that you were creating your next lifetime in this one, I think you would give more thought to what you think, say, and do in this lifetime. Everything you give out, good or bad, loops back, picks up magnitude and momentum, and comes right back at you. That is the universal law, called cause and effect or karma.

This is why it is very important to resolve your issues, because they do come back to haunt you. This is why there are no victims or martyrs, because we make or create our reality and blame everyone else. What you condemn, you become, but that might have to show up in your next lifetime. If you condemn gays, prostitutes, smoking, and evangelists or are a racist, guess what you will be in your next lifetime? What you give out comes right back at you. Each lifetime, you go through a veil of forgetfulness, so you do not remember the spirit group you were participating with in the previous lifetime. Sometimes you are the parent, and sometimes you are the child. It is okay if you do not believe in reincarnation. Do you want to take that chance? Eternity is a long time to waste on one lifetime, and if you get it wrong, you will be condemned to hell for eternity. God loves us too much for that.

The whole reason we are here is to see if we will react in faith or fear. The golden rule is "Do unto others, as you would have others do unto you." That simply means loving all people, even your enemy. Know that the enemy is you and you are the enemy. We are all one and one with God. That is why what you give out, you really do to everyone because everyone is you. So if you are putting down another religion or making a judgment of any kind, you are judging yourself. When we die, we will witness the harm we did to another. We will be them and see the negativity they gave out because of what we did. There is nothing like seeing clearly and objectively by being them. By the same token, we will also see the love we gave and how it snowballed as well. I do believe we will be our own judges because we will see and feel all of it. This is called a life review. It will be very hard for us to witness. We will not need God to judge us. He does not see the illusion. All negativity is an illusion. It does not matter how it shows up—pettiness, littleness, jealousy, revenge, hatred, etc.

God does not see it! He only sees our magnificence and love. We are all loved beyond measure, no matter what role we are playing. All of us eventually make it—it is our birthright to have joy and ecstasy. For God to be condemning anyone to hell, he would be condemning himself and us all as well. Why would God want to do that? Isn't it nice to know that no one goes to hell? If by chance we would like to see an ax murderer go to hell, we would definitely be wishing it on ourselves and everyone else. So will we think before we think, do, and say—that is, walk consciously? I like to tell people if we were that ax murderer, would we want to be forgiven and would we want to be loved? I don't know about you, but I would. So be cognizant at all times of your thoughts, words, and deeds; they will come back to haunt you. Take an inventory at the end of the day or, better yet, while you are thinking it or doing it. Offer it up immediately, clear it, then it is gone.

The universe is like a large computer. We think we can fool others and be in denial, but we do not fool the universe. What we deny we declare. If we steal from the government, no matter what excuses we come up with, do we tell the truth no matter what? That includes white lies? The truth hurts, but lies can hurt more. I believe Martin Luther King said that sentence. Live honestly with love in your heart, and there will not be any problem. Religions make you think that everything is outside you. Everything is inside you. You are the temple. Nothing is outside you! If we perceive we are going to hell, we will, but God will not leave us there; he will send us help. Everything is what we perceive even when we die. Always it is our free choice, even when we die. I believe it is even more of a free choice when we die, because no one can interfere with it. I have decided just how grand my imagination can be for my heaven. I think I will have a lot of decadent chocolate that is good for you and helps you lose weight, colors that will be brighter, and musical symphony orchestration in all things, just to name a few. Fabricate your wildest imagination—the sky is the limit. Just how much serendipity can you stand?

I think I finally figured out why my dream at the beginning of my book when I was being baptized in the Mormon religion meant. Darlene, who sent me to her biological dad, is Mormon, and so is her dad. The chiropractor is Jack Mormon. The two people that prayed over me for my blessing are Mormon. So I believe the beginning into my spiritual growth was from Mormon people. I do believe that I will be involved in Utah as well. Don't know when that will be materializing; I just think it. I knew when I had that dream that I was not turning Mormon because I had no desire to, thinking that a baptism meant a new beginning, but why was I in a Mormon gown? It was a long white gown gathered at the waist and neckline with, I believe, long sleeves that just came down the arm and out. I remembered how I extended my hand out. I brought my right arm back, fingers pointed down, extending my hand out, bringing my palm up. I walked around quite a bit after that dream, doing that same extension. I believe that I said to my dad that I will always be Catholic; that is what I was raised in. That was my beginning into spiritualism—besides, I will always be Catholic.

I did not go the following Wednesday to the Holy Ghost prayer group; went the following one after that. Everything that was said was the reason that they did not like what I had said. I waited for a whole year for the right words to come. I do feel like it would have been easier getting in front of pagans than people that knew it all. I was so passionate about those words because I thought I had given them pearls. It was obvious to me that most of them did not approve of what I had said. If I helped one person, then it was worth it. Besides, I may have planted some seeds that will come to fruition at the proper time. Between what happened to my dad and the meditation group, I really thought I was no further ahead than before I started the Dark Night of the Soul. In the movie *Pay It Forward* the little boy, Trevor, thought the same thing—that none of his good deeds worked either, and he died before he found out that they did. I actually believe no good deed goes unrewarded. I know they have the saying, "No good deed goes unpunished." Even if we pick up a piece of paper and throw it away, the universe sees all. They are blessings from heaven. So even if no one is watching, the universe always is. Do good deeds, no matter how insignificant they might seem to be. Life resolves itself in the process of life itself! Our salvation is guaranteed.

24

St. Elizabeth Catholic Church

Last Sunday Father Charles, at St. Elizabeth's, said that Bill would be giving a speech on Tuesday, Wednesday, and Thursday at 7:30 p.m. So I chose Tuesday evening—that would be the time that I would go. Also he said he was a very good healer. He played the organ and we mostly sang songs. He had a fire in him and he gave it to everyone that was there. Then he told us to choose two different people to pray with and to tell them whatever came to us. I chose the two women who sat behind me, whom I had never met, called Carol and Audrey. All three of us took our turns, saying our parts, addressing each other by names. I started off first, felt good saying what I said, plus I felt good hearing what they had to say. I went up to Bill's girlfriend and told her that I would not be able to come back and asked if he could pray over me. So we waited till most of the people had left the church. The two of them prayed over me. Bill told me that I was joyful and that I must have had a lot of friends. He told me that my relationship had healed. Then I told the two of them a little bit about the dark night of the soul. Bill said that he had the book by St. John of the Cross, but he had only read about half. He also said that he felt like he was in it as well. He said he really felt good giving praise and doing what he does, but the other times were not so good.

Theron had told me to look into his eyes, so that is what I said to him, simply that I was told to look into your eyes. Then I proceeded to tell them that most of the Holy Ghost people do not approve of reiki but that I also did reiki. He said he likewise did not think he approved—energy and all. Then this was a spin-off from the other Holy Ghost people at St. Mary Magdalene's. I told them that we have a Bible in one hand; we are righteous, and somehow we think that it is okay to judge. He said you have to judge. I said gays and other religions—did we have to judge them? I said, "Judge least thee be judged." I said that Jesus did not attack his attackers. That we were everyone on the planet and everyone was we. Unless we lead with love, we were not making it. I tapped my heart with my right hand. Plus I said, "Live and let live." The famous saying "You without sin cast the first stone" says it all. He did not like what I said and turned and walked away. I was very calm and confident; I do believe that I was effective. If nothing else, the seed was planted, coming to fruition at the proper time. His girlfriend walked me out of the church, and I told her that I had turned him off. She said no, I hadn't. I said, "Oh yes, I did." I drove home in the storm, while it was thundering and lightning, thinking that I had failed. I had to remain meek and without vanity or I was not making it. That is why the meek shall inherit the earth—the meek know that we are all one.

Right before going to California, a mother robin made a nest in the hanging plant I had on the front porch and laid four eggs. They hatched, all four, just before I left. I actually witnessed one of them cracking open, which happened to be the third egg hatched, and the baby breaking out. Seeing the babies barely lifting their heads and wings, most vulnerable in their little state. The mother would sit on the eggs while I talked to her and assured her that everything was okay and that she would not be harmed; most of the time she did not move when I went out my front door. I was hoping that they would all be there when I arrived home from California. Mike went on the front porch, the night before I was coming home, and said to the babies, "You guys look like you are ready to leave!" That very instant, all four of them took off simultaneously, scaring Mike a little from their flight. I wished I had been there to witness this phenomenon. Ever since Baby, I have enjoyed the bonding experience with birds. Mike told me that he wished he could feed babies worms and have them leave the nest in such a short period of time. I thought that was cute, with him paralleling them with children, in particular ours since we had four children.

25

Mike and I Went Up North

A COUPLE OF DAYS after I had gotten home, Mike and I took off north to our property in Roscommon. We usually went up there to work, but we also brought the boat with us. Mike had decided that the outhouse needed to be moved. The bottom of it, after twenty-one years, was breaking down. So we turned it over on its side while Mike replaced the wood with wolmanized (it is a treated wood), so it would be good for at least another twenty-one years. It all went easier and less stinky than I thought it would. Mike just dug a hole near the other one and put the dirt he dug into the other hole. He used a car jack to assist us, and we were able to do it. It was so much sturdier now that it had been replaced. Plus we cut up five trees; three were already lying on the ground. We only took down dead trees because usually every year, there were a couple of new dead trees, even if we went in surrounding lots. We have never seen anyone use their property on either side of us or in the back. They do not have anything on their property either.

I had gone to an art fair they had in Roscommon by myself, then with Cheryl, who came down from Boyne City to visit with us. She enjoys art fairs just as much as I do. I bought some dried flowers to put above the front door and a very attractive candle in a canning jar. All you do is buy oil to refill it. I have been going to fairs for quite a few years, and this was unique for me. She had put red grapes and all kinds of colorful stuff in it to make it pleasing to the eye. I also bought a boat in the shape of a canoe with little fishing gadgets on it to hang in Mike's den, where I am typing my manuscript.

Then, of course, we spent boating and swimming time on Higgins Lake. I took quite a few pictures of our property and the lake just to have on hand and to send to Pauline. It was so foggy the last time she was there that I wanted her to see it. I did my usual walk along the shore. I do my meditating—I Ams and just generally talking to my guides.

I have been doing this for years. It is just time for me to spend with me, and I like it. I haven't tried to go skiing on Higgins Lake since I was about forty-two. I had made up my mind that I was going to get up on one ski when I was forty-two and did. I had gotten up and dropped a ski when I was a teenager; I just wanted to prove that I still had it. Higgins Lake is most of the time rough, making skiing arduous at best, let alone on one ski. On the first couple of tries, I felt like I was being sprayed to death. I could not breathe; I had to let go. I knew I could do it and did. I have had a couple of bad falls where I had to lie in the water and not move when I was younger, and I definitely wanted to give up skiing altogether.

Mike had decided, before we left to come up north, that we would be going up to Mullet Lake to look for property on the water. Mullet Lake is above the forty-fifth parallel, so it is not far from the Mackinaw Bridge. The forty-fifth parallel is halfway between the equator and the North Pole. I am agreeing with this but not thinking that anything will be materializing. Everything on Higgins Lake is way out of sight. We heard that Bert Lake was also high, so we decided to look on Mullet. We had stayed at a little hotel right near the entrance of Bert State Park campgrounds. We got a room and then decided to drive around Mullet Lake looking for something within reach. After driving around the whole lake, we decided that being on the water was out of reach. But there were a few houses just on the other side of M27, a little two-lane road that had beachfront property and a very good view. Mike said he could handle that.

So we went to the Realtor the following morning. He brought up four houses on the other side of M27, all of which we had seen while driving from the road. He said this white house was neat and clean on the inside with an older kitchen. An attraction of this house was it had almost two acres of land and one hundred feet of beachfront property. This house was also on the west side of the lake, which Mike wanted. He said the water wasn't as rough and there were fewer rocks. I told Mike this house was the exact criteria that Carol, my spiritual psychic, had told me about two years ago. She said that it would have big windows—a nice white house on or near the water with the letter *M* next to it. Of course, *M* stood for M27, Mullet and Michigan. She thought the *M* might stand for Michigan. She had seen me moving in at the beginning of the year 2000, though; the middle of 2001 was the beginning. So we made an appointment to go see the inside the following day. We put a bid in for $31,000, less than they were asking for. I told the realtor that we would be getting the house because of what Carol had told me two years ago. He did not comment. He told us that he would let us know in three days whether or not they accepted the bid. When Carol told me this and it did not materialize at the first of the year, I gave up on it happening at all and doubted whether or not it would happen then. So Friday after we got home, they called us up and said they had accepted the bid. I was a little bit in shock about all of it.

This house is a five-room house with a sunroom in the front of the house that is not heated. The great room is eighteen by twenty, and that is the biggest room with the kitchen following. Both bedrooms are little smaller yet, and the one bathroom is very small. There is a basement under the great room and kitchen only. It is rather a cavernous dungeon to me; however, everyone that has seen it says that is a Michigan basement and not that bad. The furnace is a huge tank that I think was an oil-burning furnace that was converted to gas. The floor is not tiled, and the walls need to be fixed up; plus I would like a ceiling put in. Even though this house is small, relatively speaking, I know I will be very happy here. You know there are only so much rooms that you can occupy in a house and in the rest you store stuff. I would like a den to have a computer and all, but this is it. This house is really not conducive to adding on to. We are guessing that the house is fifty years old; it did not say when it was built. I never thought that I could like an older home. I always wanted a new one. This house has character, and I just fell in love with it, from the knotty pine paneling in the bedrooms and breezeway to the garage and basement, the wooden windows with no border, the wooden fireplace, to the old wooden cupboards in the kitchen. The great room, however, is my favorite place, with the curved detailed ceiling that looks regal to me. There are some very big houses being built on Mullett Lake, but I would feel greedy, when most of the world did not have a home. This is not a judgment; it is just how I feel. Besides, we were doing very good to afford this.

My friend called me up one morning—I will call her Mary—and she said she was awakened by the spirit world, and what happened this morning was strong. She told me that she felt like she was in college, taking dictation to try to get it all down fast enough; this went on for about two hours. She felt the presence of a mutual friend and was told that

Mike's mother was another; she also thought there were more. I asked her how she knew it was Mike's mother, and she said, "Because she said she was Mike's mother." She proceeded to take down three pages, all of which looked like different handwriting. She said, "You know I don't understand your spiritualism or condemn it." She said, "It is 5:16 a.m. and I am alert."

This is how it went: "Don't let your passion become an obsession! It should be a part of your life, not your entire existence. Heal only those that request healing. The purpose of your book is to heal your soul and let you prepare. It is time to let go, move on. You have grown spiritually—found your peace and serenity. Now quietly move into the next color, blue. Talk less, and just be Kathy again. Go quietly into the night. In October, do volunteer work with the elderly—give them blessings quietly so as not to alarm them by putting your hands on their shoulders. Read other books. Begin your journey and now end it. Let your new strength guide you. Only bare your soul to those that ask." She said, since she started me on my journey to recovery, "I feel obligated to tell you to let it go! You now have peace and serenity. Let your spirit rest. Stop preaching to nonbelievers. Those that need your help will find you. Find other topics to talk about." All of this was quite amazing to her and to me.

The following Tuesday, they woke her up again, only this time she said they were men that looked like colorful bouncing balls. She said she was cold. She told me that they were like the head honchos, head of the CEO, the top guns. She told them they looked like a bingo game. They said this was not a game. Then they said you are enabling this behavior that they have worked too hard to lose me now. They told her that we had talked on the phone for nine hours—guess they were keeping track. Then she told them to leave and not come back. They told her that she did not have a choice. Then she asked to talk to Mike's mother. She was impressed that she had the moxie to ask. (Freda, Mike's mother, died when Mike was fifteen.) She said she looked like a vision in light and that she was warm. She said, "I will never have peace until you find some serenity. Why are you so angry? Don't you know that I am in another place? Count your blessings, little one." Freda, Mike's mother, was talking to her son Mike here. Mary told them that if they wanted to come back, to come after 11:00 a.m., that she stayed up late and wanted her sleep. I asked her how she knew they were men—she said she just knew one had long black hair. I think that was Gray Eagle.

I have made spiritualism such a big part of my life that I wondered if I would be able to successfully do what they had asked, but I set out to try. At first I felt a little less, but now I understand most of what they were talking about. I have done bragging about my book and other things; they have let me know that isn't being meek. Pride is a problem for most people. I understand more and observe more. One thing higher dimensions do is observe more. I look to see what I see in other people and relate it to myself, offering up to the Holy Spirit what I see. I fall on my face either with reacting, preaching, or bragging, but I keep offering everything up—I feel that I cannot go wrong if I continue doing that. I do not want them to let me get away with anything; I want to strive to act like Jesus! As the saying goes, "What would Jesus do?" WWJD.

Mike and I decided that we wanted to go up north and take some pictures of the inside and outside of the house now that we knew we were buying it. Unfortunately, when we got up there, the people, for whatever reason, would not let us in; they made themselves unavailable. So our realtor went with us to take pictures of the outside. We also wanted to take care of a few other things concerning the house. Mike wanted to walk in the water to see how fast it dropped off. So I walked around the perimeter, taking many pictures of the surrounding area. We stayed in a log cabin hotel that was set back in the woods near the house. When we got home, I decided to put the roll of film in right away because we wanted to show people the pictures. When I got them back, in a close-up of the house, I saw a white horse with wings just above the roof, just about touching the roof. Then there were three other pictures that had some stuff in it that I did not see when I was taking the pictures.

Carol P. told me that I had a white horse and she did not know what it meant. It bothered me that these pictures were messed up, and I thought about taking them back. But I decided that there was more significance to these pictures than I thought and decided otherwise. I felt like the spirit world put this in, maybe my guides. Sent the pictures to Pauline in Utah, and she said whatever these pictures represented it was for me. She said she saw a lot of good energy flowing in the pictures. She also said the flying horse, as you see it, is very symbolic of power and freedom in motion. Take a ride on that energy and soar, there will be much awaiting your discovery. Betty said that we would be well protected, with nothing to worry about, and that we would be happy there. This was all was music to my ears!

We were told that we would probably not have to go up for the actual signing of the house, but because we had to do this before September 1, 2001, time was of the essence. So we ended up having to drive up on Thursday, August 30. I was not too happy about this because it was Labor Day weekend and I knew the traffic would be bad. We had to stop off in Livonia first to pick up the papers from the loan company. We stayed in a hotel right at the entrance of Bert Lake state park. I had walked to the lake from the hotel to witness the ending of a beautiful orange-red sunset. This whole weekend, for whatever reason, my stomach was bothering me a lot. So I do not know what was happening, was I making this trauma on myself or what? So once more, I thought I was dying. I finally told my guides that I had had enough suffering. I knew there was stress buying the house because all the many problems that we had. Plus my daughter Karen's wedding was coming up the following weekend.

We stopped off at our property in Roscommon to spend the night. Tyler and I walked to the Au

Sable River just to have an evening stroll, on which I wore him out. I had a ball knocking down dead little trees in the back of the lot and burning them in the fire. It was cool out, but because of the fire and the work I was doing, I did not need a jacket. I enjoyed the evening very much. I wondered if we would be spending any more nights on this property now that we had the house on Mullet Lake.

26

My Daughter Karen's Wedding

MY DAUGHTER KAREN'S WEDDING the following weekend was magic! The spirit world had visited my sister Shirley, who was at my mom's house. She had awakened first, and then the light next to her bed, which is hard to turn on, went on, on its own. Whoever the spirits were, they said to savor the magic and we were here for the celebration. The actual ceremony was glorious in every way. Karen and her new husband, Darrell, saw its grandest success. Being totally impartial, my daughter Karen was the prettiest bride I had ever seen. I had seen her wedding dress, but never did I think she would radiate that glamorously—all of the bridal party looked like models. It was held at St. Paul's Presbyterian Church in Livonia.

JoAnn agreed to let the girls all get dressed at her house near the church. The photographer was there as well, taking the girls' and family's pictures. JoAnn had set out to make Karen's day blessed for me. She did my hair and told me how beautiful I looked many times. She supplied wine and hors d'oeuvres, which I thought were marvelous. When Karen and Mike walked down the aisle and Karen got up next to me, I started choking up, and the minister said, "We have a whiner." I did not know how I would respond, but I did not think I would cry. Crissy, my daughter standing on the altar not far from me, said, "Mom, cut it out," and I was able to get a grip. Karen went between laughter and crying—I don't think she knew what to do. We both settled down, and everything went smoothly. She had two ring bearers and one flower girl that stole the show. Christopher and Cory, Crissy's two boys, and Lindsey Darrell sister Deana's daughter were the little angels participating. They acted like they were in their own little world, conversing amongst themselves, sauntering and strolling slowly down the aisle.

The reception followed immediately in Farmington Hills at Vladimir's Hall. Three hundred guests would be attending our celebration, besides the spirit world. With all that my stomach had been through recently, I needed to dance the stress off, and did. I decided I was going to savor the moment like the spirit world had said to and enjoy. While I was at JoAnn's, sitting downstairs in the dining room, I saw some stuff with my eyes closed, and I do not know if that helped me have joyous energy flowing through me or what. But it did. Many people told me how pretty I looked and commented on my dancing. saying I was the belle of the ball. I just decided to have a ball and did. It truly was the most enjoyable wedding for me that I'd ever attended, of course, being totally impartial like I said. I looked around to see everyone having a joyous time; it truly was a magical day for all.

My friend Gail told me at the reception that she felt the pain I was in last weekend. But that she also knew there was nothing that she could do for me. I said the hell I was in. And she said yes.

Helen called me up the next day and left a message on my answering machine. I did not return her call till Monday evening, the night before the attack. She also said that she felt my pain and asked what problems was I having? I told her I had a lot of pain in my stomach.

The next morning, I called my mom, not turning on the TV first. She said, "Don't you know that we are under a terrorist attack?" I immediately turned on my TV, ran into Mike sleeping in the bedroom, and told him we were under a terrorist attack. He thought I was overreacting and then proceeded to tell me WWIII had started. JoAnn, in turn, called me, and I told her. She likewise did not have the TV on; she was reading the newspaper. She said she would never forget the words that I had told her.

27

9-11-01

ON TUESDAY, SEPTEMBER 11, 2001, we had a terrorist attack on America, called America's Darkest Day. The Trade Center in New York had two airplanes taking off from Boston headed for LA; they hit both towers like fifteen minutes apart. Flight 77, departing Washington Dulles International Airport for Los Angeles, crashed into the west side of the Pentagon. Finally a fourth plane, having being hijacked, carrying passengers, went down in Pennsylvania—we believe, headed for the White House. In case some did not notice, that was 9/11—Sept. 11, 2001. This was a test for the world on how they would react—either with faith or fear. The choice was collectively all ours, with our thoughts and deeds, as to the outcome. Attack begets attack! My proposal was that we pray that President Bush would make the right decision.

I called up Carol P. and asked her if there was a correlation between my stomach bothering the attack and me. She said yes and to talk to my guides about it.

On the day of the attack or the day before, I had dried blood running down the left side of my face, at least a couple of inches. Mike had noticed it; I wasn't aware of it at all. I tried to wipe it with my fingers. It would not come off, so I washed it and it did. My face hurt at the place where it was supposedly coming from. I do not remember hurting myself. In any case, nothing showed. I also saw it in my towel that I used one time. For close to a week, I had blood smeared on both of my pillows, like I had makeup on that went all over both pillows. When I awoke in the morning, Mike told me that all the corpuscles in my cheeks and forehead were busted and I was bleeding. My face at this time did not hurt at all. When I looked in the bathroom mirror, because of my eyesight, I could barely see the bleeding. None of it looked real to me; it looked brownish purple. Mike thought it was the face cream I was using that was causing it. I never wear my makeup to bed; I always wash my face first. Plus, most of the time, I do not wear any makeup. I went in the bathroom and washed my face; I asked if my face was okay. Mike said yes. I am clueless as to what happened with my face; I just don't know. Maybe I was bleeding for the estimated five thousand people that perished. My face did not hurt at all then.

I do not think that my face bled because I meditated or prayed a lot and somehow I might be special, like the stigmata. I have difficulty in blocking out the chatter in my mind, and I do not pray that much. I say Psalm 23 every day and maybe a few Hail Marys and Our Fathers. I also like to give thanks and appreciation for everything. Plus I take an inventory—or at least try to—of what I need to clear. I believe the only reason my face bled is because I went through the dark night of the soul, clearing many lifetimes. I believe it was many lifetimes because of the unprecedented weird things that I experienced. My having my stomach be a cavity and being put on a rack, to name a couple. Also, I know we are all equal. So no one is better than anyone else. Had I known what was happening, I would have taken a new white pillowcase and pressed it against my face, like the shroud.

On the same day of the attack, Shirley and I went to the Church of Today for a Deepak Chopra seminar at 7:00 p.m. Marianne started it off by saying that Deepak was supposed to give a talk on his latest book and instead could talk about whatever he wanted. The atmosphere was somber because of the traumatic, chaotic day of events that we all had. It reminded me of the movie *The Day the Earth Stood Still*. I felt, with everyone glued to their sets and no traffic in our skies, you could certainly say that. I had worn the same clothes and sat in the same seat as I did the last time. I had brought my manuscript because I wanted to give it to Deepak to maybe assist me in getting it published. I am sure a lot of people give him a lot of stuff to read, and I know he could not possibly read it all.

So I tried communicating telepathically, seeing as it worked the last time. In fact, I wanted to say the same words, "My name is Kathy Gotz, and I have something for you." I could tell that he was too badly affected by the events of the day, so I even added stuff like "I would like you to read my book." When you set out an intent, you are then supposed to surrender the outcome by not being attached to it. I did this the last time, but I don't think I did this time. When he was walking off the stage, I came close to him, and it seemed to me like he was reaching out for my manuscript that I had in my hands but had second thoughts. So we walked up to where he was signing books and gave it to the lady that was accompanying him, and she promised to give it to him.

28

Meditation Group

Tuesday evening Shirley, Dave, and I went out to Betty's meditation group in Royal Oak. I wanted to ask Betty about my universe rock and to ask her about my white horse in the picture. My universe rock, she said, looked like the universe to her as well; she felt it was healing. She said yes, it looked like a white horse to her as well but did not say much more. We looked at the pictures of Mullet Lake and Roscommon; she saw many faces in the trees in both. She would even see the faces move or change. She pointed them out to me, but I did not see them. She also saw many extraterrestrials at Mullet Lake everywhere in the trees or sky.

Nancy did the healing exchange with me. She did me first, and while she was doing me, she said I was waving a ribbon very happily on a luxury liner. She did not think that it was a cruise but a spiritual journey. She told me that I was thinking that it was about time; believe me, I will be thinking that. I know proportionately equal to what you go through, you have gifts and opportunities on the other side. I held the universe rock in my hands while she was giving me the healing; she put her hands on top of mine and told me the rock was like a magnet and very healing. She also told me that there was an Uncle Charlie. I said, "I do not have an Uncle Charlie." She said although he said Uncle Charlie, she felt he was more like a grandpa.

The next day, I asked my mom if I had an Uncle Charlie. She said yes, she had an Uncle Charlie; he was her mother's sister Gert's husband. He was Italian, played the accordion for a living, and was very controlling.

When I was being prayed over by Carl and Shirley and I saw the tunnel crystal clear then out to the light, I think it had more significance than I had originally thought. Actually, I did not know what to think about why I was shown the tunnel, not a clue.

I went with Theron to a spiritualistic church that is in Royal Oak where Betty was in charge of a meditation group. Each person picks another person to give healing to, and then they exchange and give back to the person that gave to them. Theron did me first; while he was giving me reiki, he told me that my guides were very proud of me, then he told me, "God bless you." After that was over with, they sang a couple of songs, and then Betty channeled for each member of the group, telling each person who was coming through. I think she said that Marie was coming through for me. She told me that things would work out for me but that I needed to think before I said stuff and not react.

Afterward, we were getting ready to leave; I decided that I wanted Betty to look at my rock that was in the form of a picture of a lady that I had gotten from California. The instant that she took the rock in her hands, she said the first thing that came to her was "The Light at the End of the Tunnel." I told her that I saw the tunnel. I do believe that meant that I was reaching the light at the end of the tunnel. It has been a very long process, a process of forgiveness, nonjudgment—the good or the bad. I have slain my demons and survived—with that came inner peace and serenity! It's over, it's over—my dark night of the soul is over! Through the darkness came the light. Betty also told me that many nationalities in the spirit world took part in the forming of this rock, which would be used in my healing work, and that the rock was spiritual. All people must heal themselves by bringing peace and love into their own hearts.

I kept two of the five rocks that I had purchased in Half Moon Bay. The instant I saw both, I knew they were for me. I actually wanted to keep all five, finding them most incredulous but decided that I should share my wealth. Theron's, I knew, was his too; the other two we did not know whom to give them to and decided that I would give one to each of my daughters. Karen—I gave hers to her, and Crissy came over and actually took the one I preferred her to have while I was not at home. I just told her I had a rock for her. All the rocks were unique and special, as far as I was concerned. The other rock I had chosen for myself I took over to my mom's. Now I knew the piece of artwork was mine and incredible, but the other one was incredible also. The instant my mom took the rock, she said it reminded her of outer space then the universe. This rock swirled toward a center of white, but it had a myriad of brilliant colors such as emerald, indigo, gray, a few areas of a creamy mauve, a few dots of orange, and an earthy brownish orange, all of which were brilliant and iridescent with a magnificent shimmering glow. It also had craters that you could say represented planets and asteroids. I couldn't place what it reminded me of, but she was correct. You needed to view these rocks outside; sunlight was mandatory in viewing these rocks. This is why it was important that I saw these rocks outside when I bought them, because I would have never saw their eloquence and essence without it.

29

Taking Possession of Mullett House

AT THE END OF September, Mike and I went up to our property on Mullet Lake to take possession of it. Carl and Beverly, the people that we were purchasing it from, showed up because they had the last little bit to pick up, and they turned over the keys to us. They left the house in real good shape. While Beverly was finishing up, I had a chance to talk to her. I thought I sure would like to be friends with her and wished she lived next door. They were having a house built on Lake Huron not too far from this house. They introduced us to the people that lived next door, who were also very nice, Cheryl and Mike. I did hope I had a chance to see Carl and Beverly again. I feel as though I would because they were really good friends with the people that lived next door, so I was sure they would visit them.

I had a lot of opportunity to sit at the water because it was right across the street. I was contact papering the shelves in the kitchen cabinets, and I would take a break to sit at the water. I was truly mesmerized by the beauty and colors of this lake. I did not think I could love another lake as much as I loved Higgins, but I think I will even more, for we own this beach in front of our house. I felt like I was in heaven. My guides wanted me to let the dark night go, and this lake sure did help. Monday night, the moon looked awesome reflecting on the water, so I went to take a few pictures, hoping that they would turn out, but unfortunately, they didn't. Oh well, I gambled.

The next morning, Mike got up to go to the bathroom, and he said, "The sun is just starting to crest right now." I threw on my clothes and grabbed my camera to run outside and take pictures. I asked Archangel Michael and Raphael to assist in them turning out okay. I took one on the deck of the house then ran down to the beach, crossing M27 quickly, taking a few more pictures, one on the end of our dock. I stayed for a little bit, enjoying the moment, then went back and got into bed with Mike. The room was dark because it was in the back of the house, and the walls were that knotty pine, augmenting the darkness. Immediately after shutting the door, I saw a very vivid color show with my eyes closed, probably the most phenomenal to date. I saw a cross with Jesus on it and then with Jesus off of it—that was vague and was more sensing than seeing, but I did see. I believe that was my resurrection. Then I saw what I would say was an animated little girl, very vivid, standing at the bottom of the picture. I guess I would say that it was me, with the lack of anything else that it would represent. But I found out later that she has been a little girl guide that has been with my twin sister and me since we have been little. Then I saw this flash four different times—it appeared to be a sun with an indigo glob around it that had three humps on the top and bottom, which went more up and down than horizontally coming at me. I think those might have been spiritual gifts—I don't know. This went on for, it seemed, like fifteen minutes, just guessing though. The rest was an amazing color show of pinks and greens in different shapes but not really anything. I enjoyed it so much that I did not want it to end.

After it ended, I said to Mike, "If ever you doubt what I am doing, you won't believe what I just saw," and I told him about it.

The pictures of the sunrise that I had witnessed at Mullet Lake turned out beautiful. It is nice to show people what I saw before something happened to me. I also took several pictures of beautiful soft pastel colors of pink and blues, a peaceful sunset on that same day in the same spot my pictures are dated. It was not of the actual sun setting, though, because we get the sunrise being on the west side of the lake. In one of the pictures that I got back then of the day ending, it had a white circle of bright light sitting on the water and going below, a little right of center. It definitely was not the moon. I could not figure out at all what it could be. Of course I did not see it when I took the pictures. I asked Betty if she had an explanation. She said that she did not know, but whatever it was, it was for me. I believe that it was a beacon of bright light being reflected back at me, that I was that beacon of light. That was a glorious day for me… October 2, 2001. My spiritual psychic did verify to me that I did get the gifts of healing and knowledge.

The house in Taylor located behind me on the corner has these five scary figures that they made out of people clothes, boots, and masks that they set out each year for Halloween. Each figure stood as tall as a man and looked real in stature. The man of the house made these up himself. For several years now, I have felt that one of those figures next to the sidewalk was following me with his eyes when I went by. I would talk to him and tell him that I was not afraid of him but not going up to him. I asked Theron if I should do a blessing with holy water telling him to go to the light and that he would not be harmed. Theron told me yes, that I should. So I went out and quietly did a prayer, asking the host of heaven to assist me behind my garage in the backyard. When I walked over there to do it, he was knocked over leaning against the house. I sprinkled the holy water from the sidewalk and did my thing even though his eyes looked false. After coming back from up north, I took Tyler around the block, and this time he looked very angry with me. I could not believe an inanimate object looking angry. Theron told me that my backyard had negative energy in it and that I should do a clearing. I asked him if it was from the people's house that had the figures, and he said yes. He said, "Tell it that you cast it out in the name of Jesus and then trust that it is taken care of."

30

Prayer Meeting

IT HAS BEEN OVER a month since the attack. I went to the Holy Ghost meeting where they had mass before the meeting, but I arrived halfway through mass. It was being held in the school cafeteria, so it was somewhat informal. I got there right before communion and took a place next to Helen in the front row. The priests in front of the small audience asked if we would come up and form a circle around the altar. I noticed that there were five people kneeling down at the back that would not come up. I found this very strange. So I said to Helen, whispering in her ear, "Are they too good for us or not good enough?" She didn't know. I pondered as to why they were not participating and was very confused. I questioned myself as to whether or not I should say something to them and felt in my heart that I should. So I went up to them after and calmly said, "Why would you go to a birthday party and not eat the cake? I thought that was a slap in the face to the priest." They said this was not Catholic doctrine, everyone forming a circle around the altar, that it was more like the Protestant religion.

One lady said that in another Catholic church, they brought the choir from the choir loft onto the altar. I said, "Jesus, is every one of those people singing? How this could be dishonoring?" So then I said, "Why are you here?" Three out of the five spoke up and said their part. Helen told me that they were very dogmatic and would not change, but then I got the impression she definitely approved of what I had said. I told the people that I loved them and respected their decision and gave them a hug. They told Helen before they left that they were mad at me. I asked Helen if I should apologize; she said no. So then I told Helen what I told them. She gave me this small piece of paper with this typed out: "Here is a question that can only be answered by action. Today, God will use you to help someone in need. See to it that you obey his voice. Inasmuch as ye have done it unto one of the least of these my brethren, ye have done it unto me."

Before the meeting started, a lady that later sat next to me said that she was afraid. I said, "With Jesus standing next to you with his rod and staff to give you courage, how could you be afraid?" Then she said that her daughter's family was taking a trip to Florida by airplane soon and that she was afraid. I reiterated, with Jesus standing next to you with his rod and staff to give you courage, how could you be afraid?" She said nothing. I do believe that most of the group was not fear-based. Our collective anger, our nonforgiveness throughout this planet caused this eruption of terrorism to be acted out. We all played the part with road rage, spousal and child abuse, anger in the work forum—however it played out. We all participated as if we were the terrorists ourselves. This is why we cannot blame anyone. Deepak sure gave some food for thought when he said, "Would we feel the same for the innocent people killed in New York as for the innocent people that are killed on the other side of the planet?" I am sure the answer would be no.

Pat got up to give the message for the day's meeting. She gave a very eloquent speech on the September 11, attack. I debated as to whether or not I should share my thinking, and my answer was yes that I should. I had nothing planned whatsoever, just thought I would get up and say a few words. So first off, I thanked Pat for the very eloquent speech, and then the rest followed. Cannot remember the exact format but will try to give you the gist of it all. I started off saying that the attackers thought that they were separate from us and we thought that we were separate from the attackers. I told my husband that we should not attack. He said we must attack and that he was tired of my spiritualism. Attack begets attack. What we give out is what we will get. So what would I recommend? I would say to forgive us, forgive them, and ask for forgiveness. We think because we drop some food that we are righteous. We are not totally innocent. I said fear is spreading across this nation, and I propose that we stop watching TV. We are not here to judge the good or the bad. We are here to love one another. I do not know where the words came from; they just popped in my head when I got up there. I went to Russ when it was over to give my money; he gave me a hug and told me that he liked my words. This meant a lot to me, seeing as I admire him, but I did not respond.

I would not want to be the president and make those very hard decisions. He certainly could not please everyone no matter what he did. I am also aware that he cannot tolerate terrorism. But maybe this is an opportunity for our nation to think about why these people hate us. Maybe this is an opportunity for our nation to look at our pillaging and raping of this planet. Maybe this is an opportunity to know that the two-thirds of the world that are going hungry every night are us too. We sit in our cushy homes, clueless as to what our brothers are going through, and quite frankly, all we care about is that we get ours, even if a lot of ours don't have it. I didn't care for the spokesperson on television saying that the attackers were evil. Maybe this is where we need to think of how we are evil. Everyone mirrors us. Also the president was only responding to our collective consciousness; we cannot blame him either.

31

Mike and I Went to Vegas!

AT THE BEGINNING OF November, Mike and I went to Las Vegas to witness some good friends of ours, Bob and Debby, get married. It was their second marriage for both of them. Anyway, before we left, Theron told me over the phone that I would see something in the sky that was meant just for me in Vegas. I thought, *Okay, whatever*, and that I would be looking up. So Mike and I were at the first seats next to the window on the right hand side of the airplane going west. Mike was next to the window; I was in the middle seat. We were about twenty-five minutes or so from Las Vegas when Mike pointed to something lying on the white clouds, which would be northwest, following us along right next to the airplane. I thought it looked like a bulls-eye target. He says it was a full-circled rainbow, which surprised me; he was right. To me, it was quite poignant to have a rainbow staying in the same spot for, I would say, five minutes or so until the clouds broke up and it dissipated. I felt I would be looking up in the sky not down to cumulous clouds that were white cottony puffballs. Starting out with pastel yellow in the center, then blue, purple, yellow, orange, and purple were the first circle; around the perimeter was another rainbow—blue, yellow, and purple... Purple was the last color shown. I had flown many times and saw many clouds and there was nothing that could possibly explain something of this magnitude.

I believe that this represents that I have come full circle and that now I am at the beginning. It felt good to feel like I could walk into heaven and that there was a lot more to this three-dimensional playground than whatever any of us think. I do believe that Mike and I were the only ones to witness this phenomenon. I also believe that this rainbow came from my alien friends who had put their messages in my pictures directly. I also believe they were of a higher dimension and were helping me with my growth. I thank them from the bottom of my heart.

While we were waiting to get our seats to go on this flight, I believe synchronicity happened again. When you go to your journey within you, are definitely aware of synchronicity taking place, and you also know that there are no accidents or coincidences. Our clerk, who happened to be a cute, effervescent, petite black woman, was told by the lady next to her that two seats were just made available and to give them to us. I am impressed thinking that there must be a reason for this. The man sitting next to me on the airplane—his name was Rich—had had a stroke and seemed happy in his world but very frustrated as well. He also showed me with his right arm how strong he was by pulling my left arm. There were only a few words he could speak, and "thank you" were some of them, so he would say that over and over again. His wife Barbara sat across the aisle next to her son and his wife. I thought maybe I was supposed to privately give this man a blessing. He had his arm over in my seat a couple of times, and I quietly gave him a blessing, thinking that is why he sat next to me, but I think it was for more his wife, Barbara.

I got to talk to Barbara because of Rich, and I told her about the full-circled rainbow while I was witnessing it. She did not get up, however, to see it. I told her that I was writing a book and that this was going in my book. Then I started to explain to her a little bit about my book, about it being spiritual and about the dark night of the soul. She said that it was difficult dealing with Rich 24/7 and that she felt like she was in the dark night. I told her that I would send her my book and that I felt it would help her heal. Barbara is an attractive older woman in whom I saw joy and sadness. I also knew that we could be great friends. I looked over at Rich several times on our flight home to Detroit to see a wondrous, kind smile every time. They sat where we sat on the way out. We sat where their son and his wife sat. I told them both that I would put them in my book, and he raised his arms up in elation and joy. He seemed to totally understand everything I said; it was a joy sitting next to them.

Throughout the four-hour trip in the airplane on the way to Vegas, I was experiencing a lot of negativity in my thoughts. Knowing that everything is in us and not outside us, I thought, *What demons do I need to look at in me?* This set the tone for sadness for me on this flight trip. I had walked the night before around my neighborhood, walking past my scary friend. Theron told me not to walk past him for a while. I did anyway, but not looking at them and saying to myself that they were not real. I knew they would be taken down when I went back because Halloween was over with. Throughout the entire trip, I said, "I desire light, I do not desire darkness." I also said, "All negativity is an illusion and is not real and you have no power over me." I also said, "I bless you and thank you for the gifts that you have to offer, but get behind me, go to the light, and you will not be harmed and be better off." It took resilience, perseverance, and a tenacity to not let this overtake me. I said, "I have come too far, and I am a winner and a success." I did all this mentally in my thoughts. This all reminded me of an oxymoron, feeling light and darkness all at the same time. Maybe this is what life is about, loving and accepting every part of us… the light and the darkness. Maybe this was a battle in me. I remained in faith the entire trip.

Before I went to Vegas, I knew I would be spending a lot of time by myself. I knew Debby and Bob would be involved with both of their perspective families and would not be spending much time with us. Their wedding was very eloquent. Later, I went up to the man that married them and told him what a wonderful job he did. He even closed his eyes during the main part of the ceremony. He said he is retired now but that was his profession, that he was a minister or something. He told me that he very much enjoyed his job. I told him that he had set a wonderful tone to live by. He thanked me for saying those kind words and said it meant a lot to him. I also knew that Mike would be very busy gambling. So I set out to do my own thing, trying hard to not feel sorry for myself. I went on walks to the different casinos, taking pictures as I went along. I went up in the Eiffel Tower, seeing as I was not able to do so in Paris. I asked the elevator man how it compared to scale to the one in Europe. He said that was a good question and he said half, fifty stories high instead of one hundred. Another couple in the elevator said they had gone up in the Eiffel Tower in Europe as well. They said they had gotten engaged at the top of the Leaning Tower of Pisa. I said I had climbed that as well. They said it was like thirty years ago. I said it was like thirty years ago for me too. I found out I was a few years earlier than them. So I went shopping.

 Right across from the Rainforest Café on the way to our room at the MGM, there was a store across the street called the Grand Canyon Experience. They had a myriad of different rocks and crystals. I went nuts! Even if I knew that it might be difficult getting all this weight back to Michigan. They had a big rock crystal that looked awesome to me. Even more awesome, it was on sale at half off. Boy, that made me go tilt and was a must. It was a three-dimensional picture. I could see that I could not live without it; I still did not know how I would get it home, weighing so much. I just simply loved the earthy brown and blues in and among the crystal. I would put it on the coffee table at our picture window overlooking Mullet Lake. In case you don't know it, I like rocks and crystals. Mike won a few bucks and gave me a few hundred dollars, so I even had money to spend. I bought three of my children in Michigan gifts. I think they like rocks because of me. So I had fun in my own little world. I would occasionally find Mike at a machine and bite him on the shoulder. Of course, we would go out to breakfast and dinner together as well. I did spend some time in my room just watching a little TV or taking a hot bath.

32

Volunteering at Senior Homes

My guides told me to go donate time with the elderly. Through my friend, I called Mary in October. I went up north, and Mike was in the hospital and I did not do it. Then November came and was halfway through, and I still didn't do it. I came down sick with sinus drainage and bad sore throat, and my chest hurt, so that also prevented me. I finally decided to go and found a place near my house and my mom and dad's. Actually it was the first place that popped into my head. I called up the place and asked if they minded if I would come in and talk to the people. They said, "Come on ahead." The first time I went, I did not walk into all the rooms; I did not quite feel comfortable doing it. The next time, I asked if I could bring Tyler in, and they said, "Anytime." For the most part, Tyler was a hit, especially with dog lovers. Mostly everyone thought he was cute. They said I could even let him run around on his own. I felt more comfortable and decided to try to go to everyone in the place and spend a few minutes with everyone. Seemed like most of them were women and they were all hungry for love.

I met Loretta. She is ninety-one years old said she did not have any siblings and no children although she had been married two times. She said that she had never had a best friend. I told her that I would be her best friend. The next time I went, she apologized and said she did not remember me. I told her that I was her best friend and gave her a hug and told her I loved her. She started crying. It was very rewarding giving these young old people love. They are like two years old, crying for love. Some say they do not belong and want to go home. I am so glad that I finally listened to my guides and donated time with the elderly.

What surprised me was one of the ladies that I saw was always sitting in the same place facing the same way. I have never gone there where she was doing anything else. The time of day did not matter either. One time, she was sleeping in the wheelchair. She does not want you to bring her anything to read or anything. She does not even want visitors. If you tell her she looks nice, she shakes her head. I have tried and tried to figure out how I can break her walls down, but to no avail. She does, however, allow me to give her a hug most of the time. I feel like that is the only love she gets from anyone.

33

Jury Duty

I RECEIVED A SUMMONS to report for jury duty at the end of November, in Detroit, at the Frank Murphy Hall of Justice. I was not a happy camper and did not want to go. The last time I went, it was so boring, and I never did see the inside of a courtroom. This time seemed different from the get-go. I struck up a conversation with the lady in front of me while we were coming in and going through security. I took a seat up near the front, and I noticed someone taking a seat next to me to my right, but I did not pay attention. The gal I was talking to while coming in took a seat to the left of me. I look up to the right to see a lady that I knew, but I could not place how I knew her. She immediately said,

"You must know me from the veterinarian." I said yes, that I had Tyler, a shih tzu. Well, things immediately seemed less boring than the first time. Also this time, they immediately started calling many groups of people. Lo and behold, I was called.

While driving to Detroit, I put up my right hand to see if I had my reading glasses draped over my necklace chain. The top seatbelt would rest on the top of my glasses. When I felt to see if I had them, they were there. When I got inside the juror room, I put my hand up to see if they were there. They weren't. Sometimes when I bend over, they can fall from my chain and I do not know they had fallen. I opened the door to the jury room and asked the judge if I could look for my glasses in the bathroom and the bench I was sitting on. Even though people were sitting there, they were nowhere to be found. I did not call my husband up to ask if they were at home. I figured either they were or they weren't. When I got home, they were sitting on the kitchen table where I had left them. I thought, *What could this represent?* Maybe there was a correlation between this trial and me being positive that I had my glasses on my chain. The next day, a few of the other jurors asked me if they were at home. I told them that they were and I had been hoping they would not ask. There was speculation in this trial, with some reasonable doubt.

Neither of the women sitting next to me was called for this group. So I was instructed to go up to the sixth floor, and I followed the rest of the group to our courtroom. There were forty-four of us to choose from. I am thinking that this was a lot of people and that I would not be called. They chose the initial fourteen and went from there, eliminating many people, and there were only three of us left. The judge said, "The three of you come up to the front," then he said, "Never mind." Someone else was eliminated, and I was called to take the second chair. The judge said I looked unhappy and proceeded to ask me several questions. Actually, I was just nervous about coming up; I had never done this before. Anyway, both lawyers accepted me. I am thinking all along that maybe there was a reason for me doing this. They told us briefly about the case, and the defendant was there throughout. So I call up my spiritual psychic and asked her about this. She said it was a balancing in me, that it would be good for the other jurors that I was there.

During my lunch, I went to Greek Town by myself and had lamb with spinach and rice —my favorite dish. I still had some time, so I went to a St.

Mary's Catholic Church right across from the parking structure. I only had a few minutes for it closed at 1:30 p.m. This church was beautifully ornate and elegant. It is hard to believe you are walking into this place in the middle of Detroit. I was awestruck by the beauty; it reminded me of being at St. Peter's Basilica in Rome looking up at the ceilings. I told the priest that I would have liked to get married here. He said, "Many women say that same thing." He also told me to look at the grotto on the right hand side of the church in the front." I went up there, and the Blessed Mother was perched in the corner, encircled in a rock formation. I feel very close to the Blessed Mother. I enjoyed all of it very much and definitely wanted to make a note to come back the next day and did. I took my disposable camera from Las Vegas and used up the rest of the film. I decided that I wanted to put the film in right away to get it developed.

A black girl named Alicia was the first to take the stand. She reminded me so much of my daughter Crissy. Her height, her long hair with part of it pulled back and gathered at the top with the rest long. She also had some of it highlighted in the bun. Also her petite structure, face structure, and mannerisms were just like Crissy's. It was not obvious to me the first day, but on the second, it was obvious to me. She started crying on the stand and asked to be excused; all of it reminded me of Crissy, so much so that I started crying. I wanted to go to her and hold her in my arms. I no longer saw her as Alicia but now as my daughter Crissy. I thought, How could I be objective?

There were many things about this trial that were ambiguous to me. There was some crucial evidence that was not found or put on evidence. This would be our third day, and not too much had taken place than had been initially told to us before they started picking the jurors. On our third day for this trial, just as we were told that we could go in the courtroom, we were asked to slowly vacate the building. After we got outside, we were told that we had to go on the other side of the street. Finally, after about a half hour, we were told we could leave for a couple of hours, which turned into three and a half hours. I was so hoping that the trial would be over with today. First of all, we went to a restaurant connected to the casino in Trappers Alley. That is, I and the five other women on the jury. We took the opportunity, and all ordered breakfast. While we were there, the judge and one lawyer were also there. Then we walked around the casino, or I tried meeting up with three of the women. I decided to go back to St. Mary Church and did for a half hour or so. Several times, while walking outside I would look in the direction to the sun and close my eyes to see many things when I shut them. It seems so weird that I had never seen stuff before and now I saw quite regularly.

On the morning of the third day of the trial, I went outside in my driveway and faced west at seven o'clock in the morning to see the moon with what appeared to be a star hanging from a string near it—a little to the left and more in front, but very close. It seemed like the star was swaying slightly. This seemed very surreal to me; it definitely did not look real. I stared at it for some time, not believing what I was seeing. If that wasn't bad enough, I woke up to having this dream of my mom and me dodging bullets by running into what looked like the inside of the steps in my parking structure where I parked the car in Detroit. My mom sat on the bottom step, leaned back, and was gasping for air. I said, "You look like you are having a heart attack." Just then, three people that I knew walked in, but I do not remember who the three people were. Maybe the bullets were my mom and me dodging the bullets from our husbands—their anger. This seemed very strange to me, seeing as my spiritual psychic told me that my mom was having a problem in her chest area. Plus the correlation of a gun being in the courtroom—it was evidence of being shot four times in the direction of policemen.

I was convinced that he was guilty on all counts. We elected to give him "not guilty" on three counts and "guilty" on three counts, but not intending to kill. While Joan, the lady we chose to head this, read off the verdict, I felt good about it. The judge came in afterward and told us that he was proud of us. He told us that he would have voted the same way with the evidence and sworn testimonies. He also said that he could not do what he did and get away with it. The judge made this whole experience for us somewhat pleasurable. He added humor occasionally. He was down to earth and, I thought, very fair with everyone concerned. He said, "Now you know what I do all day every day." I had a much better idea of how our judicial system works. It might not be the best because sometimes it fails us, but it is good. I do not know, however, if all judges are as fair as this one. Then I remembered my glasses, how I had been positive I had them around my neck. There was a reasonable doubt.

This brings up another dream that I had about my mom. As I told you, she is quite heavy. In another dream a while back, I saw her flawless. She was sitting on the bed, back where the headboard is, with her legs crossed and extended out in the front. She had on a bluish gray, medium-color, form-fitting dress on that had two-inch straps over her shoulders and went straight across the chest area, gathered at the waist with, like, a three-inch waistband. I told her she looked skinny, but I remember her boobs were not lacking. She told me that she weighs one hundred pounds. My mom is about five feet now, so that would have been about right. Her hair was dark, and she looked young and pretty. This dream totally blew me away; I have only known my mom to be big, weight-wise, all my life. At one point, she did lose close to a hundred pounds, but that did not last.

34

I Went Up North

I HAD GONE UP to Mullet Lake for a few days to be by myself. My husband was still getting very angry over nothing. I went out on my deck in the front of the house at five o'clock in the morning and said, "Holy Spirit, I cannot handle my husband's anger any more. You either have to make me immune to it or eliminate it from my life." I was crying and meant every word I said. That was not good enough. I also decided that I would stand in for only him at the Holy Ghost meeting and did. I told the three people that prayed over me that I had not told them that he was a very good man. He was having some physical problems, and I told them what they were. In any case, I released it. Because he was so angry,

I decided whether or not I would even want to do this and decided unanimously that I should.

While talking to my spiritual psychic, she told me Mike was receiving healing and gentleness and that Jesus was working with him. Believe it or not, that was music to my ears. After twenty-nine years of marriage, that was singing in the rain for me. I knew that I had been perpetrator in a previous lifetime and would have wanted that for myself. During some healing that I would give Mike, I would tell him that he did not have to go to church but that he did have to invite Jesus into his heart—that that was not an option. I believe that he did, for the healing to take place. I also took to massaging his feet, which he would thank me for when I was through. It is hard on me to do it because of his size 12 feet; I am very tired when I am done.

Thinking back to when I was waiting initially to go in the courtroom, I struck up a conversation with this lady. I was telling her a little about my book and what happened. She asked me if I had written the author of *A Course in Miracles* and told them this happened because of their book. I said I never thought of that. I asked her if it would have been better for me to stay asleep and be in hell, because that is where I had been before the dark night of the soul. Although it was a very challenging experience, it was a privilege in every sense. I saw my husband relaxing and calming down. I saw my dad not having to strike out at me. I went outside many times and said, "I release you, dad." Is it better to keep banging your head up against the wall? Because that was what I had been doing previously.

Showing and giving love does conquer all; it just might take time to change the paradigm. They have to become secure so you aren't going to change your mind. I have met people that thought *A Course in Miracles* was not on the right path. All I can say is in life, you must find what works for you. All I can say is it worked for me, and they obviously did not read it! That saddens me because how can something that is so good be referred to as being wrong? One man's meat is another man's poison. It could be the Bible, the Book of Mormon, or the Koran that works for you… *A Course in Miracles* worked for me. Singlehandedly that book helped me change my mind; for that, I say "Amen."

Also, while I was talking to Carol, my spiritual psychic, she said she saw a hot-air balloon and that was good, that I was going higher. In *The Wizard of Oz*, the hot-air balloon was taking Dorothy home. The two rainbows, the one in Utah in the mountains and the full-circled rainbow in the airplane right before Las Vegas, are also in *The Wizard of Oz* in the song "Over the Rainbow." She also told me she saw an orange butterfly, which means transformation and creativity. She saw a pair of black patent leather shoes with rhinestones on them and twelve o'clock. I told her that reminded me of Cinderella. She said she saw me going to Europe but not right away. She also says she saw me signing autographs. I told her about my two previous visits to Europe when I was a teenager. She did not tell me why I would be going to Europe.

During several months of this year, I decided that I would take a look at my previous lifetimes. I would go outside and say that I take full accountability and responsibility for all of my lifetimes. Then I decided that I would say my prejudices, my racisms, my hoarding, my judgments, my jealousy, my condemnation, all my attacks no matter what form they took, my stealing, my lies, my procrastinations, my sedentary and lethargic lifestyle, my impatience, my laziness, my non-acceptance issues, my abandonment issues, my rejection issues, and just anything that would pop in my head. I figured if I looked at everything in this lifetime, why couldn't I do all of them? All I know is that I did burn more karma. It looked different. I believe it was when I saw the curved red lines going in the circle. No one told me to do this; I came up with it on my own. To this day, I do not know if it benefited me or not, but I believe it did. It owns up to the fact that you are not a victim and you made or created your reality!

Last summer—I do not know if it started when I was in Yosemite or what, but I will try to describe it. However, I do know that I had a few while I was walking in Yosemite. I started having pains shooting up my spine, throughout my torso and ending up to my neck and the back of my head. They would grab me in small sections at a time, and it was quite uncomfortable. It started on the bottom of my spine; it worked its way up slowly until it got to my neck. This went on for many months. I called up Carol P., and she said it was my body changing to accept the gifts. They were sharp pains, but they did not last very long, nor did they happen very often, just every now and then. I do not know if it was my spine opening up. The pains covered my stomach and underneath both my breasts quite a bit. Many times it happened to the back of my neck, which that is where a lot of my injuries were. I think it happened over several months because it would have been hard to take them often.

FAKE IT, IT WILL COME

    While walking in the middle of December in my neighborhood—the sun was getting ready to set in the west—I closed my eyes and stopped on three different occasions. But I did this while directly looking at the sun. I have been staring at the sun for some time throughout the past couple of years. I have convinced myself that my eyes will not be harmed. I do this because I see so much stuff when I close my eyes, although it has happened to me without looking at the sun, so that is not a prerequisite for me. I couldn't believe what I was seeing. Burning karma again, only this time, it opened up to a circle of blue like the sky, like I was going through time and space... all an illusion. It was swirling cloudlike red into a tunnel that went into the circle in the center. Sometimes the center was blue outlined in green and then sometimes green with blue on the outside. One time it was yellow and a couple times all green with two other green circles going up from the left of the center circle. Another time, it looked like the center was shaped like a house. Just guessing, but I believe it was a tunnel through an illusion and the house was my inner kingdom. I am who I really am, the "I Am." This made me want to cry because I couldn't believe it. Now more than ever, I know you can rise above the illusion. I had been burning more karma recently before this experience.

Shirley called me up from SLC and asked me to go to California for New Year's. I said there was nothing out there for me and I did not want to go. She, however, continued to put the pressure on. Mike and I immediately went out to eat after the phone call. I said, "Ha ha, Shirley wants me to go to California for New Year's Eve." About twenty minutes later, Mike says, "Kathy, I have to work for New Year's, and if you want to go, it can be your Christmas gift." I was shocked! I did not ever dream that Mike would even consider letting me go. But I thought, *I still don't want to go*. So I said, "Heaven, if you want me to go give me a sign." Now my brother Ron called me up and says he wanted me to come. I asked him if he could get my ticket for two hundred dollars. "Gary and Paul have to be nice to me, and you cannot get drunk." He says, "I guess you aren't coming then." I said, "Guess not." He called me up the next day to say he had found my ticket for $220 and asked if I would go. I was shocked because he said the first place he had gone to was American and they wanted $1,350. So now I was convinced the heavens were intervening and maybe this was my healing as well.

FAKE IT, IT WILL COME

On Christmas Eve, I awakened in the morning to this dream: four cute little girls, with staggered ages and heights, asking me to be their Holy Ghost person. But they said I had a cold sore, so they did not take me and left. Then they returned and told me that my cold sore was gone and now they were accepting me as their Holy Ghost person. Again they left, and Theron entered the house and took a seat on the coach. However, I was not in the house I lived in—it reminded me of the house on the next street which I was in once. Three of them returned—I believe the youngest took off—and I brought them in for Theron to see. I called Theron up to tell him about the dream. He said the cold sore represented the negativity in me, and he represented the patriarch because he had been counseling me. He said the four girls represented different stages of the little girl in me. I had just gotten over having a little cold sore. I medicated it right away with Campho-Phenique, so it never did get very big. This has been going on since my Halloween character looked very angry with me. I would be saying the Lord's Prayer and "Fuck you" would pop in my mind while I would be saying it or Psalm 23. I finally told Theron what was happening to me. I just told him negative thoughts were coming into my head; I did not say what negative thoughts. He told me I was still in the process of healing and this was good.

I called up Carol, my spiritual psychic, to ask her about my impending trip to California. I explained about how all four of my brothers would be there and how they all needed healing. She said as soon as I said that, she saw a sun with a ring around it, but she did not know what it meant. She said Saturn has a ring around it, and it looked similar. I felt going out to California was going to be the completion of my healing. My guides had shown me many, many symbols representing my resurrection, my wholeness, and my awakening. I think this represented my uniting with the Divine Source. The Divine Source was the sun, but we are all one with God, for we are all his sons and daughters. I knew in my heart that the heavens were sending me out west for I had no desire to go.

35

My Trip to California

ON THE TWENTY-EIGHTH OF December 2001, David and I headed out for San Francisco. While waiting in the DTW airport, I struck up a conversation with an attractive black woman. We found out right before she was boarding that we both went to the Church of Today. I thought, *There is no coincidence in this*. I told her that I was writing a book about the dark night of the soul. She said that she wanted to read it. She also told me that her thirty-year-old daughter was also writing a book. I gave her a hug before she got in line. She was going to Georgia for the holidays to be with family.

I thought that it would be nice if David and I could sit together on the flight to Pittsburg. David was sitting in the first row on the passenger side of the airplane, and I was sitting in row 19 on the other side of the airplane. It looked like we were ready to move, and I saw quite a few seats available and asked the stewardess if I could move forward. She told me yes, because they were through boarding. I could not see David, but I thought I would try to see if I could sit next to him. When I got to the front, there was a seat available next to him in the middle. This was very much a surprise to me. But even more than that, when we boarding in Pittsburg to go to San Francisco, David was in row 11 and I was in row 12. When I got to row 12, the man asked if his wife in row 11 could switch with me. Now I was shocked because I know there were no accidents or coincidences.

We got in late, California time. Ron, Dave, and Shirley came to pick us up. David actually called them on his cell phone when we immediately ran into them to go and pick up our luggage. I thought that was quite amusing. I got in the hot tub as soon as I arrived to get rid of the anxiety of the long trip. In Pittsburg, we were delayed because of the weather in San Francisco for an hour because they had to deice the airplane a couple of times, and that took an hour. So we were sitting on the airplane close to seven hours in all. They would not let us get off and walk around a little bit while we were delayed sitting at the entrance. This was rough on me, sitting all that time between two other people, and I could not move. The rest stayed up for a while, while I went to bed; however, I did not fall asleep for quite a while.

The next day, Paul came over with his two dogs, Miss Bell and Rupee. We offered him a foot massage, and he declined. After listening to my brother Ron moan over his foot massages that Shirley and I were giving him, he changed his mind. I did not think he would; neither did Shirley. While we were giving him his foot massages, he asked Shirley and me if we could do it a couple of more times before we left. It was very encouraging because he seemed to be in euphoria. We also decided to take a break and then give him a hand massage as well. After a couple of hours later and he had gone to the store, he still said that he could feel the effects of the massage. To our surprise, he stayed most of the day, which was unusual for Paul.

In the evening, they started playing poker—David, Dave my son, Greg, and Paul. Paul was losing quite a bit of money after five hours of playing. Dave said that his Uncle Paul did not have two aces. He also accused him a couple of other times, but it was not proven. Paul blew up at David and then turned against the rest that were there. Ron came out of his bedroom and told Paul that was unacceptable behavior and that he could leave if he could not act right. Paul took the two dogs and left. Luckily I was in the hot tub when this took place and did not witness it. While I was in the hot tub, I saw my son David's face bashed in and bloody. When I went into the kitchen, I told Shirley what I had seen. She said, "Because your son was just verbally bashed in." Uncle Greg said his nephew did not deserve to be treated like that from his uncle. I looked at Greg and said, "Nobody does." Greg said his rage was capable of killing someone.

The next day we called up Paul to come over, and he wouldn't. We had arranged on New Year's Eve in the day to go and visit him in Dublin. Ron had put dinner on, and we just let it set while we were gone. We drove over to get Gary at his house. His two boys, Brian and Scott, were already with us, so we had a full car with nine people. Dave my son did not come. When we got there, we walked around Paul's house, and they went into his backyard, which had great European ambiance. Greg, after like twenty minutes or so, came up to me and said, "Kathy, if you are going to give love, give it." I immediately stood up and asked if we all could join hands forming a circle and give thanks for whatever we wanted to give thanks for. Paul took my and David's hand, then he backed up and said, "I do not want to do this." Greg, who was sitting on the couch, said the same thing, but he said, "Let's do it and get it over with." I could not believe that this was taking place. I asked Shirley to start, which she immediately did. When it was my turn, I started crying and said, "Let's let the past be in the past, live in the present, be whole and love one another." I thought the heavens were definitely interceding and was very grateful. Never did I believe my four brothers would agree to this.

While David, Shirley, and I were in the hot tub, which is in Sara's house right behind Ron's house, Shirley saw a lady in light out of her peripheral vision. I asked her if she saw any of my guides and proceeded to name them. She said Gray Eagle was a gray wing, that Toshi had oriental eyes; that Jane, Bob, and Fred were more visible. So I proceeded to ask many, many questions. So I will randomly give out what I asked and said. I asked Frieda if she was happy with what I had done with Mike. She said she was elated. I asked about the other healings I had done in California. They told me the little oriental girl, Ashley, had more healing than any of us realized—she was smiling on the inside—that the old oriental woman was a shaman that wished me many blessings. I asked about the dream of the four girls that asked me to be their Holy Ghost person. They said that I had agreed to help them. They said the full-circled rainbow meant a lot to me and that it was more than an extraterrestrial that made it in the sky while en route to Vegas. They said the golden cherub and Archangel Michael were one and the same, that Archangel Michael was overlooking my guides. I asked if he was a CEO. He said he would not call him that. They said when I said "I fucking made it" on top of the mountain that it went past the chasms and was definitely appropriate.

I asked if I was fulfilling my mission on schedule. They said yes and that my children were too. I asked if it was appropriate to tell Gary about drinking alcohol. They said yes, he needed to hear it. I also asked if it was okay with what I did with my son David. They told me that I preached too much to him. They told me the top of the ladder was in sight. I said to myself that the top of the ladder would be in sight if I were at the bottom. Little Christopher and Cory were meant to come in my life, Crissy's boys. But I knew that. I asked why I was going to Europe. They said to be in joy. They also showed Shirley much of Europe—Portugal, Spain, France, and Italy. They told me that I came out to California to sing. I said, "Well, my brothers and sister do not like my singing." They said it is too dense in Michigan and that they agreed they did not like to hear me sing, but on a soul level, they were receiving healing.

I decided that I would go over to my brother Gary's and see if I could be with Mary, his estranged wife. When I got over there, Gary told me that she was upstairs and for me not to bother her. I said "Brian [Gary's son], go tell your mother that I am here." Gary said, "No, don't." I said, "Go, Brian," and he did. Mary came down, and I went out into the dining room with her and asked her if she wanted to be attuned in the first attunement in reiki because that is very healing for her mind, body, and spirit. She said yes. So we went upstairs where the four of us sat on her bed with our legs crossed in a circle with our hands joined. Mary was facing me, and Brian and Scott were facing each other. I gave all of them a blessing first, just with the joining of the hands, and then I proceeded to give them each an attunement in succession. I had them sit in a chair, probably the same chair that I gave Mary a blessing when I was there for Thanksgiving in 1999. After I was through, I told them that now they had an attunement guide, that we were all healers. We can do that with a gentle touch, a smile, or a kind word. I told them that they were all given a special gift today. Later on that day, in the evening, Scott said to me, "Thank you, Aunt Kathy, for the gift." I said, "Oh, the helicopter I gave you for Christmas." He said, "No, the gift!" I was shocked that this little boy would appreciate a spiritual gift. When Shirley was channeling in the hot tub, the spirit world told me that Scott was a cherub.

I went back over to Mary and Gary's with Gary to see if I could extend some form of healing with just their family. This was later on in the trip. I asked them if they would like to join hands again standing in a circle and give thanks for something. To my surprise, they all agreed. When Gary and I left to go back to Ron's house, he said I was too religious for him. I asked if it was because we held hands and gave thanks for something. Then he told me that he had noticed a change in Mary since I had been there. I told Gary that when you give appreciation and thanks, you get more. I said, besides you would be concentrating on the good in your life and not the

FAKE IT, IT WILL COME

negative. I also said that Brian and Scott would get excited about what they would be sharing that evening. He said, "You might have something there." When I left to go in the other room, he told Shirley that I had helped out his family a lot.

However, Shirley and I, a couple of times, asked Gary if he wanted a foot massage. But I was a little more persistent. He said no. Finally he got mad and said we were hounding him. I knew our visit was almost over and our healing time would be over. He left and went home. I called him up a couple hours later to ask him a question. He bombarded me with negative energy. I told him the only reason I came was to extend love and healing but that I could appreciate not wanting to be hounded. I felt like I did not handle the situation very well. I didn't feel like I totally did not react. He brought over a couple of boxes of Seas Chocolate, and I think it was to make up for the situation. On the phone, I told him I was not coming back. I felt if siblings cannot get along together, how we could expect the rest of the world to get along, like other countries?

The day before we would be leaving to go home, Ron, Shirley, David, and I headed for Monterey Bay. The weather in San Francisco was supposed to be bad. Going south was a good thing. It was a lovely drive that I very much enjoyed. We stopped off at a little Mexican restaurant to have lunch because we were all getting hungry. I was the first one to go into the restaurant, and there was an older couple on the other side of the room, and the rest was empty. I walked up to them and asked them if they were celebrities and if they rented the place. The women joined in and said yes. That opened the door to us talking with them throughout our meal. We found out that the man was a teacher who taught history. We asked what kind of history teacher he was. He said he couldn't remember much, but the Civil War was brought up. I asked them if they went to Virginia. And she said, of course, they did. As they were getting ready to walk out the door, I told them that we loved them and blew them a kiss. He blew one back and blessed us. They said we made their day. I know we extended love and we did not even touch them. We enjoyed them just as much as they enjoyed us. It was not an accident.

Monterey Bay was beautiful; they had a fisherman's wharf there also. We had planned on going to the aquarium and changed our minds. It was such a beautiful day that we decided to enjoy the shops, and there was a musical band out in the courtyard playing overlooking the bay. I bought their *Sol*

Latino CD. Ron liked the CD, so David burned one for him. I went and walked down on the beach; the sand was very coarse and kind of orange in color. Ron said that this bay was one of the deepest places in the ocean in the world, that it was a mountain turned upside down. The tide was coming in, so I took my shoes off to avoid getting them wet. None of the others came down with me.

We walked into the Thomas Kinkade art galleries. I found a painting that immediately drew my attention. It had a beautiful, exquisite purple tree that was quite large. For whatever reason, I put my hand up to see if I could feel energy from it; to my amazement, I could. I felt energy from the rest of the painting, but that was quite remarkable. It was only a mere four thousand dollars or so. I told the lady that when she sold the painting, to tell the people buying it about the energy in the tree. Shirley found a small painting of water and a lighthouse that was only ninety-nine dollars and told me that I must buy it for me. I did not have any more money, so I asked Ron if I could use his charge and pay it back. I would have never done it if Shirley had not adamantly insisted. I don't regret it though. It was probably the prettiest day and the nicest, enjoyment-wise, that we had in California.

The day we were leaving, I was hoping that we would make it to San Francisco. Well, we did make it but only to be driven to the airport. It seemed like we kind of sat around not really doing anything. However, I did give my son some reiki while guiding him in a meditation to his inner kingdom. He told me that he was very much at peace. Shirley and I also gave him a foot massage, so that made me feel very good. I went into the hot tub one last time. The hot tub is large, and if you go to all the seats, you feel like you have had a full massage. It was the best hot tub that I had ever been in. I felt like I had to go in there to be replenished so I could give to my brothers and son. I am grateful and appreciative that this trip was so fruitful and came to fruition. There was nothing in the skies—some pretty sunsets though. No fireworks—they had some in San Francisco for New Year's Eve, but we did not go.

I called up Carol P. to ask her if my trip to California was a success. I felt in my heart that much healing had taken place and there was love shared. I only wanted more. She told me yes, that she saw a rainbow, which means creativity and goodness. I asked about my son David. She said he was pulled into the golden circle and that was very good. However, she told me to continue praying for him. She told me that she was going on a trip to Hawaii soon because her son was getting married there. She said that for the last two days she had been in joy, but she did not like flying.

36

Back at Prayer Group

AFTER GETTING BACK FROM California, I decided to go to the Holy Ghost meeting. Mary gave the talk, and that opened a door for me to augment what she talked about. Jerry asked if there was anything to share. I raised my hand. This is what I got up and said:

"I could talk all night, but I know I cannot do that, so I will make it brief. How you get to heaven is not by taking someone that thinks like you with you. How you get to heaven is by taking someone that you struggled with with you." I had a Styrofoam cup that Mary had given us about her talk in my hand. I said, "Mary is correct—the Holy Grail is like any other cup. Its real value lies in its emptiness." I held the cup up and pointed to with my other hand. "Fourteen months ago, I decided to change my mind." I pointed at my temple area. "I changed my mind because I thought my dad was going to die; so I decided consciously each and every time that I would go over there, no matter what he did, even if he told me how vile I was or my husband got very angry, I would show and give love to him. Sometimes I would have to get in his face and calmly say something was not acceptable, however. Then six months ago, I decided to give my husband foot massages. The Bible talks about the washing of the feet. It is somewhat humbling giving a foot massage, and it somewhat exposes you to be the receiver. The unfolding of this last fourteen months no one would have believed, certainly not me. No one would have thought it possible.

"I decided to go out to California for New Year's Eve. I did not want to go because it was like going out to four of my dad. The heavens sent me, but I called up Mary from the Holy Ghost people to have them put on the prayer chain. I needed all the help I could get. I said my brothers all told me about their pain, which I did not know about. I had tried staying away from them while I was growing up. For the past twenty-five years, I think my four brothers have only been together with me on, like, four or five different occasions. After I felt their pain, I went into the throes of my own dark night. I just wanted to be left alone and cry, to release what was bubbling out of me. What came up over and over again was "This is cruel and unusual punishment." I got my brothers to all be in one room. Gary would stand on Ron's front porch; he would not come in. All nine of us stood in Paul's living room, formed a circle, and held hands. I asked Shirley to go first. When it came to me, I said, 'Let's let the past be in the past, live in the present, and just love one another,' while I was crying. I never thought something like that would take place. Love does conquer all—you just have to give it. It might take time, though. Who will you love, the lovable or the unlovable?"

Jerry came up to me after the meeting was over with and said he thought that was about the best testimony that he had ever heard. He said he knew I wanted a divorce. I did not say anything, but it made me feel good. I went in the prayer room to the right to be prayed over. I told Russ that my two brothers, Paul and Gary, were in a deep depression and could be suicidal. Plus my husband's diverticulitis was still acting up, and my son David's anthrax shot with his overactive thyroid and his heart racing were still acting up. While Russ was doing an eloquent prayer for them all, there was a feeling of joy I felt them receiving; it was more than I had hoped for. After they were through, I gave them all a hug and said I did not know what I would have done without them. Russ said he did not know what he would have done without me. It was obvious to me that maybe we both helped each other out, because what we speak, we learn. I felt like I really did have some impact on them. I also felt that it was a mutual acceptance and love being shared.

While listening to Marianne Williamson on TV one Sunday morning, she said that to go to heaven, one of the prerequisites is you must take someone with you. That someone must be the person you struggled with, not someone that thinks like you. Throughout this past year, I have tried very hard to love my dad and Mike. One thing that I needed desperately throughout the dark night of the soul was someone to hold me and say everything was going to be okay. I mean really hold me and really let me know that everything is going to be okay. So I am going out to California and let my brothers take a dump, while I listen lovingly. A dump is all their perceived pain and anger that is real to them. Then I am going to hold each one tight and tell them everything is going to be okay and how much I love them. The other thing I want is for my dad to tell me that he is proud of me. So any chance I get, I tell people how proud I am of them—it, however, must be genuine. Patronizing someone does not work. I am going to give out what I desperately want and need.

While talking with my friend JoAnn recently, she told me Doctor Easton asked about me, to which she said he never brings me up; she does occasionally. He told her that I was his biggest success story and that she was his biggest failure. JoAnn started with Ed and Easton around the same time I did. We both had similar problems, but mine were much worse. I told JoAnn what I did through forgiveness and offering my judgments and my relationships up. You can have people be catalysts; you, however, ultimately must heal yourself. She said, "I have no one to forgive." I said, "Excuse me, but you must or you would still not be in pain." It has been three years now that JoAnn still goes religiously out to Dr. Easton's office in Waterford. It is quite a hike for her also. Then she proceeded to tell me about some forgiveness and judgments that she had. I told her to offer them up. "Say that you do not know how to deal with this."

While talking to my sister Judy from Livingston, Montana, she told me that she was hearing me say that I would not react and would be removing myself but that she did not feel I was. She suggested that I might want to burn my book, that I was too attached to the outcome. She recommended doing this while I was sitting around a fire. I decided that I would burn one book three days consecutively in a row. I burned the first one that day in my backyard next to a tree, where I did a lot of meditating. The next two I did behind my garage, a great place for me. As I was burning them, I offered up all the pain and suffering that this book represented and talked during the whole process. I felt it was necessary to do it for three days because that was how long it took for Jesus to rise from the dead. I had these copies and had outgrown them and did not know what to do with them anyway. I also said, "I release you to the Universe, the Divine Source, all that is." Never is any form of release not accepted or worthless; all is invited, any form or attempt. It could be attached to a helium balloon and released. It could be your words at a river or lake. Use your imagination, which will help you help yourself. Also be in the emotion.

37

Back at Mullett Lake

IN THE MIDDLE OF January 2002, Mike and I decided to go up to the house on Mullett Lake for five days. We hung pictures and mirrors that I had bought and gotten as gifts. It was abnormally mild while we were up there. The house was really becoming a home; even Mike thought everything fit in its place. My daughter Karen and new husband, Darrell, came up with Berkley, their little over a year Alaskan malamute. He is a ninety-two-pound big boy. He enjoyed running all over the spacious backyard and the front yard. Darrell and Karen went snowmobiling quite a bit even in the dark of night. They left to go back home in Southgate on Monday. We stayed till Wednesday because a man was coming over to look into reconnecting our security system. I went out on our beach at Mullett Lake while the sun was rising and closed my eyes while looking in the direction of the sun. It was very clear to me that I was burning karma again. And I was thinking, *That is good.* When all of a sudden, white clouds from the left extended over the swirling tinted in red clouds and engulfed them, sweeping them away, so now all I saw was a sheet of white clouds. This represented a clean slate to me, like when you move an Etch A Sketch from the left to the right to erase. In any case, it felt good.

My husband, Mike, is going in to the Riverside hospital to have eight inches of his colon removed because it is gnarled, twisted, and hard. This is called diverticulitis. The doctor said that this would not repair itself and needed to be removed. When you are not walking consciously, you are walking in a labyrinth that is twisted, gnarled, and hard. It is just that—hard to get through. You feel like you are banging your head against the wall by doing the same thing but expecting a different outcome. That is the definition of insanity. We need to look at ourselves, first and foremost. We need to wake up and smell the roses—figuratively and literally. It is our obligation to seek joy by resurrecting above the illusion. Out of the guise of all illusion comes simplicity!

Mike and I decided to go up north to Mullett Lake during the first of March to do some of his recovery from his surgery. The doctor gave us his blessing and thought that this was a good thing to do. He said not to contact him unless he was having trouble. He could rest up here or down there. So we headed up, and I did most of the driving. Our house was nice and warm even though it was brisk outside with a lot of snow. I wondered what spiritual happenings might happen up north. The bottom part of his scar became red and hard, so we called up our insurance, and he told us to go to St. Ignace just on the other side of the Mackinac Bridge. The doctor was from Dearborn and our nurse from Taylor… small world, huh? She gave him a high dosage of antibiotics and wanted to see him again in two days.

On Monday, March 4, 2002, I went out on Mullett Lake for the sunrise. I walked quite a bit out, seeing as the lake was frozen, but there was much snow. I looked at the sun then to the moon to the right behind me, and brought my eyes to see what I could not explain. It looked like a second sun behind a cloud formation. I saw a very large statue from the left to right—pastel red, yellow, and blue coming down between two black parallel straight lines, coming from a point above the clouds. It had distinct definition outlined in black. Sometimes it would extend below the clouds, and sometimes the section below would disappear and reappear. What amazed me was I did not see this till I walked out on the lake, nor did I see it after I walked off the lake. I think it was Jesus or God. I did not know what to think, because it was not explainable. I had no explanation. I asked what I witnessed, "What are you?" It was quite an unprecedented phenomenon for me. I really expected for it to become alive—it was that surreal for me. I was glad that I came out for the sunrise, but I am surprised that I did not see it until I got out on the lake, for it was quite large and magnificent. It was cold and windy. I did not want to turn my back and leave, but I knew when I turned my head that it would be gone. I did think it was a gift for me to witness, but I had no idea that I would get gifts from seeing it.

I called up Theron and explained what had happened, and he told me that it was a gift of love, wisdom, and power given to me. He said it was available for all that were ready. He was told by the spirit world that it was Jesus and for him to tell me. He said we would go out to lunch and that he would give me what he had that was written about this. Unfortunately, I did not have my camera and really regretted not buying film for it. I would have brought it out otherwise. I have no pictures of my greatest unexplainable happenings in the sky. A couple of days earlier, I was out front of my house, ready to get in the car, when I shut my eyes and saw an eye with blue coming out at an angle. I had seen this same thing with white before but not blue. I did not know what to think what it could mean. Maybe that was the prelude to what happened on Mullett with the statue.

The next day, I again went out on Mullett Lake and saw pastel red, yellow, and blue this time to the left of the sun. It was in straight lines, with less vibration and was much less vivid or pronounced. I am thinking that it might turn into a rainbow, but it never did; it stopped. Maybe the feminine energy was to the right and the masculine energy was to the left. Maybe what I saw was the goddess energy instead of Jesus. I don't know.

Mike went into Cheboygan to get me some snowshoes because of the volume of snow. We were expecting some company, and I stayed home to wait for them. When Mike returned, he said they were out of snowshoes in my size but bought cross-country skis instead. They were marked down quite a bit because of an end-of-the-season sale. I went one time in Chatham in the Upper Peninsula with my brother-in-law Gary, like, twenty-some years ago. I had just had, like, my fourth kid and was not in good shape. I was little; I just did not have that much physical activity. I remember it was quite a workout. We have some railroad tracks right across the road from our house on Mullett that they took away because they no longer use it. It runs the whole length of the west side of the lake and is perfect for cross-country skiing and snowmobiling. It is quite a workout; you can definitely create a sweat. I just wanted to be able to get some good exercise.

We drove to Black Lake to visit Mike's cousin Joe and his wife, Barb. She gave us some homemade chicken soup with healthy muffins for lunch. Joe took me for a snowmobile ride, seeing as Mike could not go. I really have had zero experience on a snowmobile. Joe told me before we started on these snowmobile paths to enjoy the surroundings as well. Most of my attention was spent on looking where I was going. We went for like an hour, and I did not know if my hand could squeeze the gas for much longer. I wanted to take my other hand and see if I could help it, but that did not work. We got it up to speeds of fifty miles an hour. Plus I went up some hills, which I had to accelerate the gas to make it up. Joe stopped and told me that I did a good job. Then we came to a cliff that you had to jump. Joe got stuck and told me to go around the other way. Then I got stuck in about snow up to my knees. No one had gone off the path, and I was good and stuck. When we got back, I told Barb, "You have to do what you are not supposed to do so that you know what not to do." Maybe you could relate that same sentence to real life. When we got ready to leave, I thanked Joe for the great time and Barb for the good lunch.

On Friday, the seventh of March, I was still at the cabin, and I just closed the bedroom door, and I was getting ready to get into my bed when I saw with my eyes closed a vivid butterfly that was illumed. I don't remember the colors, but they were bright. I think it was a light yellow. It was in the center of the picture—the rest was black. After a bit, I saw a couple of other things in succession in the center but instantly forgot what they were. I guess the butterfly meant the symbol of the feminine energy, a transformation, and that I am set free. As the saying goes, "Butterflies are free." I also believe that it was a gift given to me because it appeared to come at me. I now remember that I saw an outlined—I am pretty sure one continuous line—yellowish orange circle with a panther's head outlined in it, which is the symbol for power. However, I do not know if I saw it second or third. The third was also outlined in a circle; it appeared to be an outline of a face of some sort, but I did not recognize it. I am guessing here that this represents wisdom. Now I know why I did not remember the other two; I did not know what they were. It never ceases to amaze me, the things I see, when I saw nothing before the dark night of the soul. I believe this is my witness to the love, power, and wisdom gifts given to me. When I went out with Theron for lunch, I drew what I saw in the sky, and he got that the statue I saw in the sky was Mother Mary. I was also thinking that it was feminine energy.

The night before we were leaving to go home, I went outside because Tyler needed to be let out, and we did not have a fenced-in yard. The last couple of days, they wanted people to stay off the roads because of the very windy conditions. In fact, they told us if it wasn't an emergency to not go out, and the Mackinac Bridge was closed to all trucks. When I went out, about nine o'clock, it was total calmness and serenity. The stars looked breathtaking standing out in the sky to be gazed upon. I thought that I would not be enjoying this if Tyler did not need to make a pit stop. Oftentimes I would go out and sing to the woods behind our house, like there were angels precariously perched in the trees. And I would walk out onto Mullett Lake to sing like that was the stage and the whole frozen lake was my audience. I would project my voice so the other side of the lake would hear it. I would sing the Christmas carol "Fall on your Knees," what I knew of it anyway. I know no one heard me or I would not have felt free to do it.

I envisioned Mullett Lake being cleansed of any chemicals or toxins and gave it to the violet flame. You just don't see stars down here in Lower Michigan that you see up north. Pollution, lights, or whatever causes this difficulty. I truly was awestruck at their brilliance, and I will never tire of it. We all can glow with that same brilliance if we let love into our hearts and give up the blame, shame, and resentfulness game. You take responsibility for your reality, as to why you are drawing this to you. "Embrace it and throw it away," as Wayne Dyer says. The whole planet Earth is but a stage. Sing and dance on her, the Mother Earth, for your tiptoes and song give her goosebumps of joy and ecstasy that reverberate out into the cosmos. You cannot give away what you do not have. In other words, you are bankrupt!

The next morning as soon as I got up, I got dressed and walked out quite far on Mullett Lake. I brought my camera because it looked like the start of a fantastic sunrise. If someone was with me, I really wanted to walk to the other side of the lake, just to say I did it. It, however, was cold and windy, so I went to where I could see the north and south part of the lake better. We were in the middle and the widest part of the lake. And where we were at extended out so we could not see the north or south part of the lake. I love entertaining my guides. I tell them how much I appreciate them and that I love them, calling out their names. Soon the sunrise was enveloped with clouds and taken away. I said, "Don't leave." I knew I would be spending a lot of time on this lake and just maybe silence my mind so that I could listen instead of being Chatty Kathy like the doll. I have been called that. I also have been quite an interrogator during this dark night with whomever I could clench on to. I needed to look in me and not outside me.

I got my pictures back from up north and the sunrises on Mullett Lake. They were some pretty awesome pictures. Several of the sunrises had my footprints in them, which at first I did not want. I wanted to follow the same footprints back because of the snow being deep. So it appears that the footprints left but did not return. This represents going from the darkness into the light. I also thought that some of the pictures might be a total whiteout because of all the white snow and everything. They were the exact opposite, showing my journey from darkness into the light. I went out on Mullett Lake and asked my guides to pose while saying cheese to them. When I got my pictures back, there was a picture in the clouds that looked like a mermaid when you turned the picture on its side to me. My mom, however, said it looked like a dolphin. I will take either. Theron told me that there would be stuff in the pictures but that I had to look more closely. The mermaid had a big fluffy feather in her right hand holding it up, and there is a laser of light that she is holding with her left hand down and sun next to the laser further down on the right. I saw the cloud formation and did not know what to think. I now know it is me. I could see my face smiling, and I believe my resurrection. Anyone that I would show my pictures to would laugh if I told them what they were or they would not see it at all. So the pictures are a gift to me to appreciate and love. A couple of the pictures of sunrises with footprints look like they have an illuminated cross. I also think this represents my resurrection. I am always anxious to get my film out to see what they put in my pictures. It adds extra excitement, anticipation, and pizzazz for me.

Over the weekend, my neighbor, Karen, who was like fifty-two, died of a massive heart attack. She moved in like eighteen years ago with her husband, Ron, and daughters. Over the summer, I let her read my book, then about seventy-five pages. She was a nurse and a social worker, and I thought she should read it. She read it immediately, and this was her response: She said, "I do not know if I understand or agree with your book," but she said she got a better understanding about Mike. This is coming from a lady who has heard Mike's anger and rage. She did not go into any details, but saying that, I got it, was good. Their door wall is right next to our driveway. She had ample opportunity to hear what went on. I bless her in all ways. I had a dream after she died that I looked to see one of her girls with a pool skimmer in her hands to a perfectly crystal-clear pool. They got a new pool last summer just like ours, only smaller; however, they did not put a winter cover on it or prepare it for winter, including the filter. Leaves and debris from the trees were freely allowed to fall into the pool. I looked over at our pool in the spring, in my dream, which we did prepare for winter, and it was dirty. I think this was telling me that I judged them, and in doing this, I was dirty. Over and over again, we judge, not even conscious what we are doing.

I woke up this morning to having this dream; I would say it took place when I was in the seventh grade. Two boys from my class (one I had a crush on—his name was John. He however, did not know that I existed) came over to my house. The other boys name was Leo, amazing that I can remember this. Instead of being petrified, ashamed and humiliated because of the terrible conditions of my house, I was literally flying around and happy. I was unaffected by what they thought, nor did I care. To my surprise, it appeared that they were likewise not affected. It was definitely my home in all its permeated grandeur of dumpiness. I believe I finally overcame my extreme fear of someone coming over, especially someone that I had a crush on. Again I will reiterate, I do not often remember my dreams. Make no mistake, this would normally be grounds for being ten feet under the ground, and instead, I was above. I was amazed that I even remember John from thirty-six years ago, but it was John and I with both of us being unaffected. The dream did have significance for me; I faced my fear of that house that we called home for so many years. I was set free, at that moment, from the extreme shame I felt of that house on Williams Street.

38

Waking Up!

AT THIS TIME, I want to thank all the people that participated in giving me these gifts. Without my perceived nemesis, I would not have found out fully who I really am or my journey back to my original divinity. The evil I found was the evil in me. I guess this is hardest for me to write in my book. If you loved God with your whole heart and soul and one's neighbor as oneself, there would be no struggle. For one's neighbor is myself. I just did not see they were. There would be no Satan; there would be no struggle with your brother, or you would be in hell. That is what Satan means, your struggle to return and know God. The embarrassment was I was not loving myself. This is a very hard thing to look at clearly and admit. It was easier to judge others than to look at myself. So I thought, anyway. Only to find out the truth really does hurt. When we can stand and not judge the good or the bad remaining neutral, then and only then can we truly be healed. Heaven forbid that I should take the time to look at me, instead of my brother. The abuser is abused when they are allowed to continue to abuse. All I can say is this is some game we are all playing. I know things are what you think they are, but I do not want to go through what I went through ever again. What I mean by that is the whole fifty years to date. If I get bored with joy, I will just look back at this lifetime.

Teach your children when they are two to take responsibility for what they have done and throw it away. This will eliminate an unhappy adult life by correcting their childhood as they goes along. You attract where you're at, both in marriages and relationships. There is no such thing as making him or her well and everything will be dandy. I would recommend being whole before marriage also. Victimization serves no one and is definitely not recommended. It makes you submissive and allows an abuser to abuse or the reverse. Both are abused. All are punished. The controller thinks she is happy controlling but finds out it is to his own demise. Stand calmly tall. Know that with Jesus at your side with his rod and staff giving you courage, you are safe no matter what. Then I recommend dancing. I will definitely have some input into my grandchildren's life at an early age. The greatest gift you can give your children is to love their mother or, the reverse, their father. There is no greater gift than two parents showing and giving love to one another, for then it is a learned behavior of acceptance and security and an example of how to treat your spouse. It should be God first, you, then your spouse, and last, children. Then there will be no greater example—God meaning, seeing, and being godlike. Nothing is possible without God!

The spirit world is now getting tough with what they are showing me in my dreams, now that I am nearing the end. I had this dream about my youngest son, Eric. He was about seven to nine in the dream and looked heavier than what Eric was at that age. His room has a dark-blue mattress that did not have a sheet on it. Out of where the buttons are, big red spiders with two front exaggerated long legs came folding out one by one underneath the buttons toward him. He had two beer bottles next to the bed, and I told him to go to bed, that we would deal with it in the morning. I got up after this dream and went into the front room and cried, not wanting to disturb Mike. I remember when he was, like, eighteen months, we were in the airport coming back from Utah, and he told me he was hungry. I bought him a sandwich, which was expensive, and he threw it on the floor. I got quite upset and wanted to go berserk. The funny thing is, I loved him so much. Just like my dad told me that I was his favorite. I did not protect him from his dad or his older brother either. It was a crusher, and they were playing hardball. The dark night of the soul is like a life review while you are alive. There is no cover-up; they get down to the nitty-gritty. What you do not look at and resolve, they will show you, and you will not like what you will see. I had done some work with Eric, reiki and praying over him, plus telling him I was sorry. And they still showed me that. I thought I had resolved it. Several people have told me that they felt Eric was my favorite. My dad was one, me always claiming they all were. My mom told me that I had four only children.

Mike and I went to Point Pelee National Park in Canada. It was sunny but a cool and windy day. I walked along the shoreline with inappropriate shoes on. I told Eric that he was free, that I had set him free… free to be happy, to be loved, and to be at peace. I got it in my head to go there. I had no idea why that popped in my head. It was a beautiful drive in Canada. We took the rode going along the coast, so it was a scenic drive as well. We stopped at Duffy's for a fish dinner. We love their perch. We saw Fermi, the nuclear power plant in the States. We also saw Three Sister Island. We did not take the scenic way back, so it was a faster drive. Going over the Ambassador Bridge takes patience nowadays. I would not want to do that very often.

This is what my interpretation of "The last will be first and the first will be last." We could be doing everything right, praying, going to church, and loving our families. But the moment we think we are enlightened and know all the answers and our brother decides that somehow he is not on the right path, that is when we will go from the front of the line to the back. The very second we judge, we are judged, because we are judging ourselves. It is definitely that simple. Writing the last several previous paragraphs, I cried. To take the magnitude of looking at one's self clearly hurts. After I wrote the paragraph on thanking the people that gave me these gifts, I saw a translucent flat green circle standing upright in midair moving to the right, and then it disappeared. Then I saw another one move to the right and disappear. And then another one moved to the right and also disappeared. I saw this when I was looking in the direction of Tyler floating above his head. I do not know what they symbolized, but I do know it was a healing for me. I kept on thinking that I was through being healed when one or more things showed up for me to look at. It was truly looking at every facet of me. Now I know what Carol P. meant when she said it was time to clean house. It was time to love the people that surrounded me no matter what. Jesus said, "Why have you forsaken me?" God told me that I had turned my back on him but that he had never turned his back on me. That statement sure gave me food for thought. My depression was I turning my back on God.

After visiting with Krista, the daughter of Karen that died next door, I came in the side door, and next to the landing, I saw another translucent, flat, green circle again move to the right and disappear. So I saw four different times altogether. I now know that all four represented people that I had karma with. I know Mike and my dad are two and maybe my son Eric or my father-in-law. I had just gotten through talking to Krista, offering any help that

I could give her or if she just needed someone to talk to, and that happened. I do not know if it was Krista or Karen. But I do know it was four people that I had karma with because of the four separate circles that I saw move to the right then disappear. Sometimes it takes me a while to figure out what is happening.

39

Mike's Healing!

MIKE WENT TO FLORIDA for a few days to visit with his two aunts; his uncle, his cousin Chippy, and his son Lauren were also there from Alaska. A few days after he had returned, he told me how he had given love and transformed the people while he was down there. He did not use those words; he told me what he had done. He said his Aunt Laura had broken a valuable vase and could not throw it away. Mike told her that he would fix it for what could he hurt. She loved having the vase standing tall again to admire. He talked about Chippy not going over to his uncle's until he got there and how he was on the phone when he arrived, not paying him any mind. Mike said things had changed and he was his old self again. How his son Lauren enjoyed Mike wanting to take him on at the youthful age of fourteen. How he visited his Uncle Wally often and cheered him up.

I told him that that was what life is about—showing and giving love. One thing Mike had never done with any area in his life was brag. While he was down there, Chippy, Lauren, and Mike went on charter cruise fishing for eight hours in the Gulf of Mexico. It was cloudy and windy, and the people were actually cold, some putting on sweatshirts. All three got very badly sunburned, totally oblivious what was happening to them. When Mike came home, he looked like a monster with puffiness above and below his eyes and a painfully red face. He had a severe case of sun poisoning. Even his left hand and arm were swollen. It wasn't till after he went into graphic detail on how he had transformed their lives that I realized he was actually shedding his monster mask, being unmasked literally and figuratively, right in front of my eyes. They all told him when he was leaving that they wanted him to come down every year.

Another analogy to the dark night of the soul can also be being pregnant and giving birth. Although you forget about the pain of delivery, you also know that you do not want to go back there. Plus, you are pregnant with a new life. All I know now is I am not a married United States citizen, Caucasian, heterosexual female that is a French, German, Polish Catholic. I am all of it. I am the universe, the earth and clouds and all that is. I am the Beloved, and so is everyone else on the planet. I do know that I am transformed and made new again. The purpose of life is to know and recreate who I am. I have done that now. When you abandon the concept of separation and adopt the concept of visibility, when your true relationship with God becomes visible, you are indivisible. This is some help from *Conversations with God* by Neale Donald Walsch.

Neale's books have helped me with some major transformations and were eye-openers. I thank him and all the authors I have read to help me help myself. I said to my guides, "Let's get this straight. You're going to send me down in all kinds of negative energy, and I am supposed to rise above it." They said yes, that I would be stretched emotionally, mentally, and physically to the max, where I would want to give up in all areas. Through these perceived adversities and atrocities, they said I would grow and expand, reinventing myself with strength, courage, tenacity, and resilience that I did not think

I would begin to dream to have. "You will feel tall and hold your head with honor." And I agreed! I am imagining what they said to me.

During one of Shirley's meditations, she had some questions answered about our family and hers. She was told that our parents' roles in this life are their contribution so that we did not have to. They actually did all us kids a favor by freeing us. We thought the exact opposite, thinking they were our nemesis and it was to our demise. Nothing is as it seems! My dad's role was dying unfulfilled and my mom's was carrying density. My brother Ron's success was driven by my dad's lack of fulfillment. She said mine was to be a healer and teacher, overcoming earthly denial. Kathy was denied who she was to the max most of her life, and I overcame my denial through the dark night of the soul. My dad was a big talker and, most of the time, not a doer. Although I think he became more of a doer in some areas as he got older in years. He would start a project, and if it was not perfect, he would stop then for good. Our chiropractor told me that my dad could take much pain compared to most of his clients, if not all. When he was in his sixties, he rappelled down a mountain in Utah. He flew down the mountain, burning his hands on the rope to prove he could overcome fear. My mom carried around a huge little body of density figuratively and literally from the past hurt of her mom's words. Unfortunately, the universe sends us more of what we need to overcome when we do not resolve issues.

Throughout the two years or so of the dark night of the soul, it was a very lonely time for me, and I had much time to wallow in my pain and misery. I did not have a job; my husband made good enough money. I think this made it harder for me to crawl out. I had angels sent my way, but none of them were a big part of my life. Theron was probably the biggest angel in my life, and I was addicted to him. I so badly wanted his help, and I was quite needy. He was more than patient and quite willing to help when he could. I do believe that Theron thought maybe my grand mal seizure that I had on the playground had something to do with my craziness. He did not say craziness. I did a lot of crying, and I did not know how to handle the pain and pressure. I told him I didn't think so, that it was the dark night. I felt like I did not have a life and I was very bored. So I don't know that it would probably be a good idea to donate time or have a job; this way, you would have less time to think of your pain and misery.

When I started the dark night of the soul, for whatever reason, it became very easy for me to give in all areas. I wanted to give little gifts away to everyone. I would go to the store just looking for cute things that were marked down so I could randomly give away to whomever I wanted. It also made me feel good to be so generous. I even surprised me as to how much and how freely I was able to give. Remember, what you give out is what you will get—good or bad. I also enjoyed giving compliments and saying kind words. You can really make someone's day, and they will give in return. On the Oprah Winfrey show, she had a Random Acts of Kindness Day. Think of ways that you can randomly give to others and watch others follow. But don't brag; quietly do it. The real giving is when you give to people who are not able to give back to you and you aren't expecting anything.

Support Groups

Much of what I went through was guesswork on my part. I think it would be a good idea to have a support group with other people that are in it or have been in it. The only problem is how you can weed out the depressed from those in the dark night. It would have helped me out a lot if I could have talked in a group who understood where I was coming from. Some people had heard of the dark night but really did not have a clue as to what it was all about. I felt like when I told them that I was in it that they did not believe me, so I had virtually no compassion. Many, many times I wanted to give up! Now I think that all depression is the dark night of the soul. But until I consciously decided to offer up my relationships, concentrating on what I did, nothing unusual happened. No one is exempt from the dark night of the soul—karma, if you will. We all eventually get this privilege. I am very grateful that this experience is over with, but it was a true learning adventure that I do not regret taking on. And I will definitely never forget. I think the biggest thing that I learned is the concept that we are all one and equal. The dichotomy is we are also separate. What we wish for someone else is what we will receive; there is no doubt in my mind.

I had never met anyone in the Dark Night that had the pressure and pain like I did. They wanted to die, though. My whole body hurt; pain was everywhere from head to toe. I did not know if it was physical or spiritual, but it sure felt physical. Helen told me much later that she did not think I would make it when she first met me; she said I was that bad. I met Helen like eight or nine months into the dark night. They claim that is why people in jail are forced to go within; they have no choice because they have nowhere else to go. Theron told me that he had never met anyone that was in that amount of pain and as mobile as I was. He also told me he had other clients like me but would not do the work. He said I was always willing to do the work. Plus he said he never knew anyone doing the work like I was. It was work, but I did not look at it as work—I looked at it as a process that I wanted to expedite. I like to say, "Do not procrastinate. Expeditiously expedite your expedition of your exhibition," your moment in time. However, you must have patience! This is me having fun with words, probably a little obnoxious for most people.

At the 2002 Winter Olympics in SLC, the skaters had an exhibition where the top skaters were free to perform for the audience without any pressure. Because there were many countries performing, it was like the world came together in love energy and as one. They danced in the flow of magic and unprecedented skating. They were free to express themselves in their unique way, no restrictions of any kind getting into the way. The Russian couple, Yelena Berejnax and Anton Sirarulidze, did an incredible performance. They wondered how well they would be received. And of course, they were loved. Sara Hughes was luminescent as a star out in the universe, doing a number representing the terrorist attack in New York. We all can have our unique dance that we came here to do. I think of it as your journey to your love energy unimpeded, joyously flowing through you. As Scott Hamilton said, "You cannot make it happen, you must let it." He talked about Sara Hughes not having the pressure on like the three top performers did—Sasha Cohen, Michelle Kwan, and Irena Slutskaya. The Olympics has the agony of defeat, but I think they are all winners! The majestic mountains of Utah displayed America's majesty to the max. I think also brotherhood with all nations, despite competition, was shared. I thought Utah did a great job with everything and should be congratulated for their effort.

In Canada, they had an ice skating exhibition for the Canadian couple, David Pelletier and Jamie Sale, plus the Russian couple Anton Sirarulidze and Yelena Berejnax. Both pairs did skate the performances they had done at the SLC Olympics separately. Then they did a couple of performances where the four of them were on the ice at the same time. One time in particular, both couples acted as one, joining the two countries. Both ladies glowed with such cute, effervescent smiles that were addicting to everyone. The Canadian couple did not know if the Russian couple would accept their invitation to come to Canada. Maybe the Russian couple will now invite the Canadian couple to Russia. There does appear that there is now a friendship and bond between the two couples that no one would have dreamt possible, considering what happened with the gold medal. Maybe out of the poor judging, a lot of good came for these two couples that would not have normally taken place. I am happy for both couples and wish them many blessings.

40

Canyons of Your Mind

When you go through the "canyons of your mind," take a dust mop, broom, dustpan, and mop and clean up the corridors, closets, and tangled mazes. You've got to get in there and clean, letting in the light, not hanging on to the past, facing every demon, every perceived fear that you have mustered up and made real. The dark night of the souls is a purging, cleansing, and purifying process. I do believe it is the definition of hell. I think the whole process is you changing your mind about you. Although I do not believe in suffering, I believe in humbly purging every part of you. You will be surprised how easy it becomes to say "I am sorry" even when you think you are right, because no one is totally innocent. This is not enabling; it is saying the truth. You are sorry for it taking place. Although we stumble blindly before this, it is so much fun waking up. After that, you become a Pollyanna helping everyone around you clean up his or her lives also. You do this by giving love no matter what. Everyone you assist in doing this helps your process go faster and raises the vibration for all. While reading this paragraph to my sister Shirley in Utah, she said it reminded her of the movie *Beauty and the Beast* because it talks about the corridors and tangled mazes. She also told me that I have "the heart's wisdom," which is better than knowledge. God said, "Love one another as I have loved you."

I got "the canyons of the mind" from the song "Who Will Answer?" by Ed Ames. When I was in the tenth grade in high school, our English teacher told us she wanted us to pick a record and to copy down the words. I remember what she looks like, but I do not remember her name. I chose that song and memorized it in the process. I remember my mom helping me copy the song down from a .45 record that I played many times to get the words. Throughout the years since, I would occasionally sing it but not very often. When I went to California, it popped into my head, but I did not think it would come to me. Eventually I think the whole song came to me, and I felt it was for a reason. I felt my brothers were supposed to hear it. One or two of my brothers remembered the song. While Shirley was channeling in the hot tub, they told me that I should write it down and give it to my brothers, which I never did. I felt they would pay it no mind. But I did, however, give them many opportunities to hear it if they so chose. So I asked myself how I could integrate this song in my book so that it would have my input, my expression. So that is how the previous paragraph materialized. When I first started it, I did not think I would leave it in my book.

My sister Shirley thought I should put it in my book, so here goes. So this is how I remember it from the tenth grade:

Who Will Answer?

From the canyons of the mind we wander on and stumble blindly,
Through the often tangled maze of starless nights and sunless days

While asking for some kind of clue a road to lead us to the truth, but
Who will answer?

Side by side two people stand together vowing hand in hand
With love embedded in their hearts, but soon an empty feeling starts
To overwhelm their hollow lives, and when they seek the hows and whys, but
Who will answer?

If the soul is darkened by a fear it cannot name, if the mind is baffled when the
Rules don't fit the game.
Who will answer? Who will answer? Who will answer?
Alleluia, Alleluia, Alleluia.

While watching the movie *Sergeant York* last night, an old black-and-white picture, I was very impressed with the movie. York personifies what I think is the metaphysical path to the utmost. He exemplified how you should treat people and let the universal flow, flow through you. I have seen this movie before, but I did not truly appreciate it like I do now. York leaves to meditate in the mountains to find answers, and God says, "Give to Caesar what is Caesar's and to God what is God's." This story is a true story, which made it even better. I believe the word *metaphysical* just means your spiritual search to inner peace and original divinity. Some metaphysics and metaphysical definitions are "the branch of philosophy that systematically investigates the nature of first principles and problems of ultimate reality, including the study of being (ontology) and, often, the study of the structure of the universe (cosmology). Based on speculative or abstract reasoning. Too abstract, excessively subtle. Immaterial; incorporeal. Supernatural." Some people call it New Age, but it was from the beginning of time.

A lot of people have told me that if I have cleaned up my karma, look out because I will be adding more. And I say, "Not if I keep on doing what I am doing." I will take care of my thoughts and my deeds as I do them. This is truly walking consciously if you monitor your thoughts. It all starts with a thought. You can nip it in the bud before it has time to materialize. I have even burned more karma since I was given the clean slate. In fact, it was a few days later. And for me, that is okay because I know I am taking care of business. Besides, if I have cleaned up many lifetimes, I am capable of cleaning up the moment. I will also dwell on giving praise. It is too bad that I couldn't know what I know now and have my children, a bit late at fifty. However, I know my parents did the best they could with what they had to work with; there is no doubt in my mind. Unfortunately, it is passed on from father to son; I think this is called original sin in the Catholic Church. I know you shouldn't have regrets or guilt. I do believe that you should try to become whole before having your children. Most parents do not know they aren't whole. Everything you do and say to a child is stored in their chakras—you forget, they forget; nevertheless, it is stored. Maybe I will be a better grandmother than I was as a mother. In any case, I will love my children now, no matter what!

You can be allowed to go on different tangents on your journey through the dark night. You can become obsessed and obnoxious like I was doing and almost did. Although I think a lot of good came out of my mistakes of judgment, or missing the mark as they say. Maybe the reason I was not allowed to stray very far is the magnitude of what I had overcome. Out of loneliness and desperation, I could have slept with someone. But, however, I never thought that was an option for me. For whatever reason, my guides let me know when I was doing wrong, and I wasn't allowed to get away with anything. They did this with a thought put in my head, through other people (channeling from the spirit world or through people), something I would read, through my dreams, or they would physically show me in the sky and such. I have thanked them for not letting me stray too far. I know some people are allowed to think they are doing right while doing wrong like the Pharisees or the Crusades. I believe I was guided on the right path for his namesake.

In my opinion I got a lot of mixed messages going through the dark night of the soul from all areas. From the Bible to the meditation groups, people that I felt like I was being pulled with a yin and yang effect, an oxymoron if you will. I was wishy-washy all my life. I had to weed out everything and find my truth, wondering all along if I would ever find my truth. I feel that is what we all have to do. Now that I am really coming close to my resurrection, I know that I have finally found my truth. My only problem is I desire to tell everyone to find his or her truth, to wake up and smell the coffee. But unfortunately, I have to let them find their truth in their time. And that is part of my resurrection, letting all of it go, of all outcomes. Living in this sinful world as Jesus did, not as I would have it. Not looking for good or bad, just what is. Remember, we see what we want to see and find what we want to find. See beauty in everything everywhere. I have always loved the prayer "The Serenity Prayer." I have that prayer hanging up in my kitchen. Every single word I resonate with. Contrary to some beliefs, it is not just for alcoholics.

On Good Friday, especially during the afternoon, my head hurt me, and I have not been having headaches, but I had one. I wondered if there was a correlation between Jesus being crucified and my headache from the crown of thorns. I felt this Easter Sunday was going to be me resurrection as well, and I told a few people as such. Even calling up Carol P. and telling her that I cleaned house like she told me and got the gifts of love, power, and wisdom given to me and that this Sunday, I think, was my resurrection. She said to give her a call after Easter Sunday, that she really wanted to hear from me. The morning of Easter Sunday, I woke up and sat on the couch, bringing my legs and feet in the lotus position, putting my hands out and closing my eyes. I immediately saw a little illumined cross moving upward; it was very little and high already in the all-darkened picture. Now I know it was my resurrection. But nobody would believe me if I told them. They would think it was blasphemous. All I wanted to do was cry—I guess tears of joy—that it was all over with. Alleluia! Would wonders ever cease? I called my mom, and she said now things would be hard. I said after what I have been through, everything will be easy.

This is a little strange for me. Mike had gotten me this Christmas cactus, like five Christmases ago, that I kept on my banister in the kitchen going down into the basement. I believe when he gave it to me that it had many blossoms on it. It bloomed a little while at Christmas; however, it had only a few buds on it. For Easter, it had a single purplish white iridescent flower on it. That was not strange, but for the last several months since before Christmas, it had up to four flowers on it at a time with some buds as well. Somehow I thought this was also from the heavens for me. Thinking that maybe these buds represented some clearing or special representation for what was happening to me. One time in particular, there were two on one side and parallel on the other side, symmetrically centered, adjacent to one another there were two more. While looking at them, I thought it was my two daughters on one side and my sons on the other representing their freedom. There have been many times that I wanted to throw this plant away because I did not think it looked that good, and I believe it is because it is root bound. So I am really surprised that I have kept it all these years. Each bloom that I would witness, I would go up and tell the bloom how grateful I was to witness them and how much I appreciated them. Maybe it is the case of getting more because I appreciated. I do not know the reason, but I think it is a gift from the heavens. I look for gifts from the heavens all the time and everywhere now, and guess what—they show up!

41

Surprising My Dad

I DECIDED TO GO to St. Cyril's of Jerusalem, where we went to elementary school, for Easter Mass, to surprise my dad, who sings in the choir. I was sitting up at the front, but I didn't think my dad could see me, although he was turned my way. He was standing on a platform in the back with a few other men. Finally, he waved, and I waved back. Afterward, he said he was not sure it was me. Then in front of the whole audience, he blew me a kiss with pure love. I, of course, blew him one back. No one would have guessed that knew my dad and I that this transformation could take place, most of all me. I thought he was the devil himself and definitely could not touch him. How wonderful it is to give and show love. How wonderful it is not to be in hell. I give many thanks and much appreciation. This is why the choice is ours and ours collectively as to what we want as our reality. When I sang "Alleluia" at church, I sounded like an angel to me and felt like I was in heaven. Most of the time, although I enjoy singing, I know my voice leaves a little bit to be desired, and I told my guides, "If I am supposed to sing, give me a voice."

We had eighteen people over, including ourselves, for Easter dinner feast. The house is not big, so I had people in the kitchen, front room, and family room. I really could not share with anyone but Estelle about my resurrection. I thought I was not getting any accolades, but then, I thought, *Do I need them?* Watching Crissy's two boys, Cory and Christopher, and just loving them, I was heaven and tiring. Everyone was unusually loving, and it was just a wonderful atmosphere and ambiance to be in. My son Eric ran dinner over to my mom and dad's, for which I was grateful. They knew the house would be cramped and my mom would be too uncomfortable. It was truly a blessed day for all—everyone agreed. We had a wonderful feast and shared much love. Maybe, just maybe, it was all of our resurrection. And I did not think I had a grandiose day and did. Just like the movie *Ferris Bueller's Day Off.* Ferris says this was for Cameron, who did not think he had a good day as he was on a float in the middle of town singing "Twist and Shout" by the Beatles.

I went to the Holy Ghost meeting and to mass before it started. When I took Russ's hand, when we joined hands for prayer, my hand burned, and this happened twice. I could not figure out for the life of me why my hand was burning. Then I realized that I had spent the last two days going to the senior citizens' home and putting my right hand on about two hundred people's foreheads. I thought that is quite powerful. I had really enjoyed going over there and extending love to all these people; they instantly responded and gave back without hesitation. The priest asked if anyone had anything to share. I said what I had done at the senior citizens' home that day. And I said if anyone asked what I was doing, I was giving back. He loved the sharing. I really do love this place and all that it had to offer. I also feel quite privileged to have this available to me. I had brought my spiritual pictures and showed Russ, Jim, Helen, and Don before the meditation started. I commented on what each picture represented to me.

Pat gave a rather lengthy talk, and so there was not too much time for sharing. But it was offered by Don nevertheless. I debated as to whether or not I should share because it was late, but did anyhow. This is what I said: I held up what I called my spiritual diploma and said, "This is my spiritual diploma, these are my footsteps, my beach, and it represents going from the darkness into the light." As I held the two pictures out, I moved them so they could be seen. "If I had loved God with my whole heart and soul and my neighbor as myself, I would not have had a nemesis. Jesus showed us how to resurrect with his nonattack method. I do not know if I would have made it without you all. I want to thank each and every one of you and I love you all. Thanks!" I proceeded to show a few more people, who commented on each picture that the heavens had intervened with.

Mike and I are back up north at Mullett. It is now April 16, and there is still ice on Mullett Lake. I went out on the Beach at 7:00 a.m. for a fantastic sunrise. I took quite a few pictures of the event. I do not know if they will turn out because it was quite dark from clouds, and the flash went off. I also took a picture the day before of a sunrise. This sunrise, I saw all kinds of colors that I knew would not be

FAKE IT, IT WILL COME

in the pictures. It was quite warm even though it was early in the morning. I think it ended up being 88 degrees, breaking a record from 76. Some areas had snow melting and flooding and dry with a fire hazard also. Mike and I spent the day doing odds and ends around the house. I cleaned the bathroom from too much iron being in the water, so there was rust, something that I am not very fond of. Mike changed the tractor from snow removal to grass cutting. He had to read the directions on how to do this, so it took longer. We were going to go home today, and Mike said he would be too tired for that long drive back.

Early evening, we decided to have our first real fire on the beach. Carl and Beverly already had a nice pit with rocks around it, cut-up stumps laying on their sides on all four sides of the pit to sit on, and some cut-up wood piled nearby. Actually, we think Carl and Beverly set us up quite good. We picked up debris of roots and branches from trees off of our beach left over from winter to burn also—no one to clean our beach but us. I stood at the beach watching what looked like many large amoeba to me, lying on the surface of the water. They were variegated raised three-dimensional surfaces that seemed to take a life on of their own. They were pulsating, vacillating, and oscillating while crackling and popping, randomly going off in different areas at different times. It reminded me of that movie *Close Encounters of the Third Kind* when the spaceship was landing, only this time it was a moving show on the water, both visually and with sound effects. Then all of a sudden, all the activity would stop for a little bit and then start back up, like I think the movie did. The ice was being pushed up on shore like small sheets of crystal crunching and being layered and staggered on top of each other. I had never witnessed anything like this before. When we decided we had enough because the lake stopped its activity, Mike broke the fire up. I looked in the pit to see the embers from the fire doing the same thing my amoeba were doing. So I told Mike about the correlation. He said fire and water both had a life of their own. I enjoyed it all very much, knowing this would be the first of many fires.

On the way home to our home in Taylor on I 96, all of a sudden our, '95 Chevy Tahoe, which has 115 thousand miles on it, started making a bad noise like it was dying. We were in the right-hand lane, which we normally are not in because we need to travel faster, so Mike pulled off immediately. He thought it was a hose. He got out of the car to check on the engine by raising the hood. After a little bit, he came back in and said there was nothing wrong it must have been from another car. I was thinking there must be some reason for this, and maybe we avoided an accident and to let it go. I would say we were stopped for ten to fifteen minutes. Soon after that, we were caught in a very bad traffic jam… still not putting things together. Traffic went down to one lane, so I would say like an hour's worth stopping and going. When we finally got up there, I saw the tire marks of a big Mack truck going from the right hand lane. The trailer carrying a load of dirt was on its side with the cab pinned up against the cement meridian. If we had been next to that truck in either lane, we would have been taken out or slamming into other cars because of the abrupt stop. Still, we did not put two and two together until a little later. I know there are accidents or coincidences, and I realized we were probably saved. I feel the spirit world made our car sound like that to protect us. Now I am more convinced than ever that I am protected and have nothing to fear, not even fear itself. I felt that instant that I did not care if I had died, though I cleaned up my karma and all, but I thought I would like to complete my mission.

I went to Meijer's to pick up my pictures of my sunrises up north. I put a twenty-dollar bill on my way out the door in my pocket to buy stamps and to pick up the pictures. When I got ready to pay for them, the twenty dollars disappeared, and I did not have any money in my pocket. I was shocked because I knew I had the twenty dollars. When I got out to the car, I realized that I had my charge and went back in to get them. I went home looking everywhere for my twenty dollars. I had a dream that night with my twenty dollars rolled up sitting next to one hundred dollars. The hundred appeared to be coming at me as I was giving the twenty. Maybe it means that I will be getting five times the amount that I give—I don't know. It seems weird that I am dreaming about things that have just taken place, like my cold-sore dream when I had the cold sore.

When I got my pictures of the sunrises back, I was awestruck at their beauty. I never felt like it could truly capture what I was seeing. It is so nice to be able to look back at what I saw. The pictures are getting grander. Will I top the next set of pictures? Again the dates were not on them when it was set up for them to be on. Now I was thinking maybe these pictures really might mean something, and maybe I would be a photographer as well. I have always enjoyed taking pictures since I was a young teenager, but I always made sure people were in them. Now, however, most of the time that I take pictures, no one is in them. It amazes me how it is the same beach, but with such a myriad of views. For some time, I hadn't been taking pictures at all unless I was on a trip, because my children are grown. Berkley is my only grandson; however, Christopher and Cory will always be my grandsons, whether Crissy is with them or not.

42

Back up at Mullett

MY SON DAVID CAME in from California because he is moving to Austin, Texas, and will not be able to come back for some time. Mike and I took him up to Mullet for five days. He was a big help because we were having our dock delivered and a shore station for the 20' Sea Ray. We paid them to put in the shore station but not the dock. It was quite cold most of the time we were up there. The best day was the day we were leaving. I mostly did weeding in the flowerbeds. However, I did not know which were weeds and which weren't. I chose to leave some because Mike felt that they could be flowers because of their roots after I had pulled a couple out. I felt like not too much happened for me spirit-wise. I did not take any sunrises. I was too lazy to play games with it and chose to stay in bed. Mike cut the lawn with the riding lawnmower, or tractor, as I call it. Our water has too much iron taste and rusts up appliances with rust stains and clogs them. So David and Mike installed a tank to remove some of the iron. Mike took down the shed that the roof had collapsed from the snow and an ice shanty that was old on our beach to take home in Taylor and take it to the dump. That was a plus because we had not planned on doing that. We will use the trailer to take up bikes and such, a dual purpose.

I took a roll of pictures, but it was mostly of my gardens and installing the dock and shore station. I put the film in immediately when I got home. I went to pick the pictures up the next day, thinking that there would not be anything special in them. The very first picture on the roll that I looked at, I have no explanation for. In fact, I said to the lady behind the counter, "What is this?" She said it looked like a hand to her. I agreed with her. I knew that I did not take this picture. A bright light like a sun was directly above it. Not so obvious because it was too dark, off to the middle of the right hand side was a fishing boat that I recognized as ours. A tree was in front of the boat, which is our cedar tree, which I thought was an angel. Next to the pinky was my wood-boarded-in flower garden that was in the shape of a rectangle turned at an angle. The first knuckle of the ring on the right hand finger was our collapsed roof shed with the doors open. The second knuckle on the ring finger was a pink translucent triangle that was rounded at the bottom, pointing to the center of the bright light. You could see the nails on the tips of the fingers. Both hands were extended out like you would do when praying over someone. There was pink around the light then blue. I had put this roll in my camera, had taken the whole roll on that weekend, and no one else touched it. I did not take that first picture on the roll. The heavens did. Shirley told me it sounded like a picture that was in the book *Love Without End: Jesus Speaks* by Lynda Green. Lynda spent several months painting this picture with Jesus's help.

I decided to meet with Theron to show him the picture from the heavens. He told me that the doors open on the shed, he believed, meant that the door was open for the walls to come crumbling down, walls that my dad and I were carrying. The roof was already totally caved in. As I had said, Mike took down the rest and put the fishing boat that was in the picture in its spot. I believe the fishing boat being replaced meant a solo journey. The shed had a gravel floor. We would like to replace the shed maybe with a wooden one. I know there is symbolism to everything that is in that picture, even the cedar tree, which I felt was an angel. Mike told me when I got up to Mullett on another trip that he had taken the picture from inside our bedroom window that has a storm and window. He said it is his hand and it was the reflection from the glass, and the light the flash. This, however, did not take away from this picture. The hand did not look like Mike's; it had long nails. And he doesn't, nor never has had, long nails. Plus, I could see the spirits myself.

I was thinking when I got home that I really did not have anything to write about in my book. I was taking an inventory of the whole experience, thinking it was mundane just writing about the work that we had accomplished. It was Mother's Day, and we went to Mackinaw to get some fudge and go out to dinner. On the way, we stopped off at a sawmill, but nothing really to write about. It was mostly cloudy and cool, not even exciting weather wise. If I had not gotten that picture from the heavens, I would not have written anything.

I called Carol P. to tell her about the picture. Theron had suggested that I give her a call and see what she had to say about it. She said people would be jealous of this picture. She actually did not say a whole lot, and I chose to send her the picture. Her daughter Nancy, who is a schoolteacher, gave me a call. She said that this picture was loaded with people and stuff in it. I said it was the host of heaven and my guides. Then she asked me what religion I was. I said Catholic. She said that explained a lot. She said Jesus with the thorns in his head were in it, a cross, the Blessed Mother, a young girl with blond curly hair, a white skeleton, a soul mate embracing, and much, much more. We both had the picture in front of us, and she proceeded to try to tell me where everything was. She said some stuff moved in and out of the picture while she was looking at it. She seemed to be quite excited about the picture. Carol said that she was going to take the picture into church to show her psychic friends. As I was looking more closely at the picture, I started seeing people myself on my own. I was on the phone with my sister Shirley, and we were finding them together as we talked.

One evening, while I am doing my regimented walk, I see something appear in the sky. It is dark out because it is after 10:00 p.m. It looks like a translucent, flat green or yellow diamond of sorts that was oblong in length from a side view. Around the perimeter was an aura that was oval shaped and had density like many tightly knit lines encircling it. All of a sudden, it swung down at me and disappeared right in front of my eyes a few feet away from me. I am not afraid, but I did not have a clue is to what was happening. Then all of a sudden, another one appeared, looking just like the first one; it also disappears right as it almost reaches me. I have to say another one appeared doing the same. I started to walk, and another one appeared and swung at me. I stopped again. Then another one, but this time it appeared closer to me in the sky than the first. The diamond appeared to have triangles in it or pyramids, I didn't know what it was. So all in all it happened five different consecutive times. I thought they might be gifts because they came at me. Theron and Shirley thought that it might be an extraterrestrial trying to get my attention. Carol P. thought it could be the spirit world trying to get my attention. Don't know! However, it did get my attention.

43

I'm Back at the Prayer Group!

I WAS AT THE Holy Ghost meeting again. Truly I love coming here and being with these people; it is a joy. Bridgett came in and took a seat next to me. I could not help talking to Bridgett. I told her that I knew we would be working together from the first moment that we met. She told me when it was almost over with that she was being advised to tell me to write about my experiences at the senior citizens' home. I said to her that maybe I was supposed to get in front of the group and tell them about my experiences. She said yes. Then a concern came over me, as if I could clearly tell about my experiences so that I could truly help them, and then I surrendered it. She said, "You are afraid to get in front of the mike." I said yes. She said, "Let the Holy Spirit speak through you." I said, "Okay."

So I got up in front of the mike once again, this time totally because I was being advised to by the heavens. Or so I thought anyway. This is what I said: "I have been volunteering at the senior citizens' home. They have taught me so much. I had this experience with this lady that I would like to share with you all. Two days ago, I said the Our Father and Hail Mary with this lady called Elizabeth, who is a Jehovah's Witness. However, I did not know she was a Jehovah's Witness. She said nothing to me on that day but smiled at me. However, I met her in the hall today, and this is what she said: 'What religion are you?' I said Catholic but that I was for all denominations and for no denomination. Elizabeth said, 'Well, you are going down the wrong path, and your Bible is wrong.' I said again, 'I am for all people,' taking no umbrage with what she had to say. All the while she was talking to me, she was smiling. As I was getting ready to leave, she said that she would pray for me. I said, 'Please do,' that I could use all the prayers I could get. Two days later, she waved her arms and said that she did not want me to go near her, saying I was a Jehovah's Witness. So now I stay away and do not know what to think."

"You see, I am not flamboyant when I say the Our Father and the Hail Mary. I am quiet. In fact, no one knows what I am doing except the people I pray with. Someone told me that they say the rosary. I feel that I am living the rosary because I say at least fifty Our Fathers and Hail Marys when I go; however, that is probably conservative. I also feel that I did not come alive until I started donating my time. Most of all, I just love them by giving them kisses and hugs."

I asked Bridgett how I did. She said, "Great." I knew she approved. When it was over with, she called me over to brag to a young man about my speech, saying, "Didn't you think Kathy's speech was good?" He said nothing, and I did not stick around for an answer and left.

The people that are difficult, those saying "Leave me alone, get away from me, don't touch me," are the very people I choose to help the most. In my opinion, they are the ones crying out for love. So needless to say, I have developed skills that I would not have developed if I did not try to find a way to work with them. One by one, I am breaking the walls down, and that makes me feel good when I do. Loretta from Dearborn, who is statuesque, in my opinion, every day, is like the movie *Groundhog*

Day. Every day, I tell her she is my best friend and give her a kiss and a hug. Every day she says, "I do not have any friends" and that she needs that hug and starts crying. Loretta died approximately seven months after I started visiting her. I will miss her very much. Another lady, Lottie, holds a doll that is her baby that died, and she cries. She is a joy and a pleasure to love and be with, especially how she says the Our Father and Hail Mary with me. She starts singing "la la la la," and I sing "la la la" back. Isabella is a French Canadian woman who speaks perfect English. She told me a story about helping to raise two kids next door to her that were not having their needs met. Isabella died a few months after I started visiting her. Fifi, I just love, and I enjoy her sticking her tongue out at me. She does it in love. Tonya almost cannot move at all, and I dearly love her. I mostly talk to her about spiritual stuff because she is most receptive and inquisitive.

Zetha is a black woman that is also statuesque and eloquent and sits perfectly straight. She talks to me like I am her relative or close friend from the past. Sometimes she asks me if I still am in school or remembers when we went shopping. She says I have taught her so much, but I think she is referring to someone else. She loves it when I say the Our

Father and Hail Mary. I truly love her like she is my mother. She sometimes cries in happiness for what I have meant to her. I go along with everything. I cannot express what these wonderful people have meant to me. They say I make their day, and I say they make mine—their smiles fuel me so that I am able to give freely. If anyone had said that I would enjoy something like this and it would be no labor, just joy, I would not have believed him or her. When I told Zetha that I would be gone for several weeks, she told me that I had to write her twice a week and call at least once. She teared up when I was getting ready to leave.

I also had another dream. This time, I was at St. Elizabeth's Church, and I was in the front pew, and I turn around to see Tamra at the back of the church walking toward the front. When she looked into my eyes, I knew she was being healed. My eyes lit up, and the light extended out to her; she does not come near me. I have wanted to quit going to St. Elizabeth's because Father Charles is leaving and it is out of my way to go there. I am thinking time moves on and things change—nothing stands still or stays the same. This would give me a great deal of pleasure—for Tamra to be whole and healed. Called up Theron, and he told me that he got that I still

FAKE IT, IT WILL COME

have rejection issues. I guess, because I go there and feel like I am by myself. Don't know!

I had another dream last night. I woke up feeling that I was five months pregnant with my ninth child. I actually had one baby after another in my dream. A nurse came in the room, and she told me that I was addicted to giving birth. I was thinking that nine children were far too many for this already overpopulated world. I called up Carol, who has now moved from Sedona back to Michigan, to see what she thought. She says five means change and nine means completion. She said I was feeling responsible for too many people by predicting or being attached to the outcome. I think most of my responsibility is with my parents and my four children. I feel like I need to save them, because Freda has tried so hard to come through for Mike. And I have wished that I had someone to love me as much as she loves Mike. So I am going to try to let all of it go and just live in the moment. I decided to not go to the tender care because of that dream.

44

Healing from Childhood

SHIRLEY AND I WENT over to the house we grew up in on Williams Street. The man renovating it, Ray, was nearing completion on it being done. We took a chance that we would be able to get in to see it, knowing that Ray or his daughter would not be home. However, Mike, who was finishing up the kitchen dry walling, was there to let us in. I cannot describe in words this house. We pulled up in the driveway next door and almost started crying. We could not believe our eyes. It was a very creative masterpiece that I do not think anyone would believe. Even though the house is very little, I would not mind living in it at all. It is really a two-person house because of there being really no storage room to speak of. But I really think one person would be really comfortable in it. Ray had made himself bay windows all around the house, which looked awesome. It actually reminds me of a Pillsbury Gingerbread house. It's cuteness permeating throughout. What a healing for the two of us. Shirley's guides were telling her for the last couple of days to go over there, and we finally did. We were very happy we did and wished I had brought my camera to take pictures throughout.

My brother Ron came in this last weekend because he had made a stopover after a business trip from Boston and New York. We watched the Taylor Fireworks, which were absolutely incredible. Every time I see them, they get better and better. These fireworks were dedicated to 9/11. They had an outline of the Twin Towers lit up and music to go along with the fireworks. We watched the fireworks from the deck behind my mom and dad's house. My uncle Paul and Gwen watched also. They are the best fireworks in the whole area. I cannot imagine Detroit's being any better. I also took Ron over to Williams to see if it could be healing for him as well. He got quite angry on the way and really did not want to go. I said that it would be healing for him and promised him we would not stay long. When we got there, he immediately did not say too much. Then his anger turned into joy and wonderment. He did not know if he would be jealous, seeing it redone, or what. In the car, when we were leaving, he said he did receive healing. I was happy and glad that this took place. My hope is that all my brothers and sisters have this opportunity.

    I went out at 5:00 a.m. to talk to the Universe. My husband was getting ready to leave for work, so I went out on my front porch and sat in the swing. I was fed up with a lot of things and wanted to express myself. I knew the dogs Cain and Abel, who are pit bulls, were out next door, and I did not want to disturb them. So I talked quietly. This is what I said: "Universe, you know those rejection and abandonment issues that I have—you're out of here. You know how I need acceptance and approval—you're out of here. You know the need I have to prove to people that I am going on the right path—you're out of here. I need to prove it to no one, not even myself. You know the bleeding and concerns for my children—you're out of here. I love them, but I release them. The concerns for my parents—you're out of here. I demand that my knee be healed and this body that I have abused be made new again. In my past, when I played Joan of Arc and got burned at the stake, when I thought I was doing God's work—you're out of here." I also said that we needed a less evasive and obtrusive way of life. I felt like Rhett Butler in *Gone with the Wind.* And I said, "Frankly, Universe, I don't give a damn." And I went into the house—nothing like calmly and decisively telling off the Universe. Somehow I felt better. The Universe said back, "Tomorrow is another day." When I went in the house, I closed my eyes and saw what I had seen many times before. It was a small circle with an angled shape inside like an octagon, turning and lit up in red and yellow. I thought somehow it was healing. You could call this surrendering. Suicide is the ultimate surrender, but I am certainly not recommending it.

Once again, I decided to go to the Holy Ghost meeting before I went on vacation for three weeks. Mike left at 5:00 p.m. for work, but before he left, he said a couple of mean things to me. He accused me of eating his potato chips and a tiny little piece of angel food cake. I did eat the little bit of cake, but did not feel I deserved to be treated like that. I said nothing, not telling him that I did not touch his potato chips. This upset me, but I tried to pass it off while walking around in the pool. I decided to leave, not sure that I wanted to go at all. I was bombarded with negative energy throughout the Holy Ghost meeting. I was thinking this was very strange because I usually have really good energy while I am there. So much so that I was crying; tears were uncontrollably, profusely pouring out. Most of the people keep their eyes shut or down, looking at their music books, so I could keep my pain a secret. I was going to leave as soon as it was over with and not go to the prayer room. Bridgett, however, stopped me to ask me a question about the senior citizens.

So that prompted me into going into the prayer room to stand in for a neighbor's child. Afterward, I wanted to show Mel my sunrise pictures. All of a sudden, when I was showing him the pictures, I started crying. I apologized, feeling embarrassed and humiliated. He said that that was okay, but asked what happened to prompt this. I told him about Mike and that my whole life was the dark night and I had had enough. I do not know what he thought of me. I left feeling very bad. I turned left on Outer Drive to go home, and I saw the grandest, biggest full moon I had ever seen. It was poignant and enormous in every way, taking up the whole sky. It had a little straight cloud going across the middle like it was smiling at me. After I made the right hand turn onto Allen, I never saw it again.

Carol P. had told me that she saw a full moon the last time I had talked to her. I said that explained what I had just been through and laughed a little to myself.

45

Back at Mullett

MIKE AND I ARE once again back at Mullett. We decided to take a drive into the Upper Peninsula to go to Brevoort Lake. Even though it was overcast and cloudy with some rain here and there, I could not believe this lake. It looked pristine and untouched by man, even though you could see a hint of a couple of houses on the other side. I took a few pictures, which I do not normally do under those conditions. I hoped they would turn out because it had just rained. We were bombarded with mosquitoes, and they wanted our blood. I could not move my hands around enough not to get bitten. So I did not want to stay very long. It reminded me of what you would see in Alaska. I could not understand how I enjoyed this lake so much in a cloudy atmosphere. Mike, Tyler, and I walked to the dam and stood watching the waterfall on the other side. Mike had stopped both going and coming for me to walk along the beach of Lake Michigan on the UP side. He drove alongside the road, letting Tyler and I walk as long as we wanted. I could not get over how warm and clean the water looked. It looked like the ocean to me because you could only see water with its enormous panoramic vastness. The sand had an orange color and was a little coarse but felt very good on the feet. I walked so the waves would come up and hit my feet. The sun came out while I was walking on the beach, seeing the water light up in all its grandeur.

Mike got up in the middle of the night to go to the bathroom one night. He said that I had to get up and come out on the deck for a minute. I went out on the deck to see the moon looking like it was the sun for a sunrise. And yes, it was in the east. It was not a full moon—a little more than half—the right section was missing. What was so peculiar was it was sitting right above the water, and stranger yet, it was orange. I wanted to take a picture of it, but I knew it would be a black picture with a partial orange moon in it. I wished I had anyway, even if

I would have wasted the picture. The sky was very dark. I guess because the orange made it darker and the stars were not very bright. Mike and I both found it very strange, it being a bright orange. I deliberately took note and noticed that the stars were not very bright, also contributing to the darkness. Just maybe this represented the moon turning into positive energy, because it usually represents negative. In the *Sedona Journal*, it did say the moon had been negative energy and turned into positive. I very much thought it this was a very welcome event to get up in the middle of the night to witness. I especially liked it because I did not have to freeze my but off for the occasion. And wasn't it a little strange that I had just witnessed the moon in all its glory as a moon?

It was now the first of August 2002, and I went out for another sunrise. I decided to bring my camera even though I did not plan on taking any pictures. Soon after I had gotten to the end of the dock and sat, the hint of the sun came through with a little circle of bright light at the top of the sun peeking out—like a beacon of light, a lighthouse. That stayed there for a little bit. I had seen the same thing a couple of days previously. I sat back to enjoy it and be in the moment. All of a sudden, I started seeing objects in the sky, and I will do my best to try to describe them. On the right of the sun in the center appeared to be what looked like a blue Pacman, which is what it reminded me of. It moved around the perimeter, going up left and around until it got back to where it started. And then it proceeded to go up to the right with a blue line following it, going above it and curving over the top of it, and it sat there for a moment and disappeared. Not a clue what that represented.

Then I saw many staggered blue octagon shapes appear to the left and right of the sun. There were two rows equally on both sides of the sun in the middle. Then I witnessed them swoop upward in unison into heaven—this happened several times, both on the left and right at the same time. Sometimes they would be blue circles again rising into heaven. The reason I knew they swooped was because they had blue lines exaggerating the event. I think that maybe they might be spirits that I had helped into heaven. Then I saw several small objects come down and sit to the right of me in the air or in front and disappear. I saw the sun spin—I saw colored lights flashing around the perimeter, going off at different intervals. Plus, the sun changed colors and looked different. Also I would see different shapes of red and blue around the sun that I had seen often. This was a most unprecedented sunrise for me, and I was very glad that I went out for this. This did not happen right away; I had been sitting there for a little while. I wasn't suspecting or expecting anything. How great thou art!

I now believe that the object encircling the sun was a representation of me coming full circle. I woke up the next morning to go out to another sunrise when that was what came to mind. However, it was already up some, but I was glad I went out anyway. They said on the news that it would be cloudy for this morning sunrise. Well, as usual, they were wrong. I wanted to stay in bed and was glad I had witnessed a calm, glorious morning after yesterday's stormy weather. Everything that I saw was a hazy and mostly the same color of blue even though it all had definition. The blue looked like the color you get in an eight-count crayon box. The circle that came down and sat to the right of me, I believe, was green. I never knew what I would see in the sky next. It sure has been entertaining me in the past several years. I was so engrossed in what they were showing me in the sky to even think of taking a picture. I do not know if it would have showed up anyway. I do know that it would have taken away from the moment. I truly was mesmerized with the whole sky and what they were offering obviously to me.

Mike inquired about a tender care being up here and found out there was one in Cheboygan behind the hospital. Cheboygan is approximately seven miles north of where we live at Mullett. So the next day, he drove me and dropped me off for a couple of hours. The first person I met was Gloria; she was the activities director. She totally lit up the place with her shining face. I immediately knew I was in the right place. They have approximately ninety people that are patients in this facility. I immediately felt like I was at home; I loved these young old people. It still surprises me how easy it is for me to genuinely love them. I look forward to each and every visit. I also know they are eager for me to return. Gloria came up to me on the third day of visiting and asked me if I had visited everyone in the place. I said I tried to. Gloria knows that I say an Our Father and a Hail Mary with all the people who are willing, also knowing that I do not force anything. I know the more you give, the more you will receive.

It never ceases to amaze—the people that are hanging on to anger till their last breath. They usually say they hate themselves and everyone else. This usually occurs when you bring up God or prayer to them. They usually fling their arms in disapproval. Or how two women in the same room hate each other by hurting each other physically or with words or both. They would tell me what she has done to them. You've got to feel sorry for them on how they spend their last days on earth. Then there appears that some people appear to be possessed. They are tormented and strike out at everyone by flinging their arms. Most of the people love prayer and love. And it does not matter if you are their religion or not. It appears that most people know the Our Father even if they are not in their right mind and very much welcome prayer by telling me thanks and how much it is needed. One lady told me that she was not sure if she had met anyone like me before. Often I am told how young I look and that I am not old enough to be married or have children. I have been told that I look as young as sixteen, which is very amusing to me.

I went out for another sunrise. This sunrise, the sun slowly appeared to be going to the left every time I looked up. I thought that it might represent me as I saw the Pacman go around the sun to the left. There was a lot of mist coming off the water because the water was warm and the air was cool. I

FAKE IT, IT WILL COME

took a couple of pictures of the event. Maybe all of this really did not happen and it was my imagination. It represented at the beginning. The next day, I was at another sunrise, and I saw blue octagon shapes coming at me this time. They came close enough that I tried to reach out and touch them and believe that I did. There were several little octagon shapes that I distinctly saw. I do not know what those octagon shapes mean or represent. I am also not altogether sure that they are octagon shapes, which is what they looked like to me. Again I saw many blue circles, which I believe are my guides or spirits. I took several pictures of the sunrise, hoping that what I saw would be in the pictures. I also saw a red outline encircling the sun, coming down and going into blue a few times. We will see. I always cannot wait with anticipation to see what my pictures will have in store for me.

I went again to my senior citizen place in Cheboygan. There were two people, Alice and Edward, that seemed to be tormented. I spent time with both, hoping that I could help them in some way. I was told that Alice was a good churchgoing person and that her swearing was out of character for her. She also grabs at you and pinches you even though both of her wrists are in elastic support. Probably, I am guessing, caused from carpal tunnel. She will also grab you between the legs if you don't watch out. She has the habit of swearing, using God's name in vain religiously. Alice also goes to lift her top but doesn't and attempts to grab herself between the legs. I looked her in the eyes and told her I wasn't afraid of her—meaning her demons. I kept on quietly, saying, "In the name of Jesus, I command you to be gone." In the few times that I have worked with both, they both appeared to be calming down. In fact I said to Ed, "Do you feel better?" And he said yes, without hesitation. Ed keeps his left forearm over his forehead and the right one raised at all times. He has the look that he will punch you in his eyes but never does. Or he is protecting himself. They do not appear to be very cognizant of what is going on as well. But to some degree, they are. When I put my hand on Alice's forehead, she says she does not have a headache. I do not think that Ed ever puts his arms down. I only hear him grunting and making weird noises and did not know he could talk.

This is my ninth time visiting the Cheboygan Health Care facility, my senior citizens. Alice is doing much better; she even tells me that she loves me when I tell her I love her and that I am a nice person. She appears to be much calmer and will let me put my hand on her forehead. She even stopped swearing, at least while I was there anyway. She attempted to try to pinch me once during the visit. I told her she is at peace now. Ed has put his arms down and his fist does not appear to be clenched. He tells me that he wants to marry me, but he says that to most of the women. He also allows me to put my hand on his forehead. He was still making noises, though maybe not as bad. I am so pleased that their progress has been this good before I left to go back.

I just got through dusting and vacuuming my home at Mullett Lake. And I decided to sit on the front steps for a few minutes with Tyler at my side. We have a hummingbird feeder right to the left of the front door. A hummingbird encircled me then flew off to a tree near the driveway, which was to the right as I was facing the lake. I thought, *How amusing*. I turned around and watched him looking at me as he was going. Then the hummingbird came back and sat right in front of my face, looking me in the eyes. This, I thought, was a very rare treat. The hummingbirds up here appeared to be a little larger than the ones at home in Taylor. They were really attracted to some red flowers near the deck, and I think that is why Mike went out to get the feeder. I sit in my chair in the living room and watched them this whole trip. I really have enjoyed my experience with all the birds that have come into my life. In my opinion, that is heaven. My brothers Ron and Gary both told me about their similar experiences with hummingbirds. Both claimed that they were not afraid of humans.

I now know there was symbolism in what the hummingbird had done. It came to the right of me, circled around to the front then to the left and behind, and swooped up to the trees sitting to the right. In other words, it was the same analogy as I had witnessed with my blue Pacman in the sky, only it did not come and sit to look at me, staring me in the eyes. Although stuff did swoop down at me and sit next to me and disappear in front of me. I know there is a reason for everything, so I look for it.

We were here for altogether a little more than three weeks. During those three weeks, I went swimming a lot and made many fires. You could not help wanting to go swimming because it was so hot. Carl stacked a lot of wood all over, further in the backyard, and there were many roots from trees uprooted and sitting where he had bulldozed. Plus there are many downed trees all over the woods, crisscrossing on the ground and such. This made it very difficult to walk in these woods, so I made it a passion to burn wood. I think burning the wood and going into the lake helped clear my aura from going to the seniors. I look at this as a huge enormous job. But Mike reminded me that we did not clear Roscommon overnight either. Also there was much poison ivy everywhere. So far, I have been lucky enough not to get it. Mike had a couple of leaks in the basement to fix. Plus he took down six dead trees and cut them up, stacking them further yet in the backyard. The two of us did a lot of work, but it was a labor of love.

Shirley from Utah, my brother Gary from California, and Ron from Texas, plus my mom and dad from Taylor were all coming up. Ron's friend Dave and his two kids, Jacob and Katie, were likewise coming up. So we would have a full house. I also forgot to mention that Ron's daughter Sara was coming up as well. We barbecued steaks and had summer squash and a macaroni salad. After dinner, we decided to have a campfire on the beach. While the four of us—Mike, Shirley, Gary, and I—were sitting around the fire, we saw what we thought were UFOs playing in the sky. They were blatantly playing with one another. I would say there were at least three or four of them, possibly more. However, we spent most of the time watching two of them communicating back and forth with one another in play. I felt very strongly that the display was for us. While watching it, we all heard rumbling—we were thinking it might be thunder off in the distance. However, we did not see any lightning, and we had a clear night and saw many stars, shooting stars, and space stations. Theron had told me on the phone that I was getting a surprise, and I think that was it.

During the four nights that they were there, we had many fires on the beach and many boat rides, both with the pontoon and sea ray. Also, Karen and Darrell's friends brought two brand-new jet skis up for the day. Brian was nice enough to let us all take a turn. I really do not care for jet skis and think of them as a pain. However when I got on it, I had a ball. Shirley told me that I looked like an incredible diva on it and could not believe this was my first time. Brian was actually nice enough to let me go on it twice. Considering these machines were brand-new, it was amazing he let us go on it at all. Tubing was also on the agenda. Mike pulled whomever wanted to go and guaranteed them that they could not hang on. Darrell decided to bait Mike with an open invitation in front of all of us at the campfire. We watched as he got dumped several times. Everyone thought Mullett was awesome and that we were lucky to have such a nice place.

Mike and I went back up to Mullett, and not a whole lot happened spiritually nor did I take many pictures. We did quite a bit of work, though. I wiped down the deck, and Mike sprayed the deck with an oil-base stain while I used the brush. During both of the events, it was hot, and I was wringing wet with perspiration. I had gotten down on all fours to wipe it with a wet rag, changing the water at least five times. When we got through, I did take a couple of pictures of the deck. It was a rather large deck and a lot of work. That is why I do not like decks—because they are not maintenance-free. We had Ken and Cheryl and their daughter Tracy and boyfriend Brian over for dinner. The men went fishing, and we girls took off on the pontoon boat, which ran out of gas. We were not sure how to transfer the connection from one to the other, so we flagged a boat and asked if the man could help us. And he did. Then I had a burning ceremony in my backyard of copies of my book. I said I was through with the suffering and pain and was more than ready to learn from joy.

46

Prayer Group

I WENT AGAIN TO my meditation group. I decided on my own to give another talk at the end. I got up to the mike, and this is what I said. I went to my senior citizens today, and this is what happened. There was a black lady whom I have been saying the Our Father and Hail Mary with for the past six months. Today out of the clear blue, she said, "I don't have faith" after I prayed with her. I was shocked because she never had said a complete sentence before. She also stared into space like she was not cognizant of what was going on. Her mouth greatly protruded and was not pleasant to look at; however, she had pleasant eyes. I said to her, "It is this simple—just forgive yourself, ask for forgiveness, and invite Jesus into your heart." She did not respond, so I said, "I will say it for you," and I did so and put my hand on her heart and invited Jesus in. I said, "Jesus is all color and no color. It is your right of passage for peace, love, and light. You are the Beloved and loved beyond measure. It is your birthright to have joy and ecstasy." Then I said, "You will see a very bright light. Do not be afraid of it. We cannot possibly comprehend the peace and love that will be waiting for us. Once you go to the light, come back and assist me in helping others." She still did not comment.

This is what I hear some of you people say: "I have to go to church every day. I have to drive out for this spiritual experience and that spiritual experience." I say, "What if you went to church on Sunday then found a way to serve mankind?" I could use some help, being that I visit two hundred people virtually on my own. These people are prisoners; some are not able to move virtually at all. I call them my baby girls; after all, they are helpless and needy. There are quite a few people that are always sleeping when I visit, and I wonder if they are ever cognizant. They are starved for some kind of interaction and love. I am fortunate; I do not have to work, and my husband gives me the green light to do all the donating I want. So I have the time to go and do. I really did not know what the meaning of "God helps those that help themselves" Was. Now I do. Well, that is all I had to say.

After the group had ended, I went up to talk to Mel. I told him that I knew that I would not be seeing him for a long time and had to let him know that I was okay. I did not have his number, so I knew Helen kept in touch with him and decided to give Helen a call to get his number or so that she could let him know that I was okay. I told him how I wanted to leave and was stopped by Bridgett, who asked me a question. Then I went to be prayed over and stopped to show him my pictures. I told him how I just wanted to go straight home and be miserable by myself. I told him that he must have thought I was a basket case. And he said, "Well, you were." I also told him about turning the corner to go home and seeing a full moon taking up the whole sky and how it made me want to laugh. Plus I told him how I had awakened in the middle of the night at total peace and knew that he had prayed for me and thanked him. He said, "It wasn't me." I said, "The praise and glory go to God. The thanks go to you for your prayers for me. It was through your kind words that God was able to work through you."

I had another dream last night. I had awakened around three in the morning to seeing colorful light reflecting on the crook of a couch and knew it was the Blessed Mother. The couch was a light color, and it reflected somewhat like a projector and a movie screen. I spend a lot of time on the crook of my couch, which happens to be the other side of the couch. The Blessed Mother was very much what I have seen on holy cards, often with rays of light reflecting out all around her and her arms outstretched. Then the light turned into a colorful Indian. Shortly afterward, the light of an Indian transformed into a person. I said, "Gray Eagle." He appeared to be indifferent to me and did not say much. I sensed his indifference and did not bombard him with questions like I might usually have done. I do not remember the communication at all. However, I felt at that time that the spirit world was getting me ready for me really witnessing the spirit world. I did not know the correlation of the Blessed Mother and Gray Eagle, what they had in common or what they represented. Carol said that she got the Indian was Mike. I was maybe thinking that the Blessed Mother and the Indian were also Mike.

I woke up to still another dream. This time, I had on an oversized flip-flop on my right foot.

Around the outside perimeter and heel were many baby mice. Their bodies looked like two small circles, one a little larger than the other. I sat up and started dusting these mice off my flip-flop. I looked up to see two rather large ugly cats sitting nearby, not really doing anything but looking. Normally these mice would be a time for me to go a little crazy. I think the babies are the seniors I visit at the nursing home. The cats are their loneliness and suffering without love. The director has asked me to document everything, and this is taking away from my joy. I think now that I want to go to three different homes a week. I could not figure out what this dream meant. I also had another dream about me standing on two ladies' heads. One lady is shorter, and she moved away, and I was balancing with one foot on the taller one. Then I decided to just fly as if I knew I can. Not sure what that dream meant either. I do know, however, that it has to do with what is going on in my life.

I finally told the activities director, Wendy, that if she wanted me to do her work, I wanted a paycheck. Wendy said that they weren't hiring. Wendy said that if I didn't document, I could not come in here to visit. I repeated what she said. She said yes. I told her that I loved her but that I was going over her head. She repeated what I said, and I proceeded to find out who was in charge that day. The lady in charge said that this was ludicrous and called their names over the PA. I knew I had to face this problem for I knew it was abuse; abuse is never acceptable. The abuser is abused if they are allowed to abuse. The truth is, I liked Wendy and thought a lot of her. Wendy claimed all along that Kathie was the one that demanded it to be documented. Kathie asked that in the future, I come to her and not go over her head. I did not know Kathie was the one in charge; I thought Wendy was. I assured Kathie that I would come to her in the future. I was glad that I finally faced this problem, for it loomed big in my eyes, so much so that I wanted to stop going there. Actually I give thanks to Wendy for discouraging me, because I would not have gone to Rivergate if it hadn't been for this situation.

One morning, I was talking to my sister Shirley, and she had just read the last half of my book. While reading it, she was told over and over again that this book would bless many generations to come. She said she did not know if it was my family specifically or people that would read it. She told me that my book was very well worded. I told her, the funny part was that I always felt that I was below average and could not believe that I was writing a book. I asked my twin if she would read it, and of course she would not.

Last Sunday, I went to my senior citizens. I dedicated my spreading my love or tapping into my love energy to my son Eric. I met this man whom I had seen but had spent very little time with. What little time I had spent around him, I did not think he was in his right mind. He started singing the song "Swing low, sweet chariot, I'm going to carry you home." I immediately sang with him, and he stopped and turned to look at me and gasped. I could not believe my own voice. I sounded like an angel. So I went about my business, going in the adjoining rooms. I again saw him in another hallway, and he again started singing. I again sang, and he turned his head to look up and me and gasped again. What was so unique is no one else paid us any mind. I felt for that moment that our spirits merged and some form of healing took place. Something did happen at that moment. We shared a piece of heaven. I saw him several weeks later and started singing the song, and he said, "Take you and your song and get out."

47

My Son Eric

NOTHING THAT HAS HAPPENED thus far could possibly prepare me for what happened next. I was going to the Southgate District Court to see my son Eric being sentenced to ten days in the Clare County Jail for breaking his probation. Almost a year ago, Eric got pulled over for slightly being over the level for drinking. His probation was almost up. He tested positive for marijuana. I had been waiting for some time because they could not tell me a time when he would be called. Finally, I was sitting at the last pew when he turned his head, looking downward but still looking me in the eyes. I could barely look his way but did. He looked so thin and scared. There was nothing I could do. This happened to other people, not to me. I felt like my heart was ripped out, crushed, and thrown away. I do believe that I started to take on his pain. After the judge left, the policeman overseeing told Eric he did not deserve what he was getting but that the other guy did. As a mother, you are only as happy as your unhappiest child.

That evening, I called up Don in the Holy Ghost group. Somehow I felt he would be the one to tell. He said he would immediately put it on the prayer chain and that he would be praying for the both of us throughout the next ten days. I had asked Don a month ago or so if he would pray for my children. He immediately told me to write down their names and ages, which of course I did. So that is why I chose Don. He was an angel for me, a direct line to the host of heaven. I went to bed that night and screamed. No one was home. Mike was working nights. I told God I could not handle this. I told him I wanted to die. I screamed so much that I got a pretty bad headache and had to take some Tylenol. I said the joy I was experiencing was too great and that the gifts I had been given I did not deserve. You are supposed to get what you give out; clearly, I did not deserve this. I have turned over my life to serving mankind. I did not sleep much, as you might imagine. I did not want to talk to anyone. It was also very humbling, saying what I had to say to Don.

The next day, I said, "God, you have not forsaken me," and turned my thoughts to giving thanks and joy for the healing that would take place. The next morning, I was still very much in distraught, but somehow I felt lifted, thinking the prayers from the Holy Ghost people were working. On the fourth day, I witnessed something with my eyes shut, while I was going to pee. I do not know if there was a correlation to that or not. It was an all-black picture with an illumed teardrop that stayed there for a while. I immediately said healing for Eric. Actually, I did not know it was a teardrop until I told Shirley what I described. She said it was a teardrop, and of course, that made perfect sense. I put the host of heaven in the four corners of his cell and surrounded him with a pink light. I would walk and just give praise and glory for this healing, trusting that it had already taken place. I said, "You know, Jesus, what is better for Eric than I do" and said "May thy will be done." I also said, "If it is your will." It helped when God told me that he had never turned his back on me but that I had turned my back on him. I decided that I knew that the only way I could help

Eric was if I implemented what I knew. It is only when we implement our knowledge that anything works. Trust that you will make everything right if you surrender your will. Begging and supplicating is not what they want. Trusting is everything!

Mike did not react to what was happening to Eric at all, which was a big help to me. In the courtroom from across the room, he said his car payment was due, but we did not know how to pay that. His car insurance had been cancelled; it came in the next day's mail. We did not know where his car was. In the courtroom, he said to get his car on Van Horn road and sell it. We had no keys. There was no way to get a hold of his girlfriend, Kelly. He had given me the wrong phone number. I went driving on Van Born road because that is what I thought he said instead of Van Horn, but obviously, I could not find it. Even if I had found it, I did not have keys to drive it. Finally, we both agreed that we just had to wait until he got out of jail. I think Eric felt laden with bills that he did not know how to pay. I just said, "Universe, I put all my concerns in your hands. I truly do not know how to deal with this." What if the best was yet to come that I would write in my book?

FAKE IT, IT WILL COME

When Eric arrived this Wednesday, he did not look any worse for wear to me. I immediately thought that I would not put that pain on me or bleed for my children again. I had tortured myself or maybe I did alleviate his pain. I don't know. I was feeling like I was going to pass out, and the nerve endings of my skin where going crazy. Actually, at about 9:00 a.m., I felt fine, thinking that Eric was fine. My only hope is that he had learned from this experience what not to do. I felt like I wasn't very enlightened if I was reacting the way I did. I told the heavens that I could not help it—I was a mother.

48

Volunteering Again

I FOUND A NEW place near my home to volunteer called Rivergate. They have the capacity to hold 220 patients. I talked to Essie, the activity director, and she was eager for me to start working at the facility. The first day, I went around to all the rooms on the second floor. I told Bridgett that it was time for me to move on, and she said it was time for her likewise and if I could ask about a hairdresser at Rivergate. I told her I would. I met Margaret for the first time. I asked her if I could pray with her, and she said no. But I thought she did not understand me, so I did anyway. She started screaming. The aide there said she had never seen her do that and asked if she had gotten hurt. I finally told her later what had happened. She said, "Some people do not like to be prayed with." To me, she seemed to be retarded. I gave her a hug and told her that I loved her, that I was sorry I did that and would not do that again. I said, "You do not like prayer." She said those words. I could not understand how that could bother someone like that. I told Essie what happened. I met Dorothy for the first time. She looked like she had been shoved in the corner to die very weak and frail. I asked her to pray with her, but I could not hear what she had to say, so I decided to anyway. While I was praying, looking into her eyes. She started crying, the tears just setting in her sunken eyes. Then I sang her a Christmas song, "Fall on Your Knees." I put my ear right up to her mouth and could not hear her.

Met Dorothy again a week later; I must have missed her somehow. When I see her she recognized me and was effervescent and feisty. I looked up to see her name, and it was Dorothy. They had moved her to another room. I was in shock; she was talking loud, and I could not believe it was the same person. I asked her if I had done okay when I saw her last. She said her eyes were sunken in; she was depressed because she felt that she was dying and simply did not feel like talking to anyone. There was so much joy in her at this moment. When we met for the third time, I saw her in the cafeteria, sitting up in a wheelchair. Now I really cannot believe my eyes. It also seemed like we knew each other forever. In fact, I told the lady sitting from across our table that Dorothy and I were soul mates and bonded together. She said, "I like you too." The man at the table who happened to be sitting next to me would not let me pray with him but he was very nice about it. So we prayed without him. I asked him if maybe the next time we could include him. And he said maybe. The next time, he extended his pinky finger for me to hang on to. I thought that was priceless. He did it with a big smile on his face.

Mike and I are once again up north. We had to winterize everything by getting the shore stations, dock, and boats out of the water. Ken, Mike's cousin, came over to help him get everything out on the beach. It was a lot of work, to say the least. Mike claimed I could not help with the shore stations because they were burrowed in the sand from the weight of the boats. I went again to my seniors while they were working and had a very good time. I met a few new people. People die or move on. One lady whom I met for the first time said she did not mind if I prayed with her; however, she was not

FAKE IT, IT WILL COME

religious. I said that was okay and prayed with her while holding her hands. When I was through, she thanked me. I guess she was having a hard time getting acclimated to the place. I saw Gloria again. Her smiling face was always a treat to see. I went twice while we were up there. I dove into Mullett Lake on the last day of September and the first of October. I walked out quite a ways right before we left to go home. I could not believe I did this even though it was eighty degrees out. I know you receive a different kind of healing from cold water versus tepid water. So I thanked the universe for the healing that I would be receiving from diving into cold water. I was so unaffected by the cold water I could have stayed in for hours. I drove the tractor and cut the grass while Mike was doing other things.

On Wednesday, October 9, 2002, I went out on my front porch in Taylor to say my prayers. I was staring at the sun, watching colors and the sun doing some stuff for a while, and after being out there for a while, I went in. The sun rose in the front of my house on the right hand corner at this time of year. I was looking toward the floor to the right as I stepped in the front door, when all of a sudden I saw a blue circle in the center, mint green fanning out from it and a red narrow strip around the perimeter, all having a certain shape. The green seemed to be rounded at the top but accented by the red, narrow, rectangular shape; it was straight across at the bottom but still had the red line straight across also. I put my right hand up, palm facing me, and the shape was shown brilliantly in the perimeter of my hand, then it disappeared. I went into the kitchen to get a cup of coffee, and again I put my hand up, and again I saw the same shape and colors with an iridescence and vivid brilliance in the palm of my hand. It went away. I put my hand down. I again put my hand up, and it did the same thing, three consecutive times altogether. After that, I put my hand up, and I saw a vivid circle of rich purple in the center of the palm of my hand; I did that twice. I would say it was like it was being projected on my hand. I do not think it was coming from my hand. I thought this was a pretty neat experience. I thought that it was because of my work with my seniors.

Prayer Group

That same day, I went to the Holy Ghost meeting. Don told me that I should get in front of the group and tell them about Eric. Bridgett said at the senior home that day that I should tell about my experience, what happened to me that morning, because I had shared it with her. Jerry said that I should sing when I got in front of the mike; he thought that God wanted me to sing the song "Who Will Answer?" That caught me off guard, and I thought I could do it another time. So I got in front of the group, and this is what I said:

"Two people said that I should get up in front of you guys, so here goes. The night my son went into jail, I screamed the entire night. I said, 'God, I cannot handle this. This happens to other people, not to me.' I said that I wanted to die and that I could not handle the joy I was experiencing or the gifts that I was receiving. Then the next morning, it felt like a dark cloud was lifted from me, and at that moment, I was able to flip-flop things around. I started giving praise to Jesus for Eric's healing and telling God, 'How great thou art.' Even though I was still distraught, I did this periodically throughout the day. I said I wasn't going to just call you guys. I was going to do my part. Four days later—it happened to be a Saturday in the middle of the day—while I had my eyes closed, I saw a perfectly illumed teardrop, and I knew Eric had received healing.

"I hear you guys say, when I give thanks for your prayer, 'Oh, it's not me!' You co-create with god. God is not able to do his part if we do not do ours. What is it worth, when you are down and out, to have this group at your beck and call? It is worth more than all the money on the planet and gold. It is such a privilege and honor to be a part of this group."

After that, I told them about my experience with my hand luminescent and lit up. I told them that maybe it was God's way of saying, "Keep up the good work with donating time." I said there was no greater prayer than donating time. I do not know what happened, but I do think part of the reason is being at the beginning and earning my gifts by donating time.

Before the meditation started, I met a lady that I will call Belinda. I had explained to four of the ladies in the group the previous week a little bit about the dark night of the soul. This week, I explained to the same four ladies about doing a form of exorcism on two people up north. How I quietly said, "I cast you out in the name of Jesus Christ" and told them, looking into their eyes, that I was not afraid of them, meaning their demons. Belinda said that she needed my help and told me about her experience with someone using an Ouija board in her house. She told me that a couple of people had come over to cast them out but to no avail. I said we should pray over her. So the three of us said the Our Father and Hail Mary with both of our hands on her. After the meditation was over with, I went back in the kitchen to talk to her again. I told her I would assist her but that she was the one that had to do the work, that she had to take her power back and face her fears. I told her all negativity was an illusion and nothing real can be threatened; nothing unreal exists. It was time for her to take her power back—all the power was within her. Then I told her about reiki but that people here did not agree with reiki and that I would give it to her. She agreed.

We went into the bathroom, where we would not be interrupted, so I could do the reiki. She was willing to receive any help that she could get. I had her face the mirror in the bathroom and say "I love you, Belinda," and I wrapped her arms around her. I told her I wanted her to do that every day while she was looking in the mirror under any occasion. I did the reiki symbols on her forehead then laid my right hand on her forehead, leaving it there where I looked into her eyes. This is what I said: "You've no business in here. You will be better off if you go to the light. You will not be harmed. I cast you out in the name of Jesus Christ." I said this several times.

Belinda started tearing up, like finally she would be getting some relief. As we were walking back to the kitchen, Belinda looked at me and said, "You don't even know me." I said, "That is right, you are I, and I am you." I told her that I would do some work from my house. She asked me if I would come over to her house. I said I would but that she had the power to do it herself. I told her that she had created this with her fears. What you fear, you attract. I told her that she had all the power to stand up to them.

49

My Lights

Two days later, on Friday, I had a very similar experience. I did my prayers on the front porch, around the same time as on Wednesday. After I said my prayers, I was talking on the phone with my mother. I was seeing all kinds of things with my eyes shut and open. I also saw the sky turn all red, the sun spin, and all kinds of stuff. Before now, I had never seen the whole sky turn red, and then it switched to something else. I decided to go back into the house, and at the front door, in the same spot, I saw brilliant, luminescent mint green floating in the air. I again put up my hand, and it was the size of my hand. I decided to have fun with it, transferring it from one hand to the other, moving it up and over one another in a circular motion. Sometimes it would have a little circle of blue in the center. Then it stopped, so I went in to get a cup of coffee and decided to put my hand up again. Here we went again. I was transferring from one hand to the other, having a good time. It was the same color as at the doorway. At the end, it turned all red; however, the shape went way outside my hand, and it was not luminescent; it is dull. I started moving my hands, transferring it up the wall as far as I could reach. It was a cloudy day today and darker than Wednesday. Now this was really becoming quite amusing. The green was unbelievably vivid and brilliant, like there was a lightbulb behind it.

It appears the prerequisite for this happening is looking in the sun and giving praise. If it is a cloudy day, chances are it will not work. In fact, I don't even bother looking for them. The heavens communicate with me directly, and I know the only approval and acceptance I need is from myself. Because I know my way, when it feels good, is God's way or will. I knew that I needed no one else's validation. The heavens communicated with me directly. I might not know how or what they are communicating at the time, but I eventually figure it out. I might get help from other sources, but ultimately, it remains my truth and what feels good to me. I believe this is so for everyone.

Now it is Tuesday, the fifteenth of October. I went out on my front porch for my prayers again. The sky did again some pretty neat stuff. I somewhat went into the house in a hurry. When I turned around to look in the corner, I saw a bright blue shape sitting in the air. I put my right hand up, and it only went on my fingers this time. It went above my fingers, about the length of my fingers and wider, somewhat like a circle. This was the first time I was seeing only blue; I thought this meant clairvoyance and clarity. I tried transferring it, but it wasn't happening this time. It disappeared, so I went in the kitchen where the coffee was to see if it would happen again in that corner. I had already drunk my coffee. It did the same thing, changing all different colors. This time, the orange and red were bright. I hadn't seen orange before. Plus I also saw a similar form and color show when I closed my eyes. Again, it would not let me transfer at all. Most of the time, it had a little circle in the center of the shape that was brilliant. All of it was luminescent, like a lightbulb. I now think this was the prelude to getting my gifts. All three times that this happened were within one week.

It was Saturday, October 19. I went outside my side door in the morning and walked back and forth on my driveway, looking in the direction of the sun. When I came in, I saw stuff at the top of the basement door again. Most of the shapes looked the same, and they moved to the right, disappearing into the wall. It was cloudy off and on, so I went out again on my front porch. I just started giving praise and thanks to Jesus for all the healing, blessings, and gifts. I went to let Tyler in the front door, and I saw my bright colors again on the floor and decided to go in and see what happened. So I went in and shut the front door, sat on the floor, and held it in my hands, just staring at it. The phone rang, and I paid it no mind, just stared at what was in my hands. I could not believe how brilliant it was, awesome. I got up and went back outside and came in through the front door. Same thing happened, so I sat down facing the closet, holding it my hands, but it moved toward the step. So I turned, resting my forearm and wrist on the step, and held it in the palm of my hands. The bright colors turned now to charcoal black, disappeared to dull light, and went back to charcoal black. It did this three times, just how it would look after a fire. I have seen some extraterrestrial eyes that I have heard people talk about and said I wanted them to share the essence, knowledge, and wisdom with me. That was not scary for me at all. However, this was.

I seemed a little trouble throughout the day, having a little knot in my stomach. By the end of the day, I had had enough. Mike was gone, and I was home alone. I sat on my coach in the living room and told God that I had won. I told him that I was very proud of me. I said that all negativity was an illusion and whatever my charcoaled hands represented, I could now handle. I kept on saying, "God, I've won, the game is over." We can mouth the words, but until we really mean it, by being certain—a kind of knowing, if you will—we have not succeeded. I said it with assurance and knowledge and felt my strength and power. As the *Course* says, "Reality is never frightening. It is impossible that it could upset me. Reality brings only perfect peace. I have replaced reality with illusion I made up. The illusions are upsetting because I have given them reality, and thus regard reality as an illusion." This comes from lesson 52 in the *Course*. These words have really hit home. I went to bed that night and slept like a baby and woke up well rested. Unless we implement what we know, by putting it into action while it is taking place, we are not doing! Alleluia!

50

Volunteering with Second Graders

My dad volunteered me to volunteer teaching second and third graders how to read and write. He knew that I had taught my son Eric how to read when he was a baby and my daughters before kindergarten. Anyway, I decided that I would go to volunteer. I wanted to diversify, so this would be working with young children. Marie's daughter, Pam, taught at federal school, and her mother Marie volunteered and was happy that I was volunteering. She already wanted to predict our accomplishment that we would accomplish by helping out for June at the end of the school year. We both thought we could make a difference. Marie already had, especially in one girl's life. I loved the children; they were great. I knew this place was special; from the moment I entered the classroom, I felt like I was home. I desired to develop skills that I could implement with my children that I had developed with my seniors. It truly became a passion to make a difference in these children's lives. They were the joy and light of my life; however, they did not know it yet.

I told Marie that I wanted to see if the skills I had learned to develop from visiting my seniors, I could use on these children. There were some learning-disabled children along with probably ADD children in the classroom; this situation did not make it conducive to teaching because of the disruptions. Marie said children were different and that she did not think so. I said that what was going on had to stop. I told her about several of the situations with my seniors. I told her, "What, could it hurt?" I really did believe that there was no difference. I told her that I wanted to go in the classroom and tell the children that they were the best kids on the planet, how proud I was of them, how gifted and eager to learn they all were. Marie said they would see through it. I said, "If that what you want them to be like, you have to act like that is what they are." I told her that in time, they would become what you said they were. Anyway, Pam and Marie stood back, and I jumped in and told the children what I had planned on saying. Megan rolled her eyes, but the more she rolled the more I oozed. I now have made it a passion to make a difference with these children.

Marie said she had taught in the Taylor School System for forty-five years and has never had kids as difficult to teach as these children were. The only reason she agreed to volunteer to begin with was to help her daughter Pam out, who was having an unbelievably hard time teaching. It is very rewarding, seeing these children grow in their learning and values that we were promoting daily. We are their mentors. We are a catalyst in the transformation of their lives. It is very rewarding to see your hard work pay off.

When I arrived in the classroom one day, I asked Deedy, "Where is Pam, is she not here?" Deedy said she was busy with Ashley, who was running down the hallway. When Pam arrived, she asked me if I would take Ashley out in the hall to do her work and to not let her out of my sight. Ashley is a delight for me, and this offered no stress for me at all. Of course, I said, "Sure." I talked with Ashley and asked why she was running away so much. She said because they were going to call her parents. I said, "What choices are you making that they want to call your parents? Maybe then you would not have to run." She said that her brother said she has no feelings and about her dad. I said, "Let's make a pact that we will stop in the future and make the choice that will serve you so that they will not have to call your parents so that you do not have to run away." And she agreed.

While I was tending to Ashley, I was standing in the doorway of the classroom. Kylen came running, waving his arms, and crying, saying he was running away as he threw his backpack and headed toward me at the doorway. I went to hug Kylen and said, "What is this about?" He said, "They are going to call my dad." I said, "Kylen, we know you are smart, and we know you can cooperate, so why don't you go back and cooperate, and maybe they will not have to call your dad?" He turned quietly, stopped crying, and went back and cooperated. The substitute looked at me and said, "You're good." I had prayed to the Holy Spirit that morning, offering up my relationship with Kylen, saying I did not know how to deal with him. So I was awestruck with Kylen myself. I went back to help him with his sentences that he was writing, and he totally cooperated. He normally threw himself on the floor, hid behind the blackboard, or leaned back, balancing precariously on the back two legs of the chair, staring into space. This was a new Kylen.

I have been taking a small group of the children into the computer room to read them a book that I had brought in. Because of the children's lack of respect in how they treated their peers, I decided to talk to the kids first. I said, "We have the choice to go throughout life happy or angry and sad." I asked them what they wanted to be. They, of course, said, "Happy." I said, "Then how do we treat people?" Tequila, who was African American, jumped in and said, "Like we would want to be treated." I said, "That is correct, and you are a wise little girl." She said, "My mom never says that she loves me." I said, "I will stand in right now for your mom, and I love you very much." I said this as I was hugging her. I started singing, "If you're happy and you know it, clap your hands." They all started clapping. "If you are happy and you know it, your face will surely show it, if you're happy and you know it, stomp your feet." The children stomped their feet. It was such a privilege and joy, teaching these children who were teaching me. Certainly, as we teach, we learn!

51

On One of My Walks

In the fall of 2001, during one of my walks, I was told I was the One several times throughout a two-day period. I told no one about this because I could not handle it. I told them, the spirit world, "You've got the wrong person." First of all, I did not know the magnitude of what it meant, but regardless, I thought it was too much responsibility for me. Besides, I felt like I was still reacting a little and felt I did not deserve it as well. I told them that I had been in the gutter in all areas of my life my whole life, "and you expect this out of me?" Right before Easter, I told a few people, but I had kept it to myself all that time, something I do not usually do. I wanted to at least tell one person and chose not to. I definitely was not going to write it in my book; I guess that is how healed I am getting. Maybe what "the One" simply means is I was the one that had to heal me. I do not know what my future holds, but now maybe I am ready for it. I made a collage from my most special, spiritual scenic pictures. I cried looking at it and seeing what it all represented, what I had to go through to get there. I felt like it is my diploma from the College of Evolution and given by the hand of God.

The last several months, I have been seeing different scenarios being played out more clearly while they were happening or soon after. I believe the spirit world is showing me this so I really can appreciate the true innocence of our brothers and ourselves. I am definitely having the opportunity to see clearly and not through rose-colored glasses. This is very much a privilege, and I do appreciate this awakening. I pay attention to my dreams because I know there is significance in them. Plus, I pay attention to look around in the moment and see what is really happening. The culmination—"At the beginning is the end." The fulfillment of the "am" is the birth of the "am." The choices we make dictate our life. Underneath all fear is love. Everyone is groping for the meaning of life—"Why we are here?" I guess it is to learn how to show and give love because nothing else matters.

We are once again up north for a few days. I went to my seniors in Cheboygan. I met this man for the first time. People come and go in places like these. When I was doing my rounds, I heard a man swearing, using God's name in vain. When I finally arrived at his room, he was still mumbling under his breath just how put out he was and felt. I knocked on the door and walked right over to the other side of the room to be with a man that I had prayed with before. I thought that I would not even ask him to pray with him because of his attitude, I changed my mind and asked him. To my surprise, he said okay. After holding his hands and saying the prayers, I looked at him and said, "This is an observation, not a judgment, but the words you are using are not serving you. It has become a habit with you. I see a very sweet man." The truth is, I really did see a very sweet man, so it was easy for me to say. Just then, his therapist and wife walked in. I walked out, telling his wife that she had a very sweet husband. I calmly said those words, not attacking him in any way. He agreed with my words but held back when I said he was a sweet man. I left, wishing that all situations could be this easy to rectify and that my daring to be bold made a difference. It appeared to me that healing took place at the holy, joyous moment. I also left feeling that I could be that calm in all situations.

I usually try to go to my seniors at least twice while I am up there for the weekend. I went in first to talk to Pete—that is her nickname. We had a talk about a couple of women that were nearby. One was called Alice. She would wave her arms frantically and tell me to get out of the room. This happened a few times, and I stopped going near her. I went into the cafeteria over to Pete's table. I went between Pete and another lady on wheelchairs. I asked the lady next to me if I could pray with her. She said yes. I nodded for Alice if she would like to join us. I took Pete's hand and the other lady's hand to pray. I closed my eyes and said the prayers. When I looked up, Alice was holding Pete's hand and the other lady's hand. I could not believe it. So I asked Alice if I could give her a hug. She said yes. I could not believe this lady who would not let me near her for four months was now letting me hug her. Boy, those times are the ones that are exciting. I went back to Pete after everyone had left and asked her if she believed what had taken place. She said that she had caught herself praying out loud when she was saying grace one day and noticed when she looked up that Alice and the other lady had their heads bowed.

52

Once Again at the Prayer Group

MARY TOLD ME THAT she wanted to talk to me after the meeting one Wednesday. She ended up that she ran out of time and that she would do it the following week. I was suspicious to why she wanted to talk to me. I thought that maybe Denise had told her that I did reiki on her. The following Wednesday, I stopped off at the senior home in Taylor. Bridgett was there, so I stopped in to talk to her. As I was leaving, I told her about teaching kids how to read. She said, "I hope you aren't doing reiki on them" and said I better not. I told her to get rid of her preconceived notions and invite the Holy Spirit to answer. She said, "I do not need to talk to the Holy Spirit, and that dark night of the soul you talk about—there is no such thing." I told her, "One day, you will all apologize to me." And she said she would never apologize.

That situation gave me the courage and tenacity to do what I had to do next. I called up Jerry when I got home. I told him that I wanted to quit coming to the group. He brought up reiki. He said if I had the Holy Spirit, why did I need reiki? When I went to the Holy Ghost meeting, I told a few people that tonight would be my last night. Jerry was one of them. I knew he would tell Mary. So Mary approached me after the meeting, and Russ joined in the meeting. Mary said it was a little redundant since I had already talked to Jerry. Mary said reiki was pagan and not of the Divine Source. I told her that that was her opinion. She went to say, "I know." I said, "Again, that is your opinion." I said, "You see what you want to see and find what you want to find." I told her what I did was not debatable or negotiable. I did not try to justify reiki or make excuses. Russ said only a few people knew. I told him I did not care who knew. I told them that I had judged them; I really was going to come clean. I said when we think we are enlightened and decide that someone else is on the wrong path—that is when we go from the front of the line to the back.

Mary said she just cared about me. I said "I understand" and grabbed her hand. I told them, "You guys did not believe that I went through the dark night of the soul, and that is Catholic. Russ, you read it. So why would you believe anything about me? Like it is something that I need to be ashamed of." Then Mary complained about Oprah and the metaphysical path. I said I loved Oprah, loved the metaphysical path, and said, "That's me." I think that was more than they could handle, knowing for sure that I was down the wrong path. I told them that I would come back if God wanted me to. I thought that even if they begged me, I would not return. I also told them that they could not imagine how much I loved them.

I actually felt good that it was now out in the open. I felt like I was a gay person who was going to a place that bashed gays. And now I was out of the closet, so to speak. If I returned, it would be under the stipulation that we do not look to see who is going down the wrong path, that we simply love and respect one another. It shocks me that people can put down the metaphysical path and really not know anything about it. I got a lot of my knowledge and books off *The Oprah Winfrey Show*. I feel she has helped such a large audience and cannot believe that people would downgrade her. It is truly beyond my imagination how this can take place. Even Jesus had people that crucified him. When I started reading a metaphysical book—by the way, I did not know they were New Age—life started making sense. Nothing else up until that point made any sense whatsoever. The heavens must look down at us, see our judgment of one another and how we play God, telling each other "Your Bible is wrong, your religion is wrong, your path is wrong" and so forth. It truly must be a comical sight to see. We do not even realize that it is everyone's right to have his or her truth. We do not see that the person going down the wrong path is us. We think that we are separate from each other. But I will tell you this: "God does not judge!" Who will answer? We will answer! You will answer! I will answer! And then maybe, when we point our fingers at someone, we will see the three pointing back at us.

It is now Monday, November 4. I had gone out on my front porch for another sunrise to do my usual regimented prayers. I said, "You know how well I handled the man up north and the Holy Ghost people, that is how I desire to act all the time. Jesus, I desire to act like you." When I went into the house, I saw a small luminescent circle with an octagon shape on the inside that I had seen many times before appear. It started swinging very slowly to the left and to the right like a pendulum. It swung slowly like four or five times. I would say it all had definition and was red on the outside and a type of yellow on the inside. Maybe this happened because I told Jesus that I wanted to act like him. I went back outside and then inside to witness more color at the front door and where the coffee pot was located. The color went quite a bit outside of my hands this time. The sky turned a beautiful blue then red, and then it was gray only in the section between two trees. It started clouding up, so I did not know if it was the clouds that were gray or what. I think they were showing me the clouds gray like when my hands turned charcoal black. I asked a man that I had given a blessing and reiki to called Chuck, whom I called Charlie the Cherub, what he thought of the blessing I had given him during, after, and now. Chuck died right after September 11, 2002. What popped into my head was "magnificent, magnificent, and magnificent." I also asked whom to vote for governor. They said, "Granholm, Granholm, and Granholm." She was the democratic candidate. She was forecasted to win the election. I did not vote for her.

I woke up one morning, having had another dream. Mike took me over to a house in Allen Park for me to look at. It was a long spacious ranch with large rooms. When we got inside, Mike told me that he bought the house. I said, "Why did you buy the house?" He said, "Because nobody else would." I said, "How much did you pay for it?" He said, "Fifty thousand dollars." I said, "How could you buy this house so cheap?" He said, "Because nobody else would." I thought this house must have been worth two hundred thousand to three hundred thousand dollars. I saw beautiful hardwood floors throughout. The kitchen had white and black square tiles that looked dull from age; I was thinking that I wanted to replace the floor. Over where the exterior wall would be in the kitchen was a cement valley in the floor with cement sides on either side. I asked Mike, "What is this?" He did not answer me. I did not get upset; I just thought that we could build cupboards and a sink over it. I could see a large spacious bedroom that opened up to the left of the kitchen with shiny hardwood floors and beautiful large windows. I told Mike that we should move into this house. Although you could tell this house was an older home, it was very well taken care of. The hardwood floors looked new. I know the white and black means balancing; however, I do not know what the rest means.

About My Dad

I was talking to my sister Shirley on the phone one day. She says that Dad was still talking about how I had hurt him at the reunion when he had thrown the coffee in my face and that I needed to tell him I was sorry for that occasion. I said to Shirley that I could do this, that this would be easy after what I had been through. I decided to go out and tell the universe. So I went outside and started crying when I said it. One thing that I knew was my dad had been hurt on both occasions; I also knew that he would never tell me that he was sorry. Somehow this was a release. But, however, I went over and said to my dad while I was behind him, bending over the couch, that I was very sorry for the many times that I had hurt his feelings and meant it. He seemed to accept it. What surprised me is I did not need him to say he was sorry. During this process of forgiving others and mostly yourself, you will not believe the amount you will have to do. This is why I think all people are truly innocent, because if they really knew what they were doing to themselves, I assure you, they wouldn't do it!

Mike had just made a wonderful dinner for my parents, doing everything to the nines. That evening I was lying on the couch watching TV. Mike was lying on the floor but sat up. He said the few inches of used floss I had left on the end table was disgusting. He said it was disgusting as a rag, and I knew he was referring to a used feminine product. Then he said that the sweats I was wearing were disgusting in a very angry voice. I lay there not knowing what to do. I felt sorry for him that he could correlate a short strand of used dental floss with a used feminine product. I did not know what to say. I knew I could not attack, so I chose to say nothing but knew I had to do something. The next morning, Mike took a seat at the kitchen table near the fridge, and I was at the opposite end. I had invited the Holy Spirit to be with me. He lit up a cigarette. I calmly said, "What you just did is disgusting, and living at the bar our whole married life—that is disgusting." He said, "That is my social life." I told him that he had just made that wonderful dinner for my parents and that he had ruined it for me by being so angry and that his anger was not serving him. I went outside and looked into the sun, feeling relieved. When I returned into the kitchen door, a colored light showed up at side of my right foot and followed me through the kitchen down the hallway and into the bedroom. This amazed me because my lights had never done that before. I think it was the universe validating what I had just done. My right side is my masculine side. The universe has shown up in a myriad of different ways, validating its approval of what I am doing. I know that I need no one else's validation or approval when the universe shows up wonderfully expressing itself.

53

Seniors

One day, I was doing my rounds with my seniors in Taylor, when a woman called Arlene said to me out of the clear blue: "One of your sons will marry secretly in the Catholic Church before Christmas, and the girl could be a model." She also said that I was going to be a grandma. After she told me this, she said that she had done this before. At first I thought she was making something up, then I realized that she was giving me a reading. I did not know what to think of this. I assumed that she was talking about my son Eric and his girlfriend Kelly. I was going to just pass this off but decided to share it with my daughter Karen. When I told her about it, she said, "Because you told me that, I will tell you what happened to me." She had gone to a psychic party the evening before with her mother-in-law and sister-in-law. While the psychic was ready with Tarot cards, she was told that her brother's girlfriend was pregnant, that they had an "on again, off again" relationship, and that was how she got pregnant. We had to call Eric and find out. He said that Kelly was not pregnant and that he was an atheist and would not marry in the Catholic Church even though Kelly was Catholic. I know there is a reason for everything; however, I did not know the reason for this. Maybe it was for Eric to become more responsible.

I met Margaret again at the senior home one day; I did not know if I could approach her or not. She had been in the hospital for a while, and you could not tell just by looking at her how she would respond. She looked angry, while attempting to spit, and she was always observing people passing by, by looking in their direction suspiciously. I saw her in a different room down a different hallway. I decided to gamble and approach her to just the same. I decided to use my imagination by imagining a sunrise and flowers being different colors and different varieties and so forth. She seemed to enjoy it, and I asked her if she minded if I returned. She nodded her head yes and seemed to enjoy using the imagination. She has no television, no radio, and no company that I know of. To my knowledge, she is unable to move her body. I told Essie about it, and she said to not count on that happening again, that you would never know how she would act.

The following week, I decided that that had worked out so well, so I would try it again. This time, to my surprise, she joined in. I said the flowers were singing, "Margaret is happy. Margaret is joy. Margaret is free. Margaret is love." Margaret said *happy*, *joy*, *free*, and *love*. She joined in on the colors, animals, and so forth. I told her that she was as free as an eagle. I felt her feel it. The transformation took place right in front of my eyes. I called my sister Shirley up to tell her about the situation. While I am telling her this, I realized that I had been set free to be loved, happy, and joyful. I knew that Margaret was myself and I had given myself the freedom to be free. What we give out, we receive. I was leaving to go to teach the children how to read. I had forgotten the coffee on the counter and ran back in to get it. When I ran back in, pausing a minute to look at the sun while running in the side door, at the coffee pot was a small circle of purple, lit up. I knew at that moment that the heaven liked the correlation between setting Margaret free and myself. Heaven really knows how to show up; we are the ones that have to learn how to show up in our lives. The following visit, I asked Margaret if I could pray with her, and she said yes. I held her hands and said the Our Father and Hail Mary. Awesome! Dorothy, whom I have mentioned before, was in the next bed near the window, and the drapes between them were drawn. Dorothy asked me if she understood what I was saying. I said yes. I truly have bonded with them both.

I now know that Margaret fully understands me in a simple, childlike way. While I am leaving, she will still be attempting to spit, but I also know that our souls have bonded, and what happened before, I trust, will not happen again. I told Margaret that even when I am not there that I'm loving and protecting her. I find myself not wanting to leave her because I know she is a prisoner. It almost makes me want to cry because I know her outer looks do not portray the inner her. I told her that she is my angel and that I love her very much. Margaret will forever be in my heart always. Margaret always was Margaret; I just had to look past the exterior to find her, and what I found was an angel. I do not know why she got so upset when I first said the Our Father; I do know

now that it is healed, whatever it was. The teacher always learns from the student because everyone has something to offer. I talked to Dorothy in the cafeteria, and she said that she stays away from Margaret. She says she feels sorry for her but is wary of her and thinks it is best that she stays away.

I went to my seniors at Rivergate and visited Margaret again. This time, I talked to her. I do not recall her spitting even once. She has never acted up again, and I truly enjoy her. I am truly amazed with her progress. Will wonders ever cease? I like leaving the sheep to go out and find the sheep that is lost. That is life heightened for me!

I met Elizabeth again, who swears and yells at everyone she comes in contact with. She gives the aides a very hard time, ordering them around and such. Bridgett did her hair, and she did not pay her. Now she was demanding that Bridgett do her hair again. Bridgett seemed to think that she would cause trouble for her. I told her that was abuse and for her not to do her hair. Bridgett said she loved me and that there was emptiness at the Holy Ghost meeting with me not being there. I said I could not come back yet.

Elizabeth came into her room and went into her bathroom, leaving the door open a little. I was talking with two ladies in their room, and an aide was in the room as well. I said, "The lady that is in the bathroom is so sweet and so loving." The aide rolled her eyes at me. I reiterated that she was so sweet and loving. When she came out, to my surprise, she was sweet and loving. I went up to the aide and whispered, "Fake it, it will happen!" I could not believe what I had just witnessed—was it really that simple? I walked up to Elizabeth because she asked me to come over and open up her straw. She thanked me. I said, "For a sweet lady such as yourself, anything." I was pretty near shock by now. I had been praying for the seniors that especially needed help, that were crying out for help in their anger and pain. I go to each senior home in my mind and bring up the people, but I also pray for all of them, not by name though. A few of the people I occasionally mention by name. I never did see Elizabeth again; I was told that she went into the hospital.

My Christmas cactus now has eighteen buds on it before Thanksgiving; it has never done this before. This is the same Christmas cactus that flowered for several months at the beginning of 2002 and last Christmas. The buds are iridescent purple, white and then purple again on the tips. The purple is so brilliant and appears to have a little pink in it. I do not know if the heavens are intervening in the process, but I cannot help thinking that they are. I only got a few buds in the previous years at Christmas, not eighteen buds this early. I thank the universe for its beautiful display of color, and I am truly amazed, in awe. Maybe this cactus is a keeper, and I should transplant it after all these years; I will have to look for the perfect pot to put her in. Eleven of the buds were in full bloom on Thanksgiving. My mom and dad were amazed when they came over for dinner and I showed them. Their plant has no buds on it. However, there were no blooms on mine for Christmas. Marie told me that her Christmas cactus had bloomed for several months at the beginning of 2002 also. Hers, however, was a light peach. I think it is that we both would be serving mankind this year; it is an honor and a privilege. At the beginning of 2003, my Christmas cactus had nine buds on it—I think only eight flowered, though. The spirit world is letting me know, I'm surmising, that I am going to be giving birth to creation again.

Mike and I are again at Mullett for four nights. I went out for this awesome sunrise; however, I decided not to take my camera because it was a very cloudy, overcast day. The clouds gave it a three-dimensional effect with a lot of pastel pink and such right before and during the sunrise. I knew I would not have enough time to run back in the house and decided to just enjoy the moment. But I felt sad that I was not able to capture it on film. The day before Thanksgiving, I went out for another sunrise. There was a huge, nimbusy dark cloud all by itself—nothing but clear skies all around it. It stood out very prevalently in a grandiose manner, with all its permeated darkness bigger than life, saying, "Look at me." The silent voice in my head said that this cloud was for me. I was a little confused as to why that would be the case. I took several pictures of it because it turned beautiful pastel pink right before I could actually see the sun. While driving home to Taylor that day, I remembered that they told me the cloud was for me. What was so unusual was this cloud started dissipating right in front of my eyes and transformed to whitish in color while becoming much smaller in stature. The cloud transformed in a period of ten to fifteen minutes. Maybe the cloud represented the darkness and density in me before the dark night of the soul, the pink my healing during the dark night of the soul, and the white maybe me lightening up with purity. I appreciate the heavens showing up for me. I was fortunate to take several pictures of this happening.

I am once again back at Rivergate visiting my seniors. Roy, who is African American, had asked me several months ago if I would pray with the man that was in the room with him next to the window. He said he gave him a hard time about everything, like the lights or the TV being on; in fact, that was why he was gone. He had left in a huff. I told him I would see what I could do and that I would return later. When I returned, I said he was a sweet man and asked if he would mind if I prayed with him. Roger, who is Caucasian, said that he did not mind. After several visits of praying separately, I gambled and asked if Roy would come over to pray with Roger. I drew the drapes back in between their beds, and the three of us prayed. Roger was always lying on his bed reading a book. On this visit, when we got through praying, Roy said, as he was standing over Roger, "Look at how sweet this man is, and it is all because of you." Roger, in turn, said, "I am changed, and it is because of you." Roger glowed with an incredible sweet smile as Roy and I looked on. These two men were now amicable with one another, although the drapes were still drawn. Like I said, Roger reads a lot. I like people that are in the same room to pray with me in the middle because a lot of times, people in the same room do not get along with one another. Besides, it speeds up the process.

On January 31, 2002, the year ended wonderfully for me. I went outside at approximately 3:00 p.m., looking at the sun to give glory and praise to God. And when I came in, I noticed green lights on my kitchen floor right at the top of the steps. I stood at the banister and decided to see if it would accept my right foot, which had nothing on it. The green enveloped my foot, going quite a ways outside of my foot, meaning the lights had depth to them. I could see the outline of some toes, but the light was very bright, iridescent. After a bit, I decided if I could put my left foot in it. To my surprise, it accepted my left foot, maybe not as quite as bright though. If it does not accept it, it disappears. I walked to my bedroom doorway, where it was dark because my husband was sleeping from working nights. My lights appeared, so I stood in the doorway and put my hands in it. My hands then proceeded to turn pitch black; then there was a small, bright, colorful ball of lights in between; we did this consecutively, three times in all. I knew it represented my healing. It has been almost nine months that I have been volunteering, and maybe this was my giving birth.

54

Renaissance Unity

I ALSO WENT TO the Church of Today, which is now called Renaissance Unity, for the service that would start at 10:30 p.m. The place was packed with great energy. Hayvard came in, and I remembered him, but I could not think of his name, nor could he remember mine. He said I was much brighter. And I said that is because I was in the dark night of the soul when I was with him last. We chit-chatted while I looked at the people walking in the front door looking for Carol. I sat with Carol. I had decided at the last minute to not sit home and go to the church instead. A young African American girl danced like a free spirit throughout the singing. Her smile was contagious, and you could not help being captivated by the joy that was flowing through her. I am pretty sure that I had met her one day in the chapel. I commented on her dancing, and she asked me for my telephone number. She did not say why, but I gave it. The choir was phenomenal as usual. This was Marianne Williamson last time, the leader of this church, she would return only occasionally to visit. It was a great way to end 2002. The audience gave Marianne a lengthy, well-deserved standing ovation. This New Year, 2003, will be stellar, with much serendipity for me. I cannot wait! Amen!

    This morning, I went to my seniors in Taylor. There was this lady that I had attempted to pray with many months ago. She grabbed me by the cuff of the neck and pulled me down a little bit and raised her fist. She traumatized me in that instant. An aide came over and asked me if I was okay. She would not let me give her a hug or hold her hand in any way. She also would be nice one minute and then give sarcastic remarks against you the next. On the whole, I would not see her socializing with the other woman at her table. You never knew when the other side would come out. But usually, if you talked for a little bit, it came out. For the most part I decided to keep my distance from her. For several months, I have been going outside and praying for my seniors, especially the ones that were angry. I believe this is the first time that I saw her in her room; normally, she was always in the cafeteria or in the hallway when I would see her. I gambled and asked her today if I could pray with her. To my surprise, she said yes! So I pushed her in her wheelchair over to the lady in the room that was nearby, held their hands, and prayed with them both. After I was done, I asked her if I could give her a hug. She also said yes without reservation. I really felt my prayers were working. In any case, I felt good. I still thought she could still get out a sarcastic remark, and she never did. It is times like these that make all of it worthwhile.

Back at Mullett

On President's Day, 2003, I decided that I was going to trek across Mullett Lake, which turned out to be five miles. It was an outstandingly sunny beautiful day and about 22 degrees. Because the sun was so brilliant, you did not have trouble staying warm. I was glad that the sun was at my side and back and not face on. I did not tell Mike that I planned on going. I decided while I was on the lake. I was so amazed at the glistening snow that looked like small crystals with prisms brilliantly twinkling and shining everywhere, thinking they were fairies. It looked like a desert, only whiter and flatter. I started following old snowmobile tracks that looked like they were going to the east side of the lake. There were many snowmobile tracks running parallel and perpendicular and some crisscrossing one another. Oftentimes I would see the snow looking just like the wind would be hitting the water with small swells. Every now and then, I would stop, and I would hear complete silence, especially in the middle of the lake. I had decided last winter that I wanted to do this just to say that I did it. However, last year, the ice wasn't as thick and made some noise, so I did not feel as secure. It was not very windy, which also made it conducive to make this journey.

I had on heavy sweats underneath a snowmobile suit. I also had my camera with me, which I ended up putting the strap around my neck, dangling it in the front of my chest. I took one picture of the snow looking pristine and brilliant; it was the last on the roll. I ended up taking my gloves and hat off, sticking my hat in the side of my zipped-down snowmobile outfit. I carried my gloves. I had on big heavy snowmobile boots, which I think weighed me down. When I would break stride, I would often sink in the snow, making me burn more energy walking. I started sweating. Being cold was not a factor. I wished I had on my jacket and tennis shoes; it would have been less cumbersome. The reason I followed the snowmobile tracks was so I would not have to make my own tracks in the snow. The lake runs just over ten miles north and south. It was 148' max, averaging 35.8' deep and 17,360 acres. We are at the northern section of the lake. It was the fifth largest lake in Michigan.

When the other side of the lake was becoming more visible, I wondered whether I should not turn around and head back. My hips were getting sore, and I was getting quite tired, taking small steps now. I started crying, not with tears though. I knew I could not make it back if I turned around, and I also did not know what I was going to do once I got to the shore. I did see one snowmobile with two people on it a distance away, but then they disappeared. I started panicking, not knowing what I was going to do. Then I just decided that I was burning energy and needed to save it in case I had to walk back. I said, "God, I need your help! I do not know what to do." I thought I could maybe find someone that would let me call Mike, but I did not know my telephone number. I also thought that maybe

I would see a snowmobile and ask them to take me back and I would pay them. I did not have any money on me; I would have to go into the house. So many things were running through my head. I saw a road that was coming down from a hill toward the water, and I decided that I would head for that road. It had houses on it. I was now getting very close when I saw what looked like my husband's green Tahoe slowly coming down the hill toward the water. I thought, *Could it be Mike?* I could not see the driver. Then I noticed the state park stickers on the left-hand side of the windshield. The car stopped, the door opened, and Tyler jumped out. My jaw dropped because this was so ineffable and too incredulous to believe. If anyone was a sight for sore eyes, it was Mike.

Mike told me that he had been watching me with his binoculars since I had left. Later on, he asked me, what if I couldn't make it? What was I going to do? The truth is, I had turned it over to God from the beginning. For whatever reason, I thought I was supposed to make this journey. I told Mike that there would be no threat of me repeating this. It was so hard for me to believe that we would make it to the same place at the same time. Mike, at that moment, was an angel to me—my knight in shining armor. As soon as I got into the car, I put the seat back, lay back, and closed my eyes. I was very sore, exhausted, and thirsty. The only thing that could have topped the situation off was if Mike would have had a cold drink. I was still in shock that Mike showed up at that instant.

Mike asked me if I wanted a massage in our living room at Mullett. I told him no because he presses too hard and hurts me. But I thought that I had to go through this. He started on my back, pressing with his fingers on either side of my spine, and I started screaming. There was a vertebra in my lower back that had been hurting me for some time—really forever. I really started screaming. He continued. I was near hysteria and making some grotesque noises. Because of my falls, I do believe my right hip was damaged from my falls. My lower back was unbelievably sore, and I did want him to continue. I do not know what he did, but the next day my lower back felt a lot better. Maybe this is all part of my healing and releasing. This is the second massage that Mike has given me where I felt much healing took place—the other one was in my family room in Taylor when I felt slain in the spirit.

55

Meditation Group

CAROL CALLED ME UP to invite me to her apartment, where they would be holding the old meditation group from the Church of Today. A very strong part of me did not want to go, but I thought the heavens were sending me. On the day we were to go out, a blizzard was forecasted. So that morning when I awoke, I had decided that I would not go. I went to Meijer's to get some gas and milk. When I went in to pay for the gas, an attractive black lady said she could tell that we weren't going to get any snow. I knew in my heart that we would but that I would be safe if I went. I am thinking that now maybe I should go. I called up Theron to ask if I could follow him out there because I did not know the area that

I would just feel better. He agreed. It never stopped snowing, and my visibility was greatly stifled from my windshield blades not cleaning the windows because they were iced up. Brian and Nancy were the only two others that showed up, so there was the five of us in all. Theron was going to show us a movie about his trip last summer and many pictures that he had taped on poster boards.

Nancy asked Brian to give her some healing while we were watching the movie. I, in turn, asked if I could have some healing from Brian. Carol has a reiki table, and she brought it out after the movie. Theron went first, and I went second. Theron gave me a foot massage as Brian did reiki on me at the same time. Brian asked me first if I was ready to let it all go. I, of course, said yes. Theron was a little aggressive in the massaging of my feet. Brian said that I was smoking—and I don't mean cigarettes. He gave it to the alchemical violet flame. Brian also did some toning into my lower back, which Theron, I believe, had done before. I felt so much lighter when it was done. I think we were meant to get together so Brian and I could resolve hurt feelings on my part. I was very appreciative and grateful for the extended healing by both Theron and Brian. Theron told them about my working with seniors, and then I added my kids and my book. I do not believe that I will be going back to this group again; I will be very surprised if I do. Maybe this was not only for me to receive a much-needed healing but also for Brian and I to clear our separateness.

On the way home, it was very treacherous. I followed Theron to 75, and then he left on 96 to go home. He stopped and asked me if I was okay to drive home by myself. He told me that he would follow me all the way home and then drive home. I said that I was okay and left. Theron's guides said also that I was fine. We both fishtailed often. After I left Theron, I flew home. I knew when I left that I was going to be okay. I did about forty miles an hour in the fast lane. This is going to be hard to believe, but I knew my guides were helping me. To my surprise, there were many cars on the road. One car in particular was driving in the middle of the road and was not going to let me pass. I finally made my way around him, but I came very close to the meridian. The wind and snow were so furious that my windshield iced up, and seeing was difficult. I said to myself, "Kathy, don't get too cocky on how fast you're going just because you know that you're being helped." I also remember feeling very light and gagging while driving home. Here I was on an arduous drive home and I could not stop gagging. Theron told me that I was coughing up what I had just released with the healing they gave me.

I made an appointment to do an exchange with Brian, a foot and hand massage with a little reiki. He brought his reiki table, seeing as I did not have one. He set it up in the family room. This seemed so weird to me, having Brian in my house. Brian had me lie on the table on my back and covered me with a blanket. He started on my feet. While he was massaging my feet, my left ovary started hurting, and my back felt broken where my shoulders came together at my spine. At the last meditation group that I had gone to, while I was very deep in the dark night of the soul, I asked Brian if he could do something with the pain in my back, and I showed him where. He kind of pressed with his thumb and had me fall back, and I lay on the floor for a while. From that moment on, the pain of my back feeling broken had gone away until now. I did not know why this was happening—how he took it away and why it was coming back now. I felt there was a reason for this, but now I had to deal with it. I did not tell Brian that this happened. Although when Brian put his hands on my upper back, he said my back was broken. He also told me that I was to go to a hospice. Right after this experience, I watched TV, and a commercial for a hospice came on with the telephone number; I did not even need to look up the number. Of course, I went to the Hospice of Michigan for training because I do not say no to heaven when I know it is heaven.

With the reminiscence of this experience of my back being broken, I told no one, not even Shirley, till this day. Where I was at was so horrible—mentally, emotionally, and physically, in every aspect—my dad and Mike's relationship, the nucleus of my core, that life was not an option for me. I did not even think of going to the doctor's for I felt no one could do anything for me. I think when I tell my story that many people like to trivialize what I had gone through. Brian even started his reiki with saying that many people had gone through far worse than I had, like this was a competition of sorts. In Brian's case, he said that without knowing my story. No one is more surprised than myself that I made it through this! In any case, I parallel no one; this simply is my journey to inner peace.

So I decided to call up Theron and asked him if he would like to go out to lunch before he moved out west. To my surprise, he brought two of his favorite crystals with him. I told him about my back feeling just like it had at the last meditation group before Brian had taken it away. Before we went into the restaurant, Theron put the crystal on my back to give me healing. My back was very sore, and I felt like I could use a good massage. It also felt like my spine was broken on a slant and was definitely not connected above my bra strap where my shoulder blades were connected. I told Theron that I was not going to go down the tubes now and to let fear take over. He told me to feel the pain. I did more than that, remembering when Ingalor had said my voice was small and all the horrible pain that I was in.

After doing prayers during some sunrises, my lights would appear and go to the right, having me turn slowly and sometimes fast, a certain design or different shapes all the while I was spinning. When this first happened, I thought that it was a healing of some sort. But I just decided to go along with it. I trusted! This morning, it was a little blue circle with green next and red on the outside. They are always flat, not three-dimensional. I will try to describe the shape that I saw several times. It had curved legs coming from a center that went out left and right, middle, top and bottom, and was rectangular in shape. It looked translucent but with definition. There were definitely a couple of times that I got quite dizzy. I told the universe that if this was doing good and speeding up recovery for the prayers, I said, "So be it!" But I desire not to feel sick. I have done it many times since, and I do not get sick; however, it takes me a few seconds to get my balance when I am finished.

I remember the first time this happened. One morning, my daughter Karen called me up and asked me if I would bring Vernor's over to drink for she ran out and was sick. When I got over there, I looked into the sunrise and walked back to her dark bedroom where she was sick in bed. I immediately saw my lights on her forehead. While standing next to her bed, the lights turned into a single pink rose and proceeded to come at me. When it was an arm's length away, it started moving to the right, staying an arm's length away. With my arm extended, I proceeded to follow the rose, which turned into my lights. I stopped spinning when I no longer saw the lights. I went outside on her front porch two more times so that I would see the lights. Karen did not see them and thought that I was a little strange.

I had a dream last night, and I will try to explain it. My sister Shirley and I were in a loft, sitting on a mattress that was directly on the wooden floor. I did not really see anything else in the room except a man standing near the bed facing us without a shirt on, and he had raised knobs of skin all over his torso, arms, and head. He did not converse with us nor did we find him threatening. Shirley said that I was pregnant with two, knowing that they were two single births. I knew that Mike was the father. She said to me that I agreed to do this, so I relaxed. The next scene, I walked over to my mom, who is going down the ladder, and asked her if she knew that I was pregnant. My mom did not say anything, but to the left, a cute little blond-haired boy with fair complexion appeared. He said, "I know!" The next scene, I was giving birth, and Theron and Brian had one hand on my back holding me up, the other one on my shoulder, and were telling me to breathe. This was a weird feeling, having Theron and Brian coaching me to give birth.

I called up Carol to find out what this dream could possibly mean. She said the man was Mike and the raised knobs were toxins that were coming out of him. The attic was ascension; the mattress, stability; the little boy was the little boy in me. Brian and Theron were helping me to give birth to a new life. I thought the little boy that I saw was whom I was giving birth to. I know that Mike is the man and the father of the little boy. I feel as though this little boy might be the savior. I do not know if I will necessarily be giving birth to him or that he will just come unto me. I don't know! I told Theron about the dream, and he was amused with helping me give birth also. He said, "I will know the little boy later and I will be able to correlate this dream."

Mike and I were back up north again. It was Sunday, March 16, 2003, and I was on the beach at 6:30 a.m. I was sitting on the log that was near the pit facing the water, which was still frozen. It was relatively warm out compared to what it had been, but I had on a winter jacket. I had to sit there for a while, waiting for the sun to reveal itself. For some reason, I felt like I was in heaven. Because it was a Sunday, there was only an occasional car, so it was very peaceful. Plus you could hear an occasional bird. After enjoying the sun coming up a little ways, I started seeing what I call eyes. Two blue circles appeared spaced apart and started coming at me. When they got to me, they would usually be changed to several little circles in a simple particular form. They would let me hold them, but they would move to the right and stay on my hand with my arm stretched out until I stopped looking or they disappeared. This happened several times. The last time, the circles in an L shape changed into different colors, and when I looked to the right, it was now an outlined translucent fairy with wings. It looked just like the fairies you see with her wings down. I thought I must have been seeing things or my mind was playing tricks on me. I told God that I was in heaven and enjoyed it very much.

56

The New Hope Church

BRIGITTE CALLED ME UP on Friday, March 27, 2003, in the evening and asked me to go to this new church on Racho Road called New Hope at seven o'clock. She had been complaining to me about pain in her back from doing seniors' hair for some time. In fact, she asked me to pray for her, which of course I had been doing. It was five after seven when we hung up. She said that it was not Catholic but that she had been healed and she wanted me to go. Brigitte also said that Saturday would be the last day that this evangelist Keith Johnson would be here. She said that her friend Pat would be sitting in the front right-hand side and to sit with her. So I walked right up to the front and asked the lady if she knew where

Pat was. She said Pat was the one in that brown blouse and pointed to her. I walked over to her and asked her if she was Brigitte's friend and if her name was Pat. She said yes, and we hugged. I could feel the Holy Spirit very strongly. People were shaking and jumping up and down, something I was unfamiliar with. They were singing beautiful music too with a young man playing the keyboard, on which the words were on two huge TVs high up for everyone to see. The feeling and ambiance of the church were great. I asked Pat who was going to be doing the healing. She said the man that was lying on the floor and shaking. He had been jumping up and down before this, and I was thinking, *This is strange.* She told me that he was filled with the Holy Spirit.

This was all quite unknown to me. A lot of people were speaking in tongues, so I knew that it was a good place. When I was waiting for Mr. Johnson to lay his hands on me, I waited with anticipation, thinking that nothing was going to happen. People were lying all over and shaking, and some were crying. He put his hand on me for a second. I went down but only because they were guiding me down. As soon as I went down—really probably as I was going—it felt like pain was being propelled out through my rectum like a rocket. I was concerned at this point because it was painful, and I did not know what to think. I was quietly saying, because I was in church, "Ouch, ouch, ouch." The pain, however, lasted for a while, and when it pretty much subsided, I got up. I did have residual effects from it for some time after, even to the next day. Of all things to happen, I did not think I would be in pain. I was also thinking that I would like to ask someone what had just happened. Mr. Johnson had told us to bask in it, that this was not a microwave deal, beforehand. I was thinking this was very strange. So I got up when I should have probably stayed on the floor. He came back and only said to me, "What are you doing up?" and touched my forehead again, but I did not go back down, nor did they guide me.

I went over to Pat to ask her what was going on, that something very strange just happened to me. She said, "That is strange, but I think it was a release and claim the healing." Pat also reminded me that he had said, "What are you doing up?" So now I was thinking that I should have him do it again and go over to the other side of the church. Mr. Johnson never did put his hands on me again, but he looked me in the eyes several times throughout the evening. After it was over with, people were now dancing and jumping, giving thanks for the healing that had taken place. The man who was doing this would be there again tomorrow night, and I now wanted to go back because this was his last night. We would see what happened.

When Mike got home from work he said that he did not mind if I went again tonight. So I decided to go, but I was hoping that someone would come with me. This time, when I went into the church, I did not feel the Holy Spirit as strongly. I stayed there for probably three hours and left before most of them left. I give these people accolades and applaud their endeavors, but for me, this is a little obsessive. Maybe one day I will be quivering and shaking also and feel what they are feeling. But for now, I think I would rather spend my time volunteering because this is where my calling is. My guides said to not make spiritualism my whole life, only part of it. This time, when he touched my forehead and I was guided down, nothing happened. But I decided that I was going to lie on the floor for a while anyway, just to make sure. One thing that I found out that you do not have to feel anything for healing to take place—you just have to trust and give thanks. I am grateful for this experience and glad I went. I am also now thinking that the pain I experienced was still a clearing of many lifetimes. (I do not believe the amount of pain that I had to go through for many lifetimes; it is incredible and never-ending.)

Monday evening at the end of March, I went out to watch a sunset in my backyard. There are a lot of trees in the back woods, and I usually cannot see the sun actually set. There was one huge nimbus dark cloud all by itself in the shape of a perfect bald eagle. The head was turned, and the wings were out full and quite long, latitudinal. It was resting just above the trees. The silent voice said nothing, but somehow I felt this was for me. The sun, being behind it and to the side, even made it more poignant. Then this huge cloud transformed from an eagle to a huge airplane with props in the front. I stood in awe. I was sure someone else would not see what I saw, but in my eyes, it was remarkable. I never know what I am going to see in the sky next. It has been quite entertaining, to say the least. As I was watching this, it didn't take long to dissipate almost right in front of my eyes. I called up Carol to see what this could possibly mean. She said the eagle meant that you go it alone and it is hard but that you persevere and make it. She also said the airplane was also good and means a higher path, that she saw me going to Montana and moving up to Mullett by myself.

57

Another Nursing Home

In the beginning of April, I decided to start going to another nursing home in Allen Park. I talked to Katie, the activities director, and went in for an interview. She showed me around the place and was very nice. But I did not start visiting the patients at that time. I went in a couple of days later and spent a couple hours with the seniors, mostly just praying with them. Then I decided to go back on Friday to visit them. I had a real good day singing a Christmas carol, "Oh, Holy Night" and "Amazing Grace" to people randomly throughout the building. Just when I decided to leave, I went into the office to get my jacket. Katie was there with another lady, and she offered me a homemade piece of wheat bread. I hesitated but decided to take a piece even though I was on a diet. So I said good-bye as I left eating the bread.

When I was a few feet away from the front door, I hear a lady call someone, not thinking it was me, but I turned around. This lady said, "Who are you?" very sternly. I said, "A volunteer" and that Katie knew I was here. She said, "You follow me to my office." We went into the office, where there were now a few other women. The lady was now standing across from me and said, "First off, you are not allowed to eat in the hallway." I said I got the bread from here. She said, "I'm sure." Then she proceeded to say, "Did you ask for a woman to be put to bed? You did not address yourself to my nurse." I said that a lady was in the hallway crying and said no one here cared about her and that all she wanted was to be put to bed. I quietly prayed with her and she listened, but she was still crying when I quit, so I walked a few feet over to the desk and said to the lady behind the desk, "Excuse me, is it possible for that lady to be put to bed?" She said, "No because she will be eating lunch soon." I said, "Okay" and went on my way. The lady now said, "You're judging the place." I said no, that I had no judgment. She said, "Who sent you here?" I said, "God." Then she said, "Why are you on the defensive?" I said nothing. In that moment, I was reduced to a little girl, because that is what my dad used to say to me. At that moment, I switched to an adult and said, "You're rude!" She said, "You did not introduce yourself." I said, "You get your staff together, and I will introduce myself." She walked out, saying that she would have nothing further to do with me.

As soon as she left, I started crying. I told Katie that I had never been treated so poorly at any of the other three nursing homes that I had gone to. The other lady said she treated everyone like that and to not feel bad. Katie said, "Well, I hope that this does not discourage you from coming back." I said it wouldn't. She also said that she had checked up on me a couple of times because I was her volunteer and that I did fine. I said thanks for checking up on me for I knew I had nothing to hide. I also said that I had no idea that she had checked up on me. She said she knew. Then I said that it was possible from what I had said that I would not be allowed to come back. Katie said, "She does not have control over you." Katie called me up a couple hours later and asked me how I was doing. I said fine, and then I said I couldn't come back. She said, "That's right!" She said that she did not know how to deal with the situation. I said neither did I. She told me that it was for my protection. She also said that she had to do something for this never to happen again to one of her volunteers. She said that she talked to a head person and told her it would be a loss to this facility if I was unable to return. This lady had a lot of clout, and the lady said that it didn't matter. She also said that I had a special gift and that she hoped that this would not discourage me. I told her that it was a privilege meeting her. I was now fired from volunteering in this facility.

I went outside and said to the Universe, "I am not a victim. I take full accountability and responsibility for my reality." I said, "I forgive myself, I forgive her, and I ask for forgiveness." I also said, "I do not know how to deal with this. I give it to you." This was beyond my comprehension, that any of this had taken place. I knew this lady was used to throwing her weight around and getting away with it. The abuser is abused when they're allowed to abuse; I knew I could not live with myself if I did not stand up for myself. I do not mention names because I don't know their names, nor would I, of course. Mike, my husband, said that he had this same thing happen to him all the time but that he could not do what I did, that he was manager and had to be in control at all times. Well, in my opinion, that lady was also a boss and did not show any control nor did she address who she was to me. A volunteer should be treated with honor and shown very high respect for they do not get a paycheck.

Today I went to teach the kids. For Sherry, who had been student teaching in our classroom, this would be her last day. All of us women go out of our way to help, love, and give encouragement for them to be all that they can be. At the end of class, Pam had had the kids all make up cards for Sherry, and homemade brownies were passed out to everyone. I stood next to Sherry as each kid came up and give her a hug and handed her their homemade card. Even the kids that resisted help gave her a tight embrace. I looked at her to see her tearing up. It had been hard for her to get used to this classroom like it had been for me. I told her that she would be a good teacher and that the skills she had learned would be priceless. It has been a privilege and honor to work in this classroom. Marie keeps saying that there are three kids that she would like to work with the whole summer to make a difference in their lives. That is what I would call living your truth or life fully—making a difference in underprivileged lives. I feel like Sidney Portier in the movie *To Sir with Love*. It has been that rewarding for me, and I have learned that much.

I had a dream that I was talking on the phone with Carol P. In my dream, I was telling her what Carol had said about me moving up to Mullett by myself. In my dream, Carol P. said, "That is about right." I also had a dream that I was babysitting for a man that was of Middle East descent. I was helping the kids out with healing while I was babysitting. He arrived much earlier than I expected. I was in a T-shirt and white cotton briefs. I was embarrassed that I was dressed that way when he arrived. He, however, did not react. Then in my dream next, Mike and I were following a couple that I hadn't seen in a long time but saw them today at Meijer's go into a bar. When we got in the bar, the lady was sitting on a bar stool with her back to us in black lace bikini underwear on, and dark hair was sticking out of the top of the panties. She was a little overweight, so it was quite pronounced. The only thing I could think of was having the white cotton briefs and the black lace bikini underwear mean balance with my sexuality, because they are the opposite.

Recently I have been thinking about what happened to me one cold evening while I was walking in my neighborhood. I am guessing that it was in the fall of 2001. I did not know what happened nor have I ever had an explanation for what happened, although the only person I have discussed it with was Theron and Shirley, and I did that at the time that it happened. As I turned the corner at the head of our street, I had this pain come over me from the waist down, like I was frozen. I literally could not move. What I could not get over is it came on suddenly, just like that I was in a lot of pain appearing to come from my rectum. I was literally stopped dead in my tracks. I did not know what I was going to do but decided that I had to take baby steps, like pivoting myself back and forth till I got home, which was almost two blocks away. I remembered that my dog Higgins, on a few occasions, had his back end frozen like mine did, and that came to mind when it happened. I thought it was arthritis for him. It has never happened again. Just as I arrived at my side door, it was gone, and I was fine. It has never taken place again; I still don't know what it was.

58

Progression

PROBABLY I WOULD SAY pride is our biggest downfall. It seems as though there's a fine line between love and hate, pride and meekness, and self-esteem and arrogance. Arrogance, no matter what form it takes, is to me harder than nonjudgment. It's a struggle not to brag about my book or my volunteering. I feel like I am just sharing what I am doing. But that is between God and myself. I have spent so much of my life thinking that I was a nobody that I struggled with not being able to talk about my blessings, which also included my lights and whatever. Pride is boasting you are better than someone else, and that is not acceptable in the spiritual realm. You then receive then and not in heaven. Pride could be that you know the truth and you deem someone else as wrong. Whether you are Republican or Democratic, black or white, Catholic or Baptist, beautiful or ugly, tall or short, fat or thin, energetic or lethargic. Anything that is temporarily lifting you up is you separating yourself from them and thinking you are better than them.

On the twenty-third of April, my ninth bud started blooming on my Christmas cactus. Before this bud appeared, I looked and noticed there were now no buds. I found this quite unusual to only have one. I had taken note that only eight had bloomed previously, but that the ninth bud was gone for whatever reason. It was one single bloom in the middle of the plant, which was balance. It started budding like two and a half weeks ago, before we had gone up north the last time. I knew now that I was receiving a spiritual gift. Carol P. said that I had a blue light coming down on me and I was receiving a spiritual gift. I said I knew because of my plant. On Saturday, the twenty-sixth of April, the bud was now in full bloom; however, nothing seemed to happen on this day. After the bud was in full bloom to the right of it, I notice a new bud. I was told that I would be giving birth to two separate occasions and not simultaneously. It wasn't told to me; I just knew it. The second bud is, now I know, the second birth, and I believe it represents my brother Greg's marriage saved.

Also, that same day, my lights showed up on my book on the computer. It was very little at the top in the middle of the first page. It moved to the right, sat at the right-hand side of the page, disappeared, and then reappeared in the same spot. I guessed that that means this book was ending and the next one would be starting. Also recently, my lights have been going above me and having me spin, almost looking straight up, which is a little difficult for my neck. I think maybe there is a correlation between that happening and receiving my gifts—just guessing though.

On Mother's Day, I had awakened to having this dream. I had things coming to me from out in the sky like I do during the day. I was looking at a mural like you would see in the inner city, and I know people were in it. It zoomed into this small rectangular-shaped area to the left and bottom of the mural, and that small portion only was magnified. I saw what looked like a rope starting from the inside of the outside of the perimeter and wrapped around till it got into the center, turning at each corner. On top of it was sprinkled with pastel colors. This came at me—I believe it represented my inner kingdom; the pastels, my lights. I was shown the mural again without the rectangular shape shown, not seeing how what magnified came from that section. I also saw three men's heads shown consecutively. I did not believe they had hair, and I was looking down at them. They could have been dead, but I did not recognize them. The three men could have been my father, father-in-law, and my husband and simply that I resolved my issues with them. Then I saw a rectangular shape that had lines coming from it in different directions, but I do not remember what was in the center or if there was something in the center at all. I also do not remember if this came at me or not. I know this dream has significance, but I am not sure what.

Shapes Showing up in the Sky

On Sunday, May 18, I went out for a sunrise on Mullett Lake. Initially it was so cloudy at the bottom that I did not think that I would see the sun at all. But it showed through the clouds a bright orange. The sun was going into flatter, deeper clouds that were not allowing it to be seen, so in other words, you were seeing the top and bottom cut off. Then the sun came out fully, not orange this time but bright yellow. I was sitting on the end of the dock, facing the sun, which was turning my head to the left, and I decided to call in Charlie the cherub, my friend that had died, to whom I had given a blessing. To my surprise, he showed as a flat, somewhat round shape up in the sky and swooped down close enough that I could touch him. He moved to the left and over to the right and back. I asked him if this was Charlie to go up and down, and he did, and then disappeared.

Well, this gave me the liberty to start calling in all kinds of guides and people. I started calling my guides and a few presidents like Thomas Jefferson (much admired because of the Declaration of Independence), Abraham Lincoln (for his honesty), JFK (for admiration and "Ask not what your country can do for you, but ask what you can do for your country"), and Robert his brother (also much admired). I had asked Martin Luther King to join my team a while back ago, and I, of course, called him in. A few of the other people that I called were the Blessed Mother, Princess Dian, Mother Theresa, and Loretta, my senior that I said was my best friend and whom I had told I needed a best friend. Everyone I called started out in the sky and came close enough to me that I could touch them all disappearing before I called in the next. One of them I did hold, but I do not remember which one. All of them were different shapes.

Jesus looked most unusual. He was longer than most, kind of in the shape of a small letter *J* that was outlined black, wavy, with blue on the bottom part of the *J* and red for the dot, which was an outlined circle. Most of them were quite little like the size of a quarter or a little larger. Almost generally, they were different shapes but sometimes similar. I said a few words to some of the people, not all. The only reason I stopped is because the sun went under again, and I couldn't see them anymore. I was talking to Bobby Kennedy when it stopped. I had hoped that he would be president one day, and I felt like he had been the backbone to John Kennedy.

One Sunday, I sat next to Bridgett, and she told me that I had been given the gift of song and I wasn't using it. I thought to myself that I sing to a lot of my seniors. "What do you mean by I am not using it?" Jerry said one time to get up to the mike to sing, and I said, "You want me to sing?" So I decided that I would sing "In the Arms of the Angel" by Sarah McLachlan. I had listened to her song through most of the dark night of the soul, and it always lifted me in tears. I knew that I would be singing it, and I knew that my voice was not that great and that I had fear of doing it at all. I surrendered everything to the Holy Spirit—my voice, my anxiety, and I let it go. I got in front of the mike and said that God wanted me to do this and expressed my anxiety. Jerry said, "Just do it," really not knowing what I was going to do. I got in front of the mike and did it without any help from any instrument. This was truly facing an enormous fear. Mel was at the back, and he said my voice echoed down the hallway but also asked me why I sang both verses. And I thought he did not like it. I noticed one man in the back with his eyes closed, and he was basking in it.

It was now June 11, 2003, and the kids' last day of school. I had taken some pictures of the kids, separately and in small groups, and had a few of all of us taken together. When I walked into the classroom, I realized how much I loved the kids, and wondered if I was going to be able to let them go. I passed out all the pictures, for I had kept a whole set for myself at home. I had given all the girls in the class a special name that I had mostly made up. Nakiyah, who is a beautiful African American, I called Pink Princess, for she had on pink that day.

Actually she thought of *princess*; I just added *pink*, and she liked that. This is the thank-you note that she wrote and read that touched my heart and made this all worth it:

Dear Mrs. Gotz,

> Thank you for your nice compliments, and how you wish that I were your daughter, and when you give me hugs, I feel so much better.

Sincerely,
Your Pink Princess

As Marie and I were walking out of the building, I shook my hands, letting them all go. It was a wonderful experience that I truly appreciated. The last few times leaving the school, I had a headache that progressed and accelerated to the point that I had to eventually take aspirin. I know there is a reason for everything, and I was wondering why this pain came on. I thought maybe that I could be taking on some of their pain. I went shopping, and when I got home, I took aspirin.

My Christmas cactus now has three buds on it, one pointed to the left and two pointed to the right, all at about the same stage of development. The one in the middle is higher and has progressed faster and is now the longest and biggest. I know all three buds represent three different gifts. The middle bud started opening up on June 20, 2003, and was in full bloom two days later. The two buds on either end never opened up at all, and all three fell off simultaneously. I believe the gift is that my masculinity and femininity are now balanced, which is what we are all striving for. I had to get a little graphic, to say the least. That is what we all hope to accomplish—balance. This reminded me when the bride and groom used their separate candles to light the taller candle in the middle, uniting them both.

59

Thanking the Men in My Life

I WENT OUTSIDE TO say to the universe, the Divine Source:

> Dad, thank you for going to work on your day off, when you were sick and staying over, working more overtime than most of your coworkers. I treasure you, honor you, and thank you from the bottom of my heart. I had a bed/pillow to lay my head; most of the time, food in my belly; and last but not least, a roof over my head. I know most of the people on the planet do not have those very basic

needs met, and it is all because of the grace of God and your paycheck that this was possible for me. Thank you for the joys we shared in picnics, water fights, boating, badminton, camping, and holidays. You are now an angel in my eyes, and I remember who you really are.

This is said to my strong, brave, handsome husband, Mike:

You likewise went to work on your day off when you were sick and worked many, many doubles. You also fixed everything around the house just ASAP. You were unbelievably generous to us all in so many ways, giving 150 percent. I thank you, honor you, and likewise treasure you. We went on many awesome vacations because of you. You allowed me to go on many vacations by myself. I truly thank you from the bottom of my heart for everything. I love three main men in my life from the bottom of my heart; you all have given to me endlessly, and you are my angels. I am sorry that I was asleep and did not remember who you really are. I appreciate and appreciate!

When you are playing baseball, hit to miss the ball. If you push too hard, you get the opposite. Everything contains the opposite. To have joy, you must have opposition. Expressing yourself honestly is a hard thing to do. Drama is life heightened! As a human race, it appears as though we enjoy drama, as much as we would say otherwise. The truth is that we can really shine and come through during the most dramatic times in our lives. In fact, we aren't even aware of our power or inner strength until we are presented with such an opportune moment and this experience arises. It is something, how we can correlate most life experiences and sports with how to manage life. Be vigilant against judgment and negative interpretations. Be especially vigilant against assumptions and easy answers that allow you to feel better than or separate from anyone. These last two sentences came from the February 2003 *Sedona Journal*, "God through Yael Powell."

Remove yourself from being the judge and the jury. Think of yourself as being separate from no one, and there will be no problems.

Divine transformation is concentrating on embracing the people we are, including what we do, create, and love. In other words, we are concentrating on what we want, acting like we already have it, and not wanting. Jesus was about his humanity, calmness, kindness, and tolerance. Jesus had an uncompromising tolerance for an extreme inhumanity to man when he was crucified. Jesus was often shown with his arms wide open, inviting all people. He also said, "You without sin, cast the first stone." Don't look for the pebble in someone else's eyes; see the boulder that is in your own. We are embracing all our efforts on the part of our cup that is full—having faith. We are eliminating all of the thoughts, words, and deeds in the part of the cup that is empty, deficient, bankrupt, and does not exist—all fear. Our cup can always be full if we simply allow it, by having appreciation and positive thoughts flowing about everything and everyone. Customize and execute your own plan to reinvent yourself. This paragraph came to pass after watching the movie *Chocolate*.

FAKE IT, IT WILL COME

"Seek not peace here, but find it everywhere." The peace of God is all that is real!

This I found in the book *Emissary of Light* by James F. Twyman. It is how to get to the door to the fourth dimension. I will have that door made available to me, and then I will come back and extend that light to all that will accept it. The only calamity in life is us not loving each other and thinking that we are separate. A temper is the only thing you cannot get rid of by losing it. The only thing to be combative against evil is love. *Am God* spelled backward is *dogma*. The enigmatic reversal from illusionary to what is real is called remembering. As you accept salvation, you extend salvation to all that want it. You become a beacon of light, like a lighthouse. However, you must realize no one's role is more important than another's. That is where humility comes into play. We have played the role for each other; we take turns. We all have been all of it. Because we are a part of the whole, all is available to us. It is not getting what you want but simply wanting what you have! If you want your life to fly, serve mankind; it will soar!

As the saying goes, "God helps those who help themselves." I really did not know what that meant until now. "Get busy living or get busy dying," as

Andy said in the movie *Shawshank Redemption*. What would you risk to change your life?

I feel like my whole life was the dark night of the soul. I also feel that I made it against all odds. I am no longer afraid of anything, not even fear itself. For I know there is nothing to be afraid of. We transition, that's all. We can even go back and visit a previous lifetime in our existing lifetime. I feel like once someone is in your heart, they are always in your heart. Your heart just expands and gets bigger; my cup runneth over with joy. I now have it to give to everyone. If you want abundance, opulence, and decadence, seek peace in your heart. As Kirk Douglas, in his later years, said on TV one day, "If we are not nice to one another, we will never have peace!"

I come armed, laden with love. Be vigilant on your journey through uncharted territories to indigenous inner peace. I believe that sentence sums up my dark night of the soul. Even though everyone's unique dance will be different, they will also be the same. In many ways, I felt like a pilgrim on a solo journey to my inner kingdom even though I had angels all along. In me, show thy smiling face to all that I meet, and let me see you, Jesus, in all people wherever I go. That is my greatest prayer.

FAKE IT, IT WILL COME

Remember, foreplay lasts all day long. Angels are just simply the thoughts of God. Unless we are serving mankind, we are giving lip service. "Read my lips." That is a saying from Ronald Reagan, a president I very much admired. In the circle of life, you cannot take more than you give! It is time to be "awakened savvy" and be who you really are! As President Kennedy said, "Ask not what your country can do for you, but ask what you can do for your country." So ask God what you can do for him. He will tell you! The quintessential epiphany is serving one another through volunteering with no expectations.

As in the Kellogg's Frosted Mini Wheat's commercial, we all have our other side, which could be referred to as the ego. Once you start looking at everything and realizing everyone has everything, it becomes easier and easier to admit our other side, knowing that we all have our shortcomings and weaknesses. All you have to do is look at it and throw it away, taking full accountability and full responsibility for making your reality. What you look at disappears. What you deny you declare. So what do you want to make as your reality? "Getting rid of or taking on—that is the question." Every time I see that commercial, it makes me think, *What side do I want to hear from?* It is a cute metaphor or analogy that we all have our other side, so look at it and bless it for the gifts that it has to offer and ask it to leave. Forgive yourself and everyone else, and ask for forgiveness.

60

More Progression

I AM VERY GRATEFUL that I did not leave Mike or my responsibility to clean up my house. Cleaning house is giving love to the people that surround me no matter what. The only way I can really clean my house is if I do not run away. (What we perceive as toxic people is the toxicity in us that needs to be cleared. Welcome and embrace the opportunity of amplified, accelerated growth.) Now that I have set free the people that surrounded me, I am free. I had to get in there and do the work. A lot of people would have said it would have been easier to leave. Now I know that I would have had a whole new set of problems, plus my unresolved issues to clean up. So it was definitely easier staying, and I did not know it. I take full responsibility for my reality, why I chose this experience. And now I throw it away. Sometimes what looks like the easy way out is the hardest in the long run, and what was hard then becomes easy. My children, whom I dearly love, I would not have freed either. Now what they do with their lives is up to them, but they have been set free, from their parents to their grandparents. I am forever grateful for everything.

As you're going throughout your journey of life, practice discernment and be wise. I believe discernment is not reacting to anything or anyone, staying in a calm, nonreactive place at all times, knowing that it is their right to have their opinion. In other words, you are giving people in general the room for them to have their opinion. It is also means removing yourself from any judgment of any kind. We could have many people see the same accident, and there could be a myriad of different views. Who is to say how we should interpret what they saw? We were not seeing through their eyes. Discernment is an understanding of sorts. Wisdom is to know the difference. To the degree that we separate ourselves from anyone is to that same degree that we are separated from God. All separation is judgment of any kind.

The dark night of the soul could also be referred to as an onion. It goes on in layers and must be patiently and delicately stripped layer by layer. When it is over with, it will seem like a blink of an eye. During it, however, it will seem like it takes forever. Most of us are actually born with karma, and it starts adding on layers before we are even born. When our parents fight or there is tension in the air, the baby feels the tension. Then when our parents yell at us or smack us, that all helps adding on the layers. So you can only imagine how many layers there will be at fifty. Everything is stored in our chakras, as I told you before. We forget, they forget, but it is stored nevertheless. Our perceived perils of our separateness give birth to our awesomeness. As we wander through our perceived mayhem that we have conjured up and made real, we grow in knowledge and wisdom.

To go to the top of the ladder, you cannot be of the flesh in thought, masturbation, or adultery. I feel that you will be rewarded for not doing this with your soul mate and have a wondrous relationship. It might take place on another dimension, later on in that lifetime, or another planet, for that matter. It is acceptable for you to have relations with your spouse, but that has to be in balance also. Pornography and masturbating can also become an addiction—they are not recommended, especially to any who access it or are not able to function without it. You must monitor your thoughts, which may be the hardest thing for you to do, especially when you're in such a dark place. Everyone wants that magical, romantic Romeo and Juliet experience. You must, however, earn it by having delayed gratification. I know that casual sex could never have lasting joy or fulfillment. If you are single, on the spiritual path, and have sex, it will slow your process down! I know I did not want anything to slow my progress down.

Now I am glad that I listened to my guides and did not let my passion become an obsession. I knew I wanted to go to the top of the ladder or the pinnacle of the mountain. The epiphany of my life is waking up. I wanted the option of not reincarnating if I so chose. Go out and find that one book that will help you find your truth. I knew that I had to go to the top of the ladder for that to be available to me. Once you become the "I am," after a time you go back to the "am not." This is called the cosmic wheel. Your choice, of course, but that was disheartening for me. I do not know the whole picture, so I will not make any decisions now. As they say, "Go the distance." Nothing or no one will stop me or get in my way. I am transformed. I am set free at last. I am free to soar amongst the clouds. *Amen!*

In the tapestry kaleidoscope of life, find an oasis in the recess of your mind to bathe in. Let the peace of God envelope your whole essence, taking you to heaven here on earth. Contrary to some people's belief, you can do this without drugs. Being authentic is going to your inner kingdom, calming and relaxing the mind from all fabrication that isn't real. Inhale the breadth of the Divine; exhale everything that isn't serving you. Dare to be bold by marching to a different drum down your unique road of eloquence, magnificence, and amazing grace. Be the being of all that you know you can be, in perfect harmony with nature. You know when your life is working because it feels good. And you know when you are in your ego because it does not feel good. Let the universal flow, flow through you like a pristine stream cascading down the mountainside. Open your spine, your life force, through forgiveness and serving mankind, to the joy and love that you are. Make that pivotal change to let joy in your life; some people could call it the change of life. I am an embellished Catholic made new again.

If anyone had told me that this would happen if you did this, I would not have believed him or her. There was a lot of joy in that sorrow, which made the whole experience unprecedented, exciting, unexplainable happenings. In fact, I could not wait for the next spiritual experience. But the lows were just incredible as well, me not knowing if I was crazy or what! It is a definite roller coaster ride of extreme highs and lows. It is a gripping and riveting exercise! It would be awfully mundane if we were on a merry-go-round with no highs or lows. This reminds me of the movie *Parenthood* with Steve Martin. The grandmother said that she preferred to be on a roller coaster than a merry-go-round because a merry-go-round is boring. Now I believe anything is possible, and I am open-minded and optimistic, where I was very limited and pessimistic before. The road to happiness is paved with forgiveness. You can have heaven here on earth, but you do have to make it and find it for yourself. No one can give it to you. We are all impeccable in the eyes of God.

As in *The Wizard of Oz*, you find out that you are home and had it all along and didn't even know it. You must change your mind, and the Holy Spirit will assist you in doing that. You find out that you were not in your right mind and that you were innocent all along. However, you must invite and surrender everything to the Holy Spirit for that to happen. The holy instant is real and available to all that ask. Fuel the soul by infusing and immersing in the Holy Spirit. It is a very worthwhile adventure, one that I would highly recommend for everyone. The choice is always yours. Love yourself. And then you can truly give and receive love. The only way you can be loved is to give it and show it! If I can do it, so can you! Seize the moment for it is a gift unto you. As they said in the Opening Ceremonies at SLC 2002 Olympics, "Light the fire within." In other words, strip the barriers. We all have the fire; we just have to strike the match to light it. Let your inner luminescence shine through. All are called; just a few choose to listen!

My dog, Tyler, I believe took on my pain also. I said in prayer that I did not want Tyler to take on my pain; he actually seemed to respond. I also had the Holy Ghost people pray for him as well. I knew he was having problems when he was peeing blood. At the first of this year and other times when my stomach would be really bad, he turned sick also. This last time, during the terrorist attack, he got an ear infection instead. I asked my spiritual psychic if he was responding to me, and she said yes. He very much responds to what I am going through. I do not know why I chose to get a dog in September of 1998, when I had no desire to ever own another one. It was of utmost urgency that I go out and get one right away. Maybe my guides or the heavens were sending me this desire and message. No one was more confused than I was about this. I do know that I was with him in a previous lifetime because right after I purchased him, I asked him, and he barked yes.

My tears throughout the dark night of the soul are but a glitch now. My tears now are tears of joy. I take much solace that my relationship with my dad has made such a huge transformation. No one is more shocked than I that this would be possible. Now when he dies, I will feel that I truly loved him and he loved me. I will not have regrets. I am grateful that I accomplished this while he was alive. The only regret that you will take with you when you die is the love you did not freely give to all. It will not be that you did not pray enough, go to church enough, or say the rosary enough. It definitely will not be how much schooling or career you had, how much money you had in the bank, or what materialistic goods you've acquired. The only thing that will matter is how you loved yourself and loved the people that surrounded you. This is your greatest prayer—a prayer of showing and giving love. This is called being a doer of Jesus's work. The greatest thing in life is a best friend—got that from the movie *Fried Green Tomatoes*. What do you want people to say about you when they come to visit you at your funeral?

Life before now did not make sense to me. I thought it was insane. I did not know that there was a method to this madness. My brother Ron tells me that this is all there is but that he likes my perspective. I told him to join in with me—what could it hurt? Knowing that there is a bigger picture and a grander picture sounds good to me. I feel a lot less sad when people die, knowing that they are just moving on, and when you think of them, they are with you. There is no doubt in my mind! It feels good that life makes perfect sense and I chose this experience. I have thought, what was I thinking?

I plan on doing the right thing and doing my very best not to goof up. But if I do, clear it.

I am counting on heaven! I am counting on continuing my learning process through joy. I am counting on joy and ecstasy being my new learning tools. My thoughts through the dark night of the soul and after are that the cold is too cold, the hot is too hot, and the inhumanness is too inhumane.

In my opinion, we need a kinder, gentler planet in all areas. I did not want to write that, but now I am strong enough to do it.

What I have learned through this process is: We can fly above the clouds. We can be immune to what is going on around us. We can act instead of react. We can be at peace. We can see clearly and live in the present. We can reinvent ourselves by serving mankind, praying, fasting, keeping the commandments, reading scriptures, receiving the sacrament, exercising, eating right, gratitude and thanks giving; but most of all charity (giving people the benefit of the doubt).

We are the Alpha and the Omega, so be innovative by reinventing yourself. This is an extraordinary moment in time for me by being unencumbered, unwavering, and undaunted with the three-dimensional good/bad and right/wrong philosophy. There is no right or wrong; there is only opinion. I feel like Wonder Woman and Superman by putting my right arm up in the air and shooting up to wonderment and amazement of the Universe. All of us are one, and my prayer is that everyone reinvents themselves and finds their stars. Be kind to yourself by loving all of you. There is no limit to your dream. "Dream the impossible dream." Dance

FAKE IT, IT WILL COME

in the heavens by swirling, twirling, and spinning throughout the galaxies, leaving a trail of colorful, twinkling lights as you go. Sing with the angels, playing a myriad of instruments in the orchestra of life. Listen for the poetry acoustics in the wind. See awe and wonderment at every turn and in every melody. You can have heaven here on earth; you just have to look for it and hear it wherever you go. Everything is possible with God. Nothing is possible without God. When you give praise and glory to God, you give it to yourself. Let your soul feel its worth! Earn your wings so that you can soar like an eagle on the jet stream of joy embarking from the hand of God. Feel the wind and the warmth of the sun upon your face, and know you are the goddesses' and gods' expression. Swim with the dolphins in the abyss of the inverted mountains of the cosmic oceans, and know you are the "I Am."

The only journey worth taking is the one within; if you don't go within, you go without. In Shirley MacLaine's book *Crossing the Camino*, all roads loop back to the beginning, instead of Rome. I am at the beginning; I have come full circle. The Holy Grail is an example. It is like any other cup, except that its real value lies in its emptiness. The joy comes when the cup of sorrow is emptied. So in other words, you are airing out your own closets by opening them up to the light. I have emptied my cup of sorrow through the dark night of the soul and the writing of this book. Therefore, it is a rebirth of your own soul, a baptism if you will. Take a leap of consciousness by catapulting yourself, with the help of the Holy Spirit, through to the next level or dimension. The amenities are having your cup overfilled with joy so that you can give joy freely to all that you meet. This is from the book *Medicine Cards* by Jamie Sams and David Carson: "True Power is wisdom found in remembering your total journey. Wisdom comes from remembering pathways you have walked in another person's moccasins." This means having compassion for others while remaining impartial and impersonal to all that you meet, removing all judgment. Still from Shirley MacLaine's book is that all of life is a lesson in self-knowledge. The more knowledge we have of ourselves, the more we are able to deal with anything. This is what I have learned through my experience of the dark night of the soul: "It is taking a journey in your past to set you free to move forward in the present."

61

Giving Thanks

THIS IS NOT AN ending but a beginning. My journey has led me to who I really am. This has been a test from the emergency broadcast system and only a test. On the other side of the veil, we all love one another; there is no need, lack, or disease, and we are one. Hopefully, this book will be the ingredient to help you transform your life. I thank my entourage of spirit guides; I really do not know what I would have done without them. I can only express my great magnitude of appreciation for the Church of Today and Marianne Williamson—the myriad of doors opened to me was phenomenal. Much thanks and appreciation to all of the people from the meditation group at the Church of Today, I learned so very much from all of them, and I love them all. Thanks for the Little Rose Chapel, Dian and Mother. Mother for the many times that she prayed over me so eloquently, expressing the intercession of the Little Rose. For Helen, who guided me to St. Mary Magdalene's and St. Elizabeth's, her reflexology, and her endless daily prayers for my family and myself. For all the Holy Ghost people at St. Mary Magdalene's, their uninhibited glorious praising example, and the "Wind in Fire" classes, plus all the people that prayed over me. For the group at the Church of Today that I did the Master Mind class with. In memory of Norman, who died at the beginning of 2001. Thanks to Father Charles at St. Elizabeth's Church and his joyous extension of pure love with a vengeance. What can I say about my sister Shirley other than she was always there for me and started me off on reading *A Course in Miracles* and giving blessings, a crucial part of my growth? To my husband, Mike, who provided so well that I was able to devote my time and energy in doing my work. He readily accepted any healing that I had to offer; for that, I am grateful. He also, in many ways, supported me on my adventure. I cannot imagine having gone through the dark night of the soul without Theron. He made the intolerable tolerable!

FAKE IT, IT WILL COME

It is a reflection of Mike's hand looking out bedroom window.

I condisder this as my spiritual diploma walking into the light.

KATHY GOTZ

Sunrise at mullett sideways is me as a mermaid that the spirit world put in my picture.

Me lying, in my backyard on the ground in winter taking this picture; the spirit world put in right side crown - left side cradle.

FAKE IT, IT WILL COME

Kathy Gotz at the beginning of Dark Night Soul

KATHY GOTZ

My family Eric, David, Mike
in back Christine, me, Karen on
Chistine's graduation.

My house on Mullett with stuff put in it
on the right of picture by spirit world.

FAKE IT, IT WILL COME

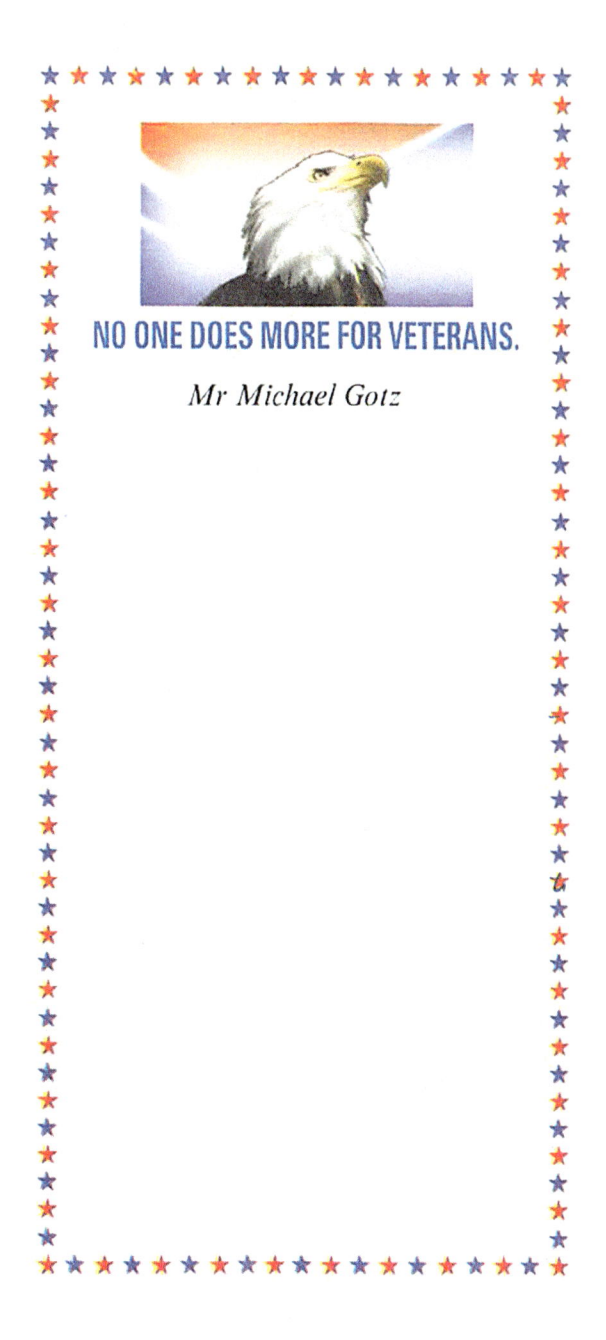

NO ONE DOES MORE FOR VETERANS.

Mr Michael Gotz

KATHY GOTZ

Me and My Dad when my children were young.

Karen's Wedding
Left to Right: David, Christine,
Mike, Karen, me, and Eric

FAKE IT, IT WILL COME

Kathy at Tender Care in Taylor, MI with
Zetha who I enjoyed very much

The Catholic Holy Ghost group at
St. Mary Magdelyn church hall

About the Author

Upon concluding my writings, I experienced more dark night events that were self-imposed! After five hospital stays, I was baptized in the Church of Jesus Christ of Latter-Day Saints, whereupon I experienced miraculous release and forgiveness.

I still attend the Holy Ghost prayer group when visiting down state. The Church of Today with Marianne Williamson has sadly ended. I do not enjoy any contact with any of the members that were there.

Mike does not attend church, but we pray holding hands with a rather lengthy prayer every morning, and he is very supportive of me. I've learned to really appreciate him and all that he does for me.

Before my last stay in the hospital, I had a great trip to traveling around China with my twin sister, Carol, in Joy. It was a worthwhile journey.

I have a rather quiet life. I walk in the woods and pray extensively. I also read scriptures over the phone with my sister Carol. I still pray in senior homes in their rooms and sing in the cafeteria, both down state and up here. It is not a burden but a joy!

I also do not give blessings or reiki attunements anymore.

Just to let you know, I no longer remember the pain of the dark night of the soul. What I wrote about has been forgotten out of my memory. But I know enough that I don't want to go back. I've been set free and enjoy life.

I'm living a blessing from the church to influence and bless my family and grandchildren. The desires of my heart are being fulfilled in life and through posterity, and I am grateful for all my experiences.

The Truth will set you free